REFUGEE STATES

Refugee States

Critical Refugee Studies in Canada

EDITED BY
VINH NGUYEN AND THY PHU

UNIVERSITY OF TORONTO PRESS
Toronto Buffalo London

© University of Toronto Press 2021
Toronto Buffalo London
utorontopress.com
Printed in the U.S.A.

ISBN 978-1-4875-0864-7 (cloth)   ISBN 978-1-4875-3867-5 (EPUB)
                                   ISBN 978-1-4875-3866-8 (PDF)

Cultural Spaces

Library and Archives Canada Cataloguing in Publication

Title: Refugee states : critical refugee studies in Canada / edited by Vinh Nguyen and Thy Phu.
Names: Nguyen, Vinh (Associate professor), editor. | Phu, Thy, 1975– editor.
Series: Cultural spaces.
Description: Series statement: Cultural spaces | Includes bibliographical references and index.
Identifiers: Canadiana (print) 20210158530 | Canadiana (ebook) 2021015876X | ISBN 9781487508647 (cloth) | ISBN 9781487538668 (PDF) | ISBN 9781487538675 (EPUB)
Subjects: LCSH: Refugees – Canada.
Classification: LCC HV640.4.C3 R438 2021 | DDC 305.9/06914 – dc23

This book has been published with the support in part by funding from the Social Sciences and Humanities Research Council.

University of Toronto Press acknowledges the financial assistance to its publishing program of the Canada Council for the Arts and the Ontario Arts Council, an agency of the Government of Ontario.

  Canada Council   Conseil des Arts
       for the Arts   du Canada

ONTARIO ARTS COUNCIL
CONSEIL DES ARTS DE L'ONTARIO
an Ontario government agency
un organisme du gouvernement de l'Ontario

Funded by the   Financé par le
Government   gouvernement
of Canada   du Canada

Contents

Acknowledgments vii

Introduction: Critical Refugee Studies in Canada 3
VINH NGUYEN AND THY PHU

Part One: Historicization

1 Shifting Grounds of Asylum in Canadian Public Discourse and Policy 23
JOHANNA REYNOLDS AND JENNIFER HYNDMAN

2 Untangling the Strands of Memory: Historicizing the 1914 *Komagata Maru* Incident and the Concept of Refugeeness 55
ALIA SOMANI

3 Erasing Exclusion: Adrienne Clarkson and the Promise of the Refugee Experience 71
LAURA MADOKORO

4 Petitions and Protest: Refugees and the Haunting of Canadian Citizenship 99
PETER NYERS

Part Two: Conjunctions

5 Where Are We From? Decolonizing Indigenous and Refugee Relations 117
JENNIFER ADESE AND MALISSA PHUNG

6 Queer and Trans Migrants, Colonial Logics,
  and the Politics of Refusal   143
  EDWARD OU JIN LEE

7 Producing the Figure of the "Super-Refugee" through Discourses
  of Success, Exceptionalism, Ableism, and Inspiration   173
  GADA MAHROUSE

8 Cross-Racial Refugee Fiction: Dionne Brand's
  What We All Long For   194
  DONALD GOELLNICHT

Epilogue: The Exceptional and the Ordinary   215
  THY PHU AND VINH NGUYEN

List of Contributors   221

Index   225

Acknowledgments

We are fortunate to be able to work closely with a number of wonderful colleagues, whose insights continue to inspire. This book was the result of a series of collaborative initiatives that began in 2017, and that culminated in the establishment of the research group, the Critical Refugee Studies Network Canada. We wish to thank members of this group, namely Edward Ou Jin Lee, Laura Madokoro, Gada Mahrouse, Anh Ngo, Peter Nyers, Alia Somani, and Y-Dang Troeung. We also wish to thank the Critical Refugee Studies Collective (based in California), whose groundbreaking work inspires our own.

We thank the contributors of this collection for trusting us with their research and for being a part of this conversation. We are grateful to the participants at the very first workshop we convened to discuss "refugee states" and "states of refuge," including Nadine Attewell, Elspeth Brown, Tamara El-Hoss, Chris Kyriakides, Shahrzad Mojab, Anh Ngo, Charmaine Nelson, and Heather Smyth, along with the contributors to this volume. For her support of this event, we thank Jennifer J. Chun. We would also like to acknowledge the support of the Social Sciences and Humanities Research Council of Canada. We benefited tremendously from the guidance of our editor, Mark Thompson, and the careful, incisive reading of our friend Eleanor Ty, as well as our two anonymous reviewers, whose suggestions helped us refine our ideas.

Donald C. Goellnicht, who was a pivotal member of the Critical Refugee Studies Network Canada and who was a dear, longtime friend, started this journey with us – indeed, without him, it's unlikely we would have made it this far. He passed away, however, before we could go to press. We dedicate this book to his memory.

REFUGEE STATES

Introduction
Critical Refugee Studies in Canada

VINH NGUYEN AND THY PHU

On 27 January 2017, US President Donald Trump signed Executive Order 13769 (Protecting the Nation from Foreign Terrorist Entry into the United States).[1] Commonly known as the Travel Ban or the Muslim Ban, the Order suspended the US Refugee Admissions Program for 120 days, placed an indefinite ban on refugees from Syria, and barred entry to anyone from seven predominantly Muslim countries in the Middle East and Africa. The next day, Canadian Prime Minister Justin Trudeau went on Twitter to proclaim: "To those fleeing persecution, terror & war, Canadians will welcome you, regardless of your faith. Diversity is our strength #WelcomeToCanada."[2] Fourteen minutes later, Trudeau tweeted a 2015 picture of himself greeting a Syrian refugee child at the airport.

These two Tweets, a declaration of hospitality and visual evidence of this hospitality, exemplify Canadian "humanitarian exceptionalism," a belief that what sets Canada apart from the US and other nation-states is its distinct benevolence and commitment to human rights. The well-timed public pronouncement was a strategic and politically expedient response to the devolving political situation in the US, which has gone on to implement Immigration and Customs Enforcement raids, separate border-crossing parents from their children, and indefinitely detain asylum seekers in concentration camps. Trudeau draws on a tradition that defines Canadian liberal nationalism – qualities of generosity, hospitality, and tolerance – against our southern neighbour's restrictive and ruthless actions. The president's widely condemned racist and xenophobic Order provided the prime minister with an opportunity to exalt Canada as an open and welcoming haven to the global public. At a moment of American humanitarian failure, Canada asserted itself as a leader in refugee humanitarianism. The subsequent trending of the hashtag #WelcomeToCanada on Twitter attests to the ways that the narrative of Canadian humanitarian exceptionalism proliferates in the age of viral social media.

A belief in and promotion of the nation's exceptionalism is not new. Canada's international reputation has long been pegged to a narrative of beneficence towards refugees and migrants fleeing oppression, persecution, and unfreedom, which begins, so this story goes, at least as far back as the nineteenth century, when Canada served as a terminus in the Underground Railroad, providing freedom to fugitive slaves, and extends into the twentieth century, with the offer of sanctuary to displaced people from Europe fleeing the turmoil of the Second World War and American draft dodgers protesting the war in Vietnam, to highlight just a few signal moments.[3] Indeed, this narrative was consolidated in 1986 when the UN awarded the nation with a Nansen medal in recognition of aid to refugees in the aftermath of the wars in Southeast Asia. The narrative persists despite numerous moments when Canada turned away rather than welcomed the people who arrived on its shores, including Indian migrants aboard the *Komagata Maru* in 1914, Jews fleeing Nazi persecution on the MS *St. Louis* in 1939,[4] Chinese stowaways aboard container ships in 2001 and 2017, and Sri Lankan Tamils seeking refuge on the MV *Sun Sea* in 2010, to list just a few examples. A notion of exceptionality thus shapes national and global perception of the nation's character, recently confirmed in a Pew Report, which noted that, in 2018, Canada "surpassed" the US for the first time, and "now leads the world" in refugee resettlement.[5]

To be sure, at certain moments of crisis, disaster, and war, Canada *has* opened its door, if only slightly, to many refugees.[6] Rather than dismiss the nation's humanitarian tradition – which has benefited generations of refugees, including the co-editors, who came to Canada as refugees – we are concerned with addressing the limits it poses for understanding refugee history and assessing the political in Canada. The humanitarian tradition is limited because it obscures exceptionality's varied operations, the terms in which refuge has been provided, the contexts in which it is denied, and the complex roles that refugees have played in nation-building or in the critique of state-centred notions of sovereignty. These varied operations demonstrate a vital point: Canada needs refugees to advance its cultural and political ends. The significance of the relationship between exceptionalism, dependence, and political expediency, between the Canadian nation-state and refugees, lies at the core of this book.

Refugee States: Critical Refugee Studies in Canada explores "refuge" and "refugee" as complexly related concepts that pivotally influence nation-building both within and beyond the nation's borders. We focus on how Canada has engaged, historically and in the present moment, with people seeking refuge and highlight the multiform ways that refugees have responded to Canada. The book examines the fraught yet generative encounters that produce refuge and refugees, explains the impact of these encounters in shaping "exceptionality" in Canada, and accounts for the ways that refugees themselves have critiqued official state narratives and sought different political alignments and forms of relationality.

The exception is central to the political problematic that subjects like refugees pose, for they both press at the limits of and also come to define state sovereignty and nationhood. As Giorgio Agamben famously asserts, the state of exception is formed when the law is, paradoxically, suspended so as to preserve sovereign authority.[7] Drawing on Agamben, Peter Nyers argues that "refugees are included in the discourse of 'normality' and 'order' only by virtue of their exclusion from the normal identities and ordered spaces of the sovereign state," that they are, in other words, formed through "the sovereign relation of the exception."[8] Nyers examines the manifold ways that refugees grapple with and attempt to create other modes of community beyond the state of exception. Our book draws inspiration from this foundational work, which has nuanced refugee agency to shed light on assertions of subjectivity that are not wholly constrained by notions of biopolitical state sovereignty.

By centring the figure of the refugee and the concept of refuge, this book builds on and expands well-established critiques of Canadian nationalism, nation-building, and settler colonialism.[9] While we seek to understand and interrogate state sovereignty, our methods do not reproduce the state as the singular locus of knowledge production or source of subject formation. That is, our approach is less concerned with critiques of the state, and more with the ways in which refugees take up, work with, challenge, and transform state directives and agendas, asserting their subjectivities variously in opposition to and in parallel with other categories and subject positions as well as carving out ways of living and being with others. Of course, the state does not disappear, and humanitarian exceptionalism remains a key shaping force for refugee lives and articulations.

But, because of the unique conditions of statelessness, the refugee is a key figure for rethinking social and political organization beyond the unit of the nation-state.[10] This is why, although we recognize and acknowledge the importance of key historical markers – most notably, the ratification of the 1951 UN Convention Relating to the Status of Refugees, which Canada signed in 1969, and the 1976 official addition of "refugee" as a new class of immigrant in the Immigration Act of Canada – our explorations are not bound to the narrow terms and linear temporality set by these documents.

This book develops "refugee states" as an organizing rubric for explaining the meanings of refuge(e), the rationales for its denial, and the contexts in which it is reclaimed and renarrated. In including the term "state" in our conceptualization of this rubric, we underscore the nation-state's role in producing refugees, in determining the basis for legal recognition, and in structuring the conditions in which refugee lives are made (im)possible. Just as importantly, we conjoin "refugee" to "states" to highlight the irreducible presence of refugees in these definitional and executive processes. Attending to the existence of these subjects and their actions brings to light the state's attempt to monopolize control of asylum and political subjectivity, unsettles the teleological determinism of the state, and points to the possibilities of other life-worlds. At the same time, the tension between refugees as political subjects and states as political organizations plays out in the conjunction "refugee states," which opens up alternative frameworks for analysis and critique. Thus, while the state undeniably influences understandings of refuge(e), neither refuge nor refugee can be fully understood in terms of state formations alone.

"Refugee states" names the conditions of psychic experience, everyday modes of living, challenges to the state, and articulations of sovereignties beyond nationhood. Unfolding in varied forms and manifestations, "refugee states," as our contributors demonstrate, are refugee relations, voices, imaginaries, memories, subjectivities, communities, and protests. They describe how refugees and those seeking asylum experience social and political processes of bureaucratic management – how they negotiate these processes, the fraught ways that they experience state power, and the extent to which the everyday world is marked by historical collisions and conjunctions that call into question discrete categories of identity and community.

What is the relationship between Canada and refugees? To what extent might Canada's differing response to refugees lay bare the state's own stakes in these encounters? In what ways have refugees negotiated this narrative of humanitarian exceptionalism and how have they crafted responses that unsettle its conventions? In other words, how are refugees "solutions," as Yến Lê Espiritu provocatively puts it, to the quandaries of statecraft rather than "problems" to be managed?[11] Moreover, how have these possible solutions opened potential alliances with, as well as provided a means of taking account of possible intersections between, other minoritized subjects in Canada? These are just some of the questions that our contributors take up in their interdisciplinary and situated analyses of Canadian refuge(e) formations.

Through the framework of "refugee states," this book provides two related insights for the study of refugees in Canada. First, we emphasize the importance of reconsidering historical and contemporary moments to contextualize understandings of refuge(e) that are produced at certain points in time. In revisiting key events and historicizing discursive terms and political forms, our contributors in the first half of the collection demonstrate the slipperiness or pliability of political definitions and categories. "Refugee" and "refuge" are not definitive and uncontested categories, but instead become legible alongside and in tension with a range of other terms such as "migrant" and "immigrant," which are sometimes conflated with, and at other times considered distinct from, "refugee."

Consider, for example, "migrant," a term that intersects with and yet is often considered distinct from "immigrant" and "refugee." Indeed, not all migrants are immigrants, the latter usually understood as subjects who enter the nation-state through legally sanctioned mechanisms and who are expected to contribute to the economic and social development of the nation and to remain indefinitely – a process that refugees can also undergo. "Migrant" is a term often employed to designate those who are undocumented, or stateless, or holding temporary or precarious legal status, among other categories. Refugees are, at times, understood as migrants. At highly politicized moments, however, refugees are considered distinct from migrants. The relationship between the two categories is contentious. The term "economic migrant" is used in many instances to deny refugee claims, according to national protectionists who seek to disqualify applicants on the grounds that migrants who move for better economic opportunities cannot be considered refugees, who are deemed to be politically persecuted. Given these conflations, refuge(e) must be considered neither in hermeneutic isolation nor as historically fixed categories, but rather as porous concepts and flexible subjectivities.[12] As a method, *historicization* allows us to examine overlaps, contradictions, and ambiguities that attend the management and articulation of refuge(e). Whereas legal definitions, derived from the UN model, provide normative and positivistic explanations of who a refugee is, the analytic of "refugee states" illuminates the difficulty of containing refugee experiences.

Our second insight focuses on the *conjunctions* that constitute refuge(e). To account for "refugee states" is to understand refugees through multiplicity, as subjects who occupy, negotiate, and respond to multiple time-spaces, contexts, and positionalities. Accordingly, we conceptualize refuge(e) relationally, as categories that are in contact and intersection with other groups and subject positions. Adopting a range of methodologies, our contributors draw attention to the constructed and contingent unfoldings of refuge(e). Taken together, the book argues that refuge and refugee are constructions that gain their significance in relation to other categories such as migrant, immigrant, undocumented, irregular asylum seeker, bogus refugee, citizen, and Indigenous. Moreover, refugee is never just singular, but is ontologically produced through and with other identities such as race, gender, class, sexuality, and ability. We contend that constructions of refuge(e) do not occur in isolation, but instead are situated in conjunction with historical, social, political, and cultural contexts that bring varied subject positions together in ways that have the potential to be epistemologically and politically generative.

Critical Refugee Studies in Canada

In foregrounding refugee states, we take inspiration from and seek to contribute to critical refugee studies, an interdisciplinary field that distinguishes itself from policy-oriented approaches to the study of refugees by opening up new theoretical orientations and foregrounding different – crucially non-state centred – political concerns. In his survey of refugee studies, Richard Black notes that the field has been dominated by policy developments and considerations. A danger that arises from this approach, however, is that "refugee research will lead to work that is not only undertheorized and oriented towards particular bureaucratic interests, but also fundamentally unsuited even to the task of influencing the policy world in which it is mainly situated."[13] While the policy impact of refugee research is debatable, B.S. Chimni argues that refugee studies has contributed to the containment of refugees from the global South into the global North.[14] That is, policy-oriented research, which primarily views refugees as objects of study and as "problems" to be managed instead of agential subjects, supports Western state agendas and neo-imperial policies.

In contrast to traditional refugee studies, scholars in critical refugee studies take up issues of forced migration by foregrounding a refugee-based perspective and by developing theoretically grounded methods for analysis. The field is concerned with the underlying and structuring conditions that produce the need to seek asylum and with the ways that refugees negotiate these conditions. Instead of studying refugees in order to produce knowledge to manage them, research in critical refugee studies seeks to understand the larger political, historical, social, and cultural forces that shape how we view and ultimately treat refugees. The criticality of critical refugee studies, then, comes from fundamental critiques of violent bureaucratic processes and state ideologies rather than the production of knowledge to further support and perpetuate them.

As it has developed in the US context, critical refugee studies focuses on the extensive impact of American empire, specifically the imperialist and racial projects that connect foreign wars as well as transnational refugee passages in their wake. Yến Lê Espiritu's work, which is at the forefront of developing this framework for the study of Southeast Asian diasporas in the aftermath of the war in Vietnam, builds on the insights of Hannah Arendt and Giorgio Agamben to posit that the refugee radically calls into question the "established principles of the nation-state and the idealized goal of inclusion and recognition within it."[15] Critical refugee studies, according to Espiritu, reverses popular assumptions, for "it is the existence of the displaced refugee, rather than the rooted citizen, that provides the clue to a new politics and model of international relations."[16] Rather than instrumentalize or pathologize refugees as "objects of knowledge," critical refugee studies employs "the figure of the refugee" as an analytic lens through which to understand and challenge the workings of state power, which inextricably link the enactment of violence with professions of benevolence, of destruction with rescue.

Accordingly, an ideological critique of the "national order of things," to draw on Liisa Malkki,[17] is central to the project of critical refugee studies, so that, as Agamben notes, the refugee becomes the "sole category in which it is possible today to perceive the forms and limits of a political community to come."[18] In various ways, scholars such as Yến Lê Espiritu, Mimi Thi Nguyen, Cathy Schlund-Vials, Viet Thanh Nguyen, Khatharya Um, and Eric Tang, among others, have attended to forces such as imperialism, nationalism, war, and race, which produce the conditions and dynamics of refuge and refugee, in the forms of displacement, asylum seeking, and resettlement.[19] Although derived from an interrogation of US empire and American militarization in Southeast Asia, their insights about the violence that produces refugees and refuge resonate elsewhere and have broader implications for an examination of refugees in Canada.

Refugee States develops the field of critical refugee studies for the transnational Canadian context, understood as a history that celebrates peaceability rather than the conquest and militarism so manifestly characteristic of the US, and where this celebration is predicated on obscuring settler colonial violence and the British Empire's legacy of race-based exclusion.[20] In so doing, the book contributes to exciting research already underway in Canada that highlights the necessity of attending to refugee perspectives, in particular Peter Nyers's landmark study, which expands the realm of the political and subjectivity when it comes to "rethinking refugees." Other scholars and activists such as Sherene Razack, Harsha Walia, Sunera Thobani, Y-Dang Troeung, Carrie Dawson, Alison Mountz, David A.B. Murray, Craig Fortier, and many of the contributors in this collection, working in a variety of fields and contexts, have also undertaken critical analyses of refugee politics and culture in Canada.[21] While they may not be contained under the "critical refugee studies" rubric per se, these scholars and their work have informed our thinking about Canada as a specific context for doing critical refugee studies.

Canada's exceptionality is unique and important to consider for two major, interrelated reasons. First, the fact that Canada presents itself as a more liberal and enlightened solution to the problems posed by the US obscures its own complicity and involvement in projects of empire building. Indeed, the nation's abetting of wars, most notable in the form of arms supply and its economic incursions overseas, has both produced refugee populations and greatly benefited the country.[22] A focus on Canada enables critical refugee studies to explore the functions of imperialism in a national context that has disavowed such insidious histories of imperialism.

Second, Canadian exceptionality is all the more striking given that American exceptionalism – understood as a belief in the nation's uniqueness as champion of individualism and defender of democracy and a related faith in its solemn mission to transform the world in accord with these values – is a more prevalent and powerful concept. Indeed, while American exceptionalism has been the subject of sustained examination for several decades, not least because this belief masks the underlying objective of imperial expansion, the notion of Canadian exceptionality has yet to be fully recognized as such, nor has its function in constituting refuge(e) been adequately interrogated.[23] Consideration of the shared logics between British Empire and settler colonialism and their significance for establishing the early infrastructure for refuge(e) widens the historical and geographical purview of critical refugee studies beyond the reach of American empire and complements important research that has helpfully revealed the importance of the Second World War and the global Cold War in forming refugee subjects. What makes critical refugee studies in Canada *critical*, then, is careful attention to how refugees and refuge are embedded in and inextricable from settler colonialism and imperial histories, which have been integral to discourses of humanitarian exceptionality. This is the case even when there are supposedly no histories of overseas empire.

Settler Colonialism, State Sovereignty, and Refugee Conjunctions

To explain the contexts for the formation of refugee states, this volume engages in the tasks of historical re-examination as well as refugee conjunctions. These tasks require exploring the connections and intersections that determine the variegated meanings of refuge(e) and broadening frameworks for analysis beyond widely accepted timelines and commonplace understandings of refugees, mainly derived from the United Nations High Commissioner for Refugees (UNHCR)'s oft-cited definition of a refugee as someone who is forced to flee their country because of "well-founded fear of persecution." Without denying the continued relevance and influence of legal approaches to the term refugee, we move beyond these official formulations to take account of the term's discursive complexity. As Laura Madokoro observes in her chapter for this book, Adrienne Clarkson, a former governor general and prominent public figure, self-identifies as a refugee even though her family arrived in Canada well before 1976 and even though their circumstances accord with an entirely different category of immigration, namely, civilian exchange. Similarly, migrant justice advocates have revisited the *Komagata Maru* Incident as a touchstone for understanding refugeeness in Canada, a fascinating phenomenon that Alia Somani takes up in her chapter. While these moves clearly diverge from linear histories of refugees in Canada, simply labelling them as anachronistic misses a crucial point: These assertions of refugeeness are deliberate and highly self-conscious strategies meant to do vital cultural and political work – to claim belonging and to establish parallels between the experiences of disparate groups at seemingly discrete moments as evidence of a larger pattern of exclusion. Rather than dismissing these moves as erroneous, we take seriously the underlying challenge that they pose, which is to reconsider the histories of refugees in Canada and their entanglement within the intertwined logics of settler colonialism and British empire.

Any study of refugees in Canada must first acknowledge and reckon with the fact that the Canadian settler state's capacity to grant political asylum to refugees – and assert its sovereign power – is contingent on its centuries-long colonial suppression of Indigenous sovereignty over land, natural resources, and people.[24] Underlying "refuge" in settler states like Canada is a form of "structured dispossession" of territory, where the state's power of domination "has been structured into a relatively secure or sedimented set of hierarchical social relations that continues to facilitate the dispossession of Indigenous peoples of their lands and self-determining authority."[25] In this way, migrants, immigrants, and refugees participate, however unwittingly, in the ongoing colonization of Indigenous peoples and lands, even when they may themselves face forms of state-sanctioned violence, exclusion, and injustice such as racism and economic marginalization.[26]

Moreover, state sovereignty and settler colonialism in Canada is rooted in its history as part of the British Empire. The legal mechanism for refuge, for entry into or exclusion from the nation's borders, can be traced to varying extents to this history. Prior to 1947, Canada shared with other colonies its foremost duty to extend loyalty to the monarchy as a settler colony on the outposts of British Empire. Legally, British subjects were afforded the protection of the Crown, and were granted the right to migrate throughout the empire. Canada was a key, if remote, node in the routes of imperial migration that connected Hong Kong with India and colonies in the West Indies, and, as such, became a destination for British subjects. Xenophobic politicians, however, sought to restrict these rights by invoking the concept of imperial citizenship, most notably through infamous race-based laws such as the Chinese Immigration Act (first introduced in 1885 and revised in 1903 and 1923), which levied an increasingly expensive head tax on immigrants of Chinese origin, and the Continuous Journey Regulation, an amendment to the Immigration Act of 1908, which prohibited migrants from landing in Canada who did not travel directly from their country of origin. (This Regulation was tested by the migrants aboard the *Komagatu Maru*.)

Discernible here are early forms of national immigration control, significant precisely because they emerged in response to the tensions and pressures of existing within the British Empire. These forms of control sought to manage migration by limiting the movement of racialized British subjects across empire. Indeed, imperial citizenship was an unofficial discourse of nationality that emerged *before* Canada achieved complete autonomy as a nation-state, at a moment when belonging was not yet codified in formal citizenship but nonetheless influenced the terms of inclusion and exclusion.[27] The migration of British subjects deemed undesirable compelled Canada to develop procedures to address immigration, and eventually to deal with Convention refugees, even though race and other forms of exclusion were invoked implicitly instead of overtly.[28] This context of bounded nationhood helps to shed light on how the refugee was defined and came into being, in a process that began long before the term gained official recognition in Canada in 1976.

At the same time that imperial citizenship was concerned with controlling entry of racialized others, settler administrators were preoccupied with the management and violent suppression of Indigenous peoples in Canada. Imperial citizenship was thus a two-pronged discourse inseparable from settler colonialism. Settler colonialism and empire set in motion overlapping – yet at times distinct and incommensurate – forms of displacement of Indigenous peoples, who were dispossessed of their land, and of diasporic subjects, who were compelled to work this very land as "coolie" indentured labourers and as enslaved peoples. The legacies of this process persist into the present era of globalization and neoliberalism, forces which have uprooted refugees, disrupted their lives, and displaced them for prolonged periods in sites of detention. Although this enduring process further drives a wedge between Indigenous peoples and diasporic subjects, including refugees, division is not the only effect. As Daniel Coleman reminds us, "Indigeneity and diaspora are proximate cultural formations."[29] In other words, Indigeneity and diaspora are cultural formations shaped by experiences of displacement, one under settler colonialism and the other through (neo)imperial forces, which bring them in relation to the racial nation-state.

In these ways, historical reconsideration, as an approach that grapples with, while remaining unconstrained by, legal definitions and rigidly linear timelines, helps illuminate how routes of imperial migration have influenced today's systems of immigration management – systems that have sought to delimit refuge(e). We see the trace of imperial citizenship in the passport, visa, and points system, which are ways of discriminating on the basis of race, sexuality, and class without directly naming these categories.[30] The discriminatory foundations that the concept of imperial citizenship helped fortify are also manifest in refugee policies such as the Safe Third Country Agreement, quotas, detention, and deportation, as well as in discursive constructions of refugees as "irregular," "queue jumpers," and "bogus refugees," the logics and effects of which are examined in Johanna Reynolds and Jennifer Hyndman's co-authored chapter for this volume. Refuge and refugees are, it follows, embedded in and inextricable from Canada's ongoing assertion of national domination through the violent logics of settler colonialism and its imperial histories, understood in terms of its development within the British Commonwealth and, as critics are beginning to show, its complicity in more contemporary neo-imperial projects, especially as a US ally during and after the global Cold War.[31]

These intertwined imperial and settler colonial logics set in motion overlapping processes that variably produce refuge(e) – processes to which refugees respond in complex ways. Exploration of conjunctions between disparate subjects and between identity categories provides a means of reflecting on the political potential of multiform responses to the state. Such conjunctions, as our contributors show, draw attention to the ways that refugee and refuge are lived and embodied in complexity, that forces such as race, gender, sexuality, and disability crucially shape how we understand them. By exploring select conjunctions, *Refugee States* illuminates the sometimes surprising and often revelatory linkages between subject positions and lays bare the state's attempts to isolate refuge(e) and thereby pre-empt epistemological and subjective profundity as well as potentially threatening alliances.

Our framework of critical refugee studies expands debates beyond progressive narratives that emphasize the journey from displacement to resettlement, and which construe refugees as a "problem" of the global South for which liberal states in the North provide solutions through gestures of hospitality, in the process absolving themselves of any responsibility for the conditions that produce refugees. *Refugee States* disrupts these binaries, revealing how Canada's history as part of the British Empire intersects with settler colonialism so as to continue to delimit and obstruct routes of migration and define freedom and unfreedom for differentially racialized subjects. The volume also attends to the varied forms in which refugee narratives unfold in response to these histories. Taken together, the chapters in this volume explain how concepts of refuge and refugee shape the state, and critically describe the material conditions in which refugees articulate their relation to and defiance of official discourses.

Chapter Outlines

The first section of this book focuses on historicization, situating seemingly discrete moments to demonstrate parallel processes that have defined and sought to constrain refuge(e) as formations integrally related to the logics of empire and settler colonialism. Johanna Reynolds and Jennifer Hyndman examine the emergence of "irregular" categories of refugees such as "queue jumpers" and "bogus refugees" and their correlation to restrictive policies and tightening borders. In doing so, they also provide a helpful overview of the current context of asylum and refugee resettlement in Canada. The next two chapters reorient our temporal understanding of the refugee category by exploring historical case studies of subjects seeking refuge before "refugee" was codified into law in Canada. Laura Madokoro examines the cultural and political significance of former Governor General Adrienne Clarkson's framing of her family's history of displacement from Hong Kong to Canada during the Second World War as a "refugee" experience. Alia Somani further considers the impact of imperial routes of migration by investigating the political stakes of invoking refugeeness as a framework for re-examining the *Komagata Maru* Incident (1914), which was at the time understood as involving "migrants." Finally, Peter Nyers extends these analyses by re-examining the larger historical context for the emergence of petitions, a centuries-old political genre, for articulating and performing protest, which, as his chapter shows, has been revised and adapted for the ends of migrant justice advocacy.

The chapters included in the second section of the book elaborate on the productive potential of conjunctions, whose stakes are nothing less than refugees' capacities for expressing agency. Specifically, they show how refuge and refugee are made and remade through race, sexuality, disability, and Indigeneity. The four chapters included in this section reveal that, though the inextricable concepts of refuge(e) are mediated constructions, they nonetheless exert material consequences. At the same time, the chapters attend to the various forces of power, identity, and community that shape imaginaries and prompt careful reconsideration of the potential for new alliances and radical refusals. In their co-written chapter, Jennifer Adese and Malissa Fung consider how a "genealogy of disclosure" might offer a method for locating refugee and Indigenous relationality, and a pointedly ethical rejoinder to white nationalist demands that racialized subjects explain their origins. This analysis offers an important way to approach the difficult issue of refugee positionality vis-à-vis the Canadian settler colonial state and to assess the possibilities for alliances between refugee settlers and Indigenous peoples. Building on these insights, Edward Ou Jin Lee draws inspiration from Indigenous political theory to consider how LGBTQ migrants navigate their way across closed borders and contest state sovereignty through acts of refusal. Gada Mahrouse draws further attention to intersectionality, by considering convergences between critical refugee studies and critical disability studies, focusing in particular on the discursive function of the figure of the "super-refugee" and its impact in consolidating ideologies of exceptionalism. We conclude with Donald Goellnicht's reflections on the potentialities activated by cross-racial representation. Focusing on Dionne Brand's *What We All Long For,* Goellnicht meditates on how creative artists might write different stories that avoid the coercions of conventional refugee narratives, as compelled by refugee regimes and the nation-states that they serve.

The two sections of this volume develop a critical refugee studies framework to nuance "refugees" as agential subjects rather than simply passive objects of study; to consider the ways that "refuge" marks an intersectional process imbricated with the politics of race, gender, sexuality, and class; and to assess the varied forms with which the concepts of "refuge" and "refugee" are articulated. Through close examination of refugee movements, contexts, and subjectivities, *Refugee States* reveals how Canada has relied upon the rejection and inclusion of refugees as a means of statecraft – a process that the pandemic has further laid bare. The "critical" orientation of the project illuminates the historical, political, and cultural conditions that produce refugees, the narrative of humanitarian benevolence that persists nationally and internationally, and offers alternative modes of understanding refugee passages to and within Canada. Taken together, the chapters illuminate not just how the state influences displacement and resettlement but, more pivotally, how refugees themselves navigate their fraught passages.

NOTES

1 The US Supreme Court upheld this order in June 2018.
2 Justin Trudeau, "To those fleeing persecution, terror & war, Canadians will welcome you, regardless of your faith. Diversity is our strength #WelcomeToCanada." 28 January 2017, 3:20 pm. https://twitter.com/JustinTrudeau/status/825438460265762816.
3 Nelson, "The Canadian Narrative about Slavery Is Wrong"; Hendrick and Hendrick, *Black Refugees in Canada*; Squires, *Building Sanctuary*; Roberts, *Discrepant Parallels*; Kelley and Trebilcock, *The Making of the Mosaic*; Knowles, *Strangers at Our Gates*.
4 The case of the nine hundred Jewish refugees turned away in 1939, on the cusp of the Second World War, was the subject of one of the most influential books on refugee history in Canada. See Irving Abella and Harold Troper, *"None Is Too Many": Canada and the Jews of Europe, 1933–1938* (Toronto: Lester and Orpen Dennys, 1982).
5 That this report disregards the fact that 80 per cent of the current 70.8 million displaced people in the world live in neighbouring countries in the global South demonstrates how Canada continues to receive a disproportionate share of the humanitarian spotlight when the assistance it actually extends is meagre compared to less wealthy nations such as Lebanon, Jordan, and Turkey. See Jynnah Radford and Phillip Connor, "Canada Now Leads the World in Refugee Resettlement," *Pew Research Centre*, 19 June 2019. https://www.pewresearch.org/fact-tank/2019/06/19/canada

-now-leads-the-world-in-refugee-resettlement-surpassing-the-u-s/ Accessed 27 June 2019.
6 See the Government of Canada's website: https://www.canada.ca/en/immigration-refugees-citizenship/services/refugees/canada-role/timeline.html. For a helpful history of Canada's treatment of refugees, see Marlene Epp's *Refugees in Canada: A Brief History*.
7 Agamben, *The State of Exception*.
8 Nyers, *Rethinking Refugees*, xiii.
9 See, for example, Himani Bannerji, Glen Coulthard, Smaro Kamboureli, Eva Mackey, Arun Mukherjee, Rinaldo Walcott, Sunera Thobani, Asha Varadharajan, and other scholars, who have drawn attention to what Bannerji describes as "the dark side of the nation." These studies have drawn attention to the limits of the so-called cult of multiculturalism, as a form of governmentality that has managed racial difference and paid lip service to tolerance as a liberal ideal, without substantive consideration and redress of unequal structures that perpetuate injustice.
10 Giorgio Agamben, "We Refugees," trans. Michael Rocke, *Symposium* 49, no. 2 (1995): 114–19; Arendt, "We Refugees."
11 Espiritu, *Body Counts*, 2.
12 Um, *From the Land of Shadows*; Vinh Nguyen, "Refugeetude."
13 Black, "Fifty Years of Refugee Studies," 67.
14 Chimni, "The Birth of a 'Discipline.'"
15 Espiritu, *Body Counts*, 10.
16 Ibid., 10–11.
17 Malkki, "Refugees and Exile."
18 Agamben, "We Refugees."
19 Espiritu, *Body Counts*; Mimi Thi Nguyen, *The Gift of Freedom*; Schlund-Vials, *War, Genocide, Justice*; Viet Thanh Nguyen, "Refugee Memories and Asian American Critique"; Um, *From the Land of Shadows*; Tang, *Unsettled*.
20 Price, *Orienting Canada*. For a more general discussion on theories of empire in the Pacific, see Kuan-Hsing Chen, *Asia as Method: Toward Deimperialization*.
21 Razack, *Looking White People in the Eye*; Walia, *Undoing Border Imperialism*; Thobani, *Exalted Subjects*; Troeung, "Witnessing Cambodia's Disappeared"; Dawson, "'Treaty to Tell the Truth'"; Fortier, "No One Is Illegal"; Mountz, *Seeking Asylum*; Murray, *Real Queer?*.
22 Engler, *The Black Book of Canadian Foreign Policy*.
23 What makes Canada unique are precisely the conjunctions between British Empire and settler colonialism, which are continuous with, rather than separate from, humanitarian exceptionalism. Canada is unique insofar as, unlike settler colonial states such as Australia, which has a parallel history in relation to the British Empire, it actively *defines itself* as tolerant and

would not these days, according to government officials, condone the extreme patriotic protectionism of white nationalism.
24 For an important discussion of the topic of refugees and Indigeneity, see Coleman et al., *Countering Displacements*.
25 Coulthard, *Red Skin, White Masks*, 40–2.
26 Byrd, *The Transit of Empire*; Thobani, *Exalted Subjects*; Lai, *Slanting I, Imagining We*; Phung, "Are People of Colour Settlers Too?"
27 Gorman, *Imperial Citizenship*. See also Sukanya Banerjee, *Becoming Imperial Citizens: Indians in the Late-Victorian Empire* (Durham, NC: Duke University Press, 2010); Gabrielle Moser, "Photographing Imperial Citizenship: The Colonial Office Visual Instruction Committee's Lantern Slides, 1900–1945," *Journal of Visual Culture* 16, no. 2 (2017): 190–224.
28 Mongia, "Race, Nationality, Mobility."
29 Coleman, "Indigenous Place and Diaspora Space," 73.
30 Backhouse, *Colour-Coded*; Abu-Laban, "Keeping 'Em Out."
31 Whitaker, *Cold War Canada*; Robert Teigrob, *Warming Up to the Cold War*.

REFERENCES

Abu-Laban, Yasmeen. "Keeping 'Em Out: Gender, Race and Class Biases in Canadian Immigration Policy." In *Painting the Maple: Essays on Race, Gender, and the Construction of Canada*, 69–82. Vancouver: University of British Columbia Press, 1998.
Agamben, Giorgio. *The State of Exception*. Translated by Kevin Attell. Chicago: University of Chicago Press, 2005.
Arendt, Hannah. "We Refugees." In *Altogether Elsewhere: Writers on Exile*. Edited by Marc Robinson, 110–19. Boston: Faber and Faber, 1994.
Backhouse, Constance. *Colour-Coded: A Legal History of Racism in Canada, 1900–1950*. Toronto: University of Toronto Press, 1999.
Black, Richard. "Fifty Years of Refugee Studies: From Theory to Policy." *International Migration Review* 35, no. 1 (2006): 51–78.
Byrd, Jodi. *The Transit of Empire: Indigenous Critiques of Colonialism*. Minneapolis: University of Minnesota Press, 2011.
Chimni, B.S. "The Birth of a 'Discipline': From Refugee to Forced Migration Studies." *Journal of Refugee Studies* 22, no. 1 (2009): 11–29.
Coleman, Daniel. "Indigenous Place and Diaspora Space: Of Literalism and Abstraction." *Settler Colonial Studies* 6, no. 1 (2016): 61–76.
Coleman, Daniel, Erin Goheen Glanville, Wafaa Hasan, and Agnes Kramer-Hamstra, eds. *Countering Displacements: The Creativity and Resilience of Indigenous and Refugee-ed Peoples*. Edmonton: University of Alberta Press, 2012.
Coulthard, Glen. *Red Skin, White Masks: Rejecting the Colonial Politics of Recognition*. Minneapolis: University of Minnesota Press, 2014.

Dawson, Carrie. "'Treaty to Tell the Truth': The Anti-Confessional Impulse in Canadian Refugee Writing." *Canadian Literature* (2017): 14–31.

Engler, Yves. *The Black Book of Canadian Foreign Policy*. Halifax: Fernwood Publishing, 2009.

Espiritu, Yến Lê. *Body Counts: The Vietnam War and Militarized Refugees*. Oakland: University of California Press, 2014.

Fortier, Craig. "No One Is Illegal: Movements in Canada and the Negotiation of Counter-National and Anti-Colonial Struggles from within the Nation-State." In *Producing and Negotiating Non-Citizenship: Precarious Legal Status in Canada*. Edited by L. Goldring and P. Landolt, 274–90. Toronto: University of Toronto Press, 2013.

Gorman, Daniel. *Imperial Citizenship: Empire and the Question of Belonging*. Manchester: Manchester University Press, 2007.

Hendrick, George, and Willene Hendrick. *Black Refugees in Canada: Accounts of Escape during the Era of Slavery*. Jefferson, NC: McFarland Publishing, 2010.

Kelley, Ninette, and M.J. Trebilcock. *The Making of the Mosaic: A History of Canadian Immigration Policy*. Toronto: University of Toronto Press, 1998.

Knowles, Valerie. *Strangers at Our Gates: Canadian Immigration and Immigration Policy, 1540–2015*. Toronto: Dundurn, 2016.

Lai, Larissa. *Slanting I, Imagining We: Asian Canadian Literary Production in the 1980s and 1990s*. Waterloo: Wilfrid Laurier University Press, 2014.

Malkki, Liisa H. "Refugees and Exile: From 'Refugee Studies' to the National Order of Things." *Annual Review of Anthropology* 24 (1995): 495–523.

Mongia, Radhika. "Race, Nationality, Mobility: A History of the Passport." *Public Culture* 11, no. 3 (1999): 527–55.

Mountz, Alison. *Seeking Asylum: Human Smuggling and Bureaucracy at the Border*. Minneapolis: University of Minnesota Press, 2010.

Murray, David A.B. *Real Queer?: Sexual Orientation and Gender Identity Refugees in the Canadian Refugee Apparatus*. Lanham, MD: Rowman and Littlefield, 2015.

Nelson, Charmaine. "The Canadian Narrative about Slavery Is Wrong." *Walrus* (2017). https://thewalrus.ca/the-canadian-narrative-about-slavery-is-wrong/.

Nguyen, Mimi Thi. *The Gift of Freedom: War, Debt, and Other Refugee Passages*. Durham, NC: Duke University Press, 2012.

Nguyen, Viet Thanh. "Refugee Memories and Asian American Critique." *Positions: east asia critique* 20, no. 3 (2012): 911–42.

Nguyen, Vinh. "Refugeetude: When Does a Refugee Stop Being a Refugee?" *Social Text* 37, no. 2 (2019): 109–31.

Nyers, Peter. *Rethinking Refugees: Beyond States of Emergency*. London and New York: Routledge, 2006.

Phung, Malissa. "Are People of Colour Settlers Too?" In *Cultivating Canada: Reconciliation through the Lens of Cultural Diversity*. Edited by Ashok Mathur,

Jonathan Dewar, and Mike DeGagné, 289–97. Ottawa: Aboriginal Healing Foundation, 2013.

Price, John. *Orienting Canada: Race, Empire and the Transpacific*. Vancouver: University of British Columbia Press, 2011.

Razack, Sherene. *Looking White People in the Eye*. Toronto: University of Toronto Press, 1998.

Roberts, Gillian. *Discrepant Parallels: Cultural Implications of the Canada-US Border*. Montreal and Kingston: McGill-Queen's University Press, 2015.

Schlund-Vials, Cathy J. *War, Genocide, Justice: Cambodian American Memory Work*. Minneapolis: University of Minnesota Press, 2012.

Squires, Jessica. *Building Sanctuary: The Movement to Support Vietnam War Resisters*. Vancouver: University of British Columbia Press, 2014.

Tang, Eric. *Unsettled: Cambodian Refugees in the NYC Hyperghetto*. Philadelphia: Temple University Press, 2015.

Teigrob, Robert. *Warming Up to the Cold War: Canada and the United States' Coalition of the Willing, from Hiroshima to Korea*. Toronto: University of Toronto Press, 2009.

Thobani, Sunera. *Exalted Subjects: Studies in the Making of Race and Nation in Canada*. Toronto: University of Toronto Press, 2007.

Troeung, Y-Dang. "Witnessing Cambodia's Disappeared." *University of Toronto Quarterly* 82, no. 2 (2013): 150–67.

Um, Khatharya. *From the Land of Shadows: War, Revolution, and the Making of the Cambodian Diaspora*. New York: New York University Press, 2015.

Walia, Harsha. *Undoing Border Imperialism*. Oakland: AK Press, 2013.

Whitaker, Reginald. *Cold War Canada: The Making of a National Insecurity State, 1945–1957*. Toronto: University of Toronto Press, 1994.

PART ONE

HISTORICIZATION

1 Shifting Grounds of Asylum in Canadian Public Discourse and Policy

JOHANNA REYNOLDS AND JENNIFER HYNDMAN

Introduction

Public discourse about refugees is made, remade, and unmade by elected officials who are both political leaders and policy makers, civil servants, media organizations, and a range of civil society actors. It both responds to events or "crises" and shapes the conditions of possibility for policy making and legislation by governments. As the introductory chapter has argued, Canada has a record of enduring humanitarian practices, but also an underbelly of racialized exclusion, settler colonial violence, and selective, prejudicial policies in relation to newcomers. In this chapter, we seek to trace the ways in which Canada's humanitarian reputation is destabilized by political leaders through quotidian tactical tropes, like the "bogus refugee" – throwing into question the fundamental legitimacy of asylum seekers making claims for protection in the country.

The 1999 boat arrivals off Canada's West Coast created a political hot potato for the Liberal government of the day, especially given the clear involvement of smugglers. In the Canadian context, refugees and asylum seekers in Canada have faced a wide range of responses to and public debate about their plight – from highly positive to acutely negative. Such discourse is critical to the making and passage of law and the opening of political and social space in Canada for refugees, asylum seekers, and other migrants in precarious situations. We also aim, then, to trace contemporary Canadian refugee policies and practices in relation to the denigrated constructions of the "refugee" to see what effects, if any, they might have on displaced people themselves.

This chapter begins with an overview of the current context of asylum and refugee resettlement in Canada, followed by an analysis of original research on the rise of the "bogus refugee" and "queue jumper" using a content analysis of Canadian newspapers, and a subsequent discourse analysis of salient terms that emerge. We juxtapose the rise of anti-refugee rhetoric with the introduction of draconian laws against "irregular arrivals," such as asylum seekers who arrive by boat, who are deemed "designated foreign nationals" or DFNs.

What are the conditions for creating and implementing more draconian laws and regulations to exclude asylum seekers or select particular groups of refugees? We turn to a short section that examines the importance of paying attention to what might seem like banal bureaucracy, but instead represents the prioritizing of certain regions of the world and nationalities over others. Drawing on the anti-racist theory of scholars like Radhika Mongia and Etienne Balibar,[1] we expose more ways in which racist policy enacts exclusions that are highly racialized, both in the context of refugee resettlement and through the expansion of the Canadian Temporary Resident Biometrics Program (TRBP). Just as critical refugee studies must examine how humanitarian exceptionalism acquires potency by amplifying the exception as the norm, as Vinh Nguyen and Thy Phu show in the Introduction, research in this field must also look at the messaging of political leaders and the media that reiterate their sound bites. One must pay attention to the prosaic, even banal bureaucratic targets and tables that embody plans to include newcomers but also hide racialized exclusions. In short, we analyse the implications of discourse and "policy crit" – a play on "lit crit" – for critical refugee studies.

Setting the Scene: Canada the Good, Bad, and Ugly

In a global context, Canada is historically and somewhat paradoxically both a welcoming country for resettled refugees chosen abroad by the government and a relatively exclusionary place for asylum seekers who arrive on their own, with some exceptions. One cannot discuss displacement or exclusion in Canada without acknowledging the cultural genocide of Indigenous peoples[2] – the legacies of which are discussed by Jennifer Adese and Malissa Phung in their chapter for this volume – and exclusionary immigration policies including, but not limited to, the 1923 Chinese Exclusion Act, the internment of Japanese Canadians during the Second World War, and the exclusion of Jews who tried to land in Canada during this same period.[3] Despite a progressive metanarrative of Canada's immigration history, and tacit celebration of the settler state, these instances reveal what Himani Bannerji calls the "dark side[s] of the nation."[4]

While resettled refugees have often been represented by the government and media as *good* refugees, that is, the deserving ones who wait in camps to be resettled, asylum seekers (also known as refugee claimants), by contrast, arrive spontaneously at Canadian ports of entry and have been cast as threats or fraudsters.[5] Recent legislation and changes to the regulations introduced in 2010 and 2012 embed such assumptions in their provisions and serve to securitize refugees as potential threats, a point to which we return in the following section.

Canada has been praised for its commitment to refugees, primarily based on its role as a resettlement country.[6] The latest Global Trends report produced by the United Nations High Commissioner for Refugees (UNHCR) confirms that Canada resettled the largest number of refugees worldwide in 2018.[7] Resettlement, however, is a completely discretionary act and form of protection, one that can wax and wane in relation to a government's political or ideological positions.[8] Moreover, the vast majority of resettled refugees come from a small number of countries. By contrast, asylum seekers have rights and entitlements codified under the 1951 Convention Relating to the Status of Refugees and its 1967 Protocol, as well as protection against return if torture or other cruel and unusual punishment is probable. More importantly, these protections are incorporated into the law and regulations of the Immigration and Refugee Protection Act (IRPA), as Canadian law. Despite these legal protections, asylum seekers are continuously framed by both media and public discourse as "jumping the queue," a term that, as we explain in greater detail shortly, has no legal meaning.

While the way that resettled refugees are selected abroad and brought to Canada is very planned and predictable, the arrival of asylum seekers, refugee claimants, and other unexpected migrants is not. Many migrants will utilize the asylum seekers' pathway, since it is the only way to legally enter the country without a visa and/or passport. These latter groups are often called "spontaneous arrivals," a term that suggests that they were not invited, are not welcome, and may not be as legitimate. And yet asylum seekers are protected by far more legislation than resettled refugees. They are commonly referred to as "irregular border crossers," and much media attention has focused on the current government's curated Tweets and photographs exhibiting Canada's benevolent nature and generosity towards asylum seekers at the border, in contrast with the behaviour of the United States. The choice of language, labels, and categories for those seeking protection, as other authors show (Lee, this volume; Nyers, this volume),[9] is critical in constructing the legitimacy of the person entering Canada. It is also vital to reinforcing an acceptable "victim" narrative: as Jan van Dijk reminds us, we lose empathy for victims when they act in "un-victim-like" ways.[10] Unlike the *good* refugees waiting to be resettled, border crossers flip the passive script. We are not suggesting that refugees in camps are passive or without agency, but rather that arrival at the border challenges the dominant narrative that tells the story of seeking refuge through a saviour-victim lens, one that reinforces particular expectations of how refugees must act. At the same time, fear and "crisis" narratives abound, again "testing" the perceived benevolent nature of the Canadian state.

Whatever the word choice, language is instrumental in shaping public discourse about people on the move in need of protection. In turn, negative public opinion, or at least wavering support for refugees, can be exploited with the introduction of more exclusionary policies.

While distinctions between asylum seekers and refugees can be used for political gain and exclusionary policies, so too is the distinction made between "migrants" and "refugees": "Migrants hope for honeypots; refugees need havens" is one such an example.[11] Such a facile and insulting binary insinuates that migrants and refugees are discrete groups of people that never overlap. This binary suggests that migrants are simply shopping for a better life in one of the world's wealthy countries, while refugees legitimately seek protection in "haven" states – large refugee-receiving countries in the global South. Much more has been written about the stakes of using the "migrant" versus the "refugee" label (see, for example, Roger Zetter and Heaven Crawley).[12] In 2015, at the height of the war in Syria and increased migration across the Mediterranean to Europe, the choice of terminology also became a political debate by major news outlets, with Al Jazeera refusing to use "migrant" because of the highly charged, state-centric, and inaccurate assumptions of the catch-all term in reference to the Mediterranean boat arrivals, while Western media used it liberally.[13] The stakes are high in defining who *should* be protected, and who should not.

As Audrey Macklin contends, through a blurring of categories, Canada has witnessed the "discursive disappearance" of potential refugees through such policies.[14] The Safe Third Country Agreement (STCA) between the United States and Canada is one example of such policy. This Agreement requires individuals seeking refugee status to make their claim in the first "safe" country they arrive in, to avoid what some have called "asylum shopping" between these two countries; asylum seekers are the main subjects of this disappearing act.[15] Other specific policies and legislation introduced in 2010 and 2012, after the rise of the "bogus refugee" in public discourse,[16] contributed to the externalization of asylum by intercepting would-be asylum seekers before they could land on Canadian soil. Specifically, biometric visas, which use digital fingerprints in all visa applications, are now required for all visitors from countries where visas are required as of December 2018. Such visas actively work to keep people out.

At the beginning of 2020, more people were displaced from their homes on a global scale than at any other time since the Second World War. An estimated 26 million people were refugees, at least two-thirds of them in conditions of extended exile for more than five years.[17] Those in *protracted refugee situations* (PRS) – a term designated by the UNHCR – include Afghans, Somalis, Sudanese, South Sudanese, and Syrians who fall under the auspices of UNHCR. Some 5 million Palestinians who have been displaced for more than two-thirds of a century have faced protracted displacement for even longer.[18] The government of Canada has been an advocate for solutions to address the problem of protracted displacement: "[t]he consequences of having so many human beings in a static state include wasted lives, squandered resources and increased threats to security."[19] While resettlement is not a comprehensive response for these displaced groups, it does provide one permanent pathway to protection for some. In 2017, however, only 102,800 refugees were referred for resettlement, a 54 per cent decline over the previous year, owing to a steep drop in the resettlement spaces available; the dramatic decline occurred primarily in the United States under President Trump.[20] In 2018, the US announced that it would cap refugee resettlement at 30,000, and most observers note that federal funding is likely to support not more than 20,000 refugees.[21] Later this target fell to a mere 15,000 refugees in the US. Canada became the lead resettlement country globally in 2018 and again in 2019, albeit with only 30,100 people coming to Canada in 2019.[22] In February 2021, President Biden announced a dramatic increase in the US resettlement target: 125,000 refugees in the first year of his presidency.[23] This backdrop is important to appreciate the rise in asylum seekers worldwide, and the high premium on the few discretionary resettlement spaces that remain.

Refugees Resettled to Canada

Canada has a relatively strong record of refugee resettlement since the Second World War, despite, as noted above, the egregious exclusions, internments, and refusals in the early part of the twentieth century. In 1956, more than 100,000 Hungarians fleeing communist rule were welcomed in Canada.[24] Its first large-scale group processing occurred in the late 1970s as part of the Comprehensive Plan of Action in Vietnam,

Laos, and Cambodia.[25] At that time, a serendipitous alignment of government policy, public opinion, and citizens' action brought some 74,000 refugees to Canada in a five-year period from those countries. Many of these refugees were assisted through private sponsorship.[26] The 1976 Immigration Act took full effect in 1978 and founded the concept of *designated class*.[27] This new legal structure added capacity for resettling refugees beyond the 1951 Convention's refugee definition by affirming that "in accordance with Canada's humanitarian tradition ... any Convention refugee or any person who is a member of a class designated by the Governor in Council as a class" could be eligible for resettlement.[28] In 1978, the Governor in Council adopted the Indochinese Designated Class Regulation.[29] Key to the success of this massive resettlement program was the fortunate alignment of Cold War geopolitics, Canadian public opinion (as shaped by the politicized media coverage of the conflict in Southeast Asia), and government policy.[30]

This remarkable show of solidarity was largely predicated on superpower alliances and a geopolitical landscape in which refugees were evidence of (capitalist) ideological superiority over the (communist) enemy. And yet, even during this period of extraordinary generosity, Canada began to exclude asylum seekers if they did not fit this superpower political logic. For example, in 1979, Canada imposed visas on people leaving Chile, many of whom were fleeing Pinochet's violent military regime, to which human rights atrocities were widely attributed and documented. Today, these tenacious Cold War politics have faded, and a more defensive posturing between the wealthier, global North and the global South characterizes refugee geopolitics.

Whereas refugees once provided proof of Canada's ideological superiority in a Cold War context, in the current context, concerns about terrorism, national security, and the sustainability of the welfare state prevail. The conflation of terrorist and refugee is a convenient way to securitize and problematize the refugee. By "securitize," we mean the process that deems refugees and asylum seekers as threats, declares a crisis of national security, and then addresses these threats with extraordinary measures.[31] Fear is a powerful emotion and political resource; state production of such anxiety can allow for extraordinary measures to prevent, for example, perceived invasions of home. Such fear is used to underwrite the allocation of resources to fortify particular regions and manage risk. Three main elements are associated with securitization: an entity, such as a government or sovereign, which makes the securitizing statement or assertion of threat; a referent object, normally the people or place being threatened and needing protection; and an audience, who is the target of the securitization act and who must be persuaded to accept the issue or security threat as genuine.[32] In the context of the securitization of immigration and asylum, Jeff Huysmans writes about the ways in which security threats are created for an insecure public that unites around eliminating the threat, in this case by excluding migrants/asylum seekers. Canada had largely sealed its own borders against asylum seekers to exclude them from its territory and in so doing manage the perceived risk they pose. Pre-emptive risk management approaches began in earnest after the attacks of 9/11. After the events of 11 September 2001, foreigners – including refugees – became the focus of heightened security screening and measures in both the US and Canada. Politicians and media in the US characterized Canada as the weak link in terms of security, and the US government convened meetings with its Canadian counterpart to discuss elements of the Smart Border Accord that would serve to enhance a continental perimeter around both countries to keep the war on terror out.

Preclusion was ushered in by Canada's Multiple Borders Strategy, an approach espoused by the Canadian Border Services Agency (CBSA), a Canadian corollary to the Department of Homeland Security in the US, which were both inventions of the post-9/11 period.[33] The Multiple Borders Strategy conceives of the border not merely as a territorial boundary or geopolitical line between the US and Canada. Rather, as the CBSA clarifies,

> [t]he strategy strives to "push the border out" so that people posing a risk to Canada's security and prosperity are identified as far away from the actual border as possible, ideally before a person departs their country of origin. Admissibility screening occurs prior to the arrival of an individual in Canada or after they have entered the country in order to ensure that those who are inadmissible do not enter or cannot remain in Canada.[34]

The border is reconceived as any point at which the identity of the traveller can be verified.[35] Pre-emptive screening by airline liaison officers – through visa and biometric requirements – potentially *precludes* a lot of people from coming to Canada, especially from refugee-producing countries.

Governments in the global North learn migration management strategies from one another and regularly copy and transfer pre-emptive policies designed to restrict access to sovereign territory.[36] Access to Canadian territory is highly managed. Canada's legal obligations under the 1951 Convention Relating to Refugees and the 1967 Protocol state that asylum seekers who arrive on sovereign Canadian territory have the right to seek asylum. Yet if they cannot arrive on Canadian territory, they cannot seek asylum. The preferred refugees, therefore, are the ones who can be screened, selected, and welcomed in an orderly fashion. Wars, human rights atrocities, and related human displacement, however, are not so predictable.

The Rise of the "Bogus Refugee": A Content and Discourse Analysis

The war in Syria, beginning in 2011, has generated "one of the biggest refugee and displacement crisis of our time," according to the UN High Commissioner for Refugees, Filippo Grandi, with more than 11 million forced to flee their homes.[37] The Canadian response to the Syrian "refugee crisis"[38] was arguably prompted in part by the death of a Syrian boy, Aylan Kurdi, in September 2015, which became an iconic representation of the "crisis" and deaths in the Mediterranean. The Canadian public, along with Justin Trudeau's newly elected government, responded favourably to large-scale resettlement. In October 2015, the Liberal government pledged to resettle 25,000 Syrian refugees, both government-assisted and privately sponsored, by December 2015, a deadline that was extended to and met by February 2016. An additional 25,000 government-assisted Syrian refugees were scheduled to arrive by the end of 2016. As of August 2018, more than 56,000 Syrians had arrived in Canada, either as government-assisted refugees (GARs), privately sponsored refugees (PSRs), or blended visa office-referred refugees (BVORs).[39] More than 40 per cent were privately sponsored by groups of Canadian residents, some through faith-based organizations and others through sponsorship groups formed in workplace, school, and other civil society sites.[40] While the government's increased resettlement target was greeted positively by refugee advocates, it was clear that the same treatment would not be extended to other regions in Africa, where two-thirds of the world's refugees wait in limbo, as the Canadian Council for Refugees argues in a public statement.[41] We return to the issue of prioritizing certain regions and nationalities for resettlement in the final section of this chapter.

Yet before the advent of Operation Syrian Refugees in 2015, another government framed asylum seekers and refugees in a much different light. An analysis of newspaper content from 1996 to 2004 traces the frequency and use of the terms "bogus" and "queue jumper" in Canadian newsprint media. Use of these terms spiked with the Chinese boat arrivals of 1999, when "bogus refugee" and "queue jumper" emerged in public discourse as terms for asylum seekers.[42]

The term "bogus refugee" appeared, and an anti-asylum seeker discourse emerged quickly, evident in newspaper cartoons, political debate, and talk radio. The Canadian state's response to this "crisis," not to mention its manufacturing, is telling. Notably, the invocation of "snakeheads" was a way that government vilified human smugglers from China. Moreover, the detention of asylum seekers in remote locations in British Columbia was used to prevent their disappearance – and made legal representation difficult, given the geography. While a small number of these asylum seekers were granted refugee status, the vast majority were not, and, unless they were detained, they did not stay in Canada long to find out their fate at the Immigration and Refugee Board. Reporters found evidence that most of these Fujianese people were destined for New York City.[43] The federal government immediately sought to prevent similar incidents.

No more boats landed until a decade later, when the *Ocean Lady* reached Canada's west coast on 17 October 2009. It carried 75 Sri Lankan Tamil men plus one minor, all of whom sought asylum upon arrival after first being arrested, jailed, and interrogated.[44] In August 2010, after three months at sea, the MV *Sun Sea* arrived on the same stretch of Canadian coast, this time carrying 492 Sri Lankan Tamil men, women, and children.[45] On 13 August 2010, the day after the ship was boarded by the Canadian authorities but before it even docked, then-Public Safety Minister Vic Toews said that those on board would be investigated to determine who among them were "human smugglers or terrorists."[46] Toews went on to say that Canada has been "very welcoming" of refugees, but that the government "must ensure that our refugee system is not hijacked by criminals or terrorists." In these ways, aspersions were cast on the people on these ships before they ever arrived.[47]

On 1 January 2017, unofficial data from the Immigration and Refugee Board showed that 61 of 76 claims had been finalized in relation to the *Ocean Lady*, with 36 positive and 21 negative decisions made. A lawyer shared unofficial Refugee Protection Division data from the Immigration and Refugee Board with us regarding the *Sun Sea* as of February 2019. Thirteen cases remained pending, but of the 479 claims finalized, 335 people had positive decisions and 107 had negatives ones (a 70 per cent recognition rate). The *Sun Sea* carried 380 men, 63 women, and 49 minors, whereas the *Ocean Lady* transported 75 men and 1 minor on board. This appears to have mattered. In 2018, for asylum cases from Sri Lanka heard in the new system (after the 2010 and 2012 changes noted above), the recognition rate was 71.7 per cent overall. Positive decisions for Sri Lankan asylum seekers on the *Sun Sea* are commensurate with the overall decision rate in 2018, but the men on the *Ocean Lady* faced a much lower acceptance rate: less than 50 per cent.

On more than one occasion after their arrival, Public Safety Minister Toews called the Tamil asylum seekers from Sri Lanka "queue jumpers."[48] As lawyers and refugee advocates note, "queue jumping" is an incorrect term and has no meaning in refugee law. There is no sequential order required in making a refugee claim. Indeed, there is no queue, for under Canadian and international law a person is entitled to cross the border without authorization and seek asylum. The suggestion that asylum seekers engage in illegal activity by securing irregular access (i.e., via *smuggling*) to sovereign Canadian territory for the purpose of claiming asylum is also spurious. The 1951 Convention Relating to Refugees is clear on this point, stating in Article 31, section 1 that

> [t]he Contracting States shall not impose penalties, on account of their illegal entry or presence, on refugees who, coming directly from a territory where their life or freedom was threatened in the sense of article 1, enter or are present in their territory without authorization, provided they present themselves without delay to the authorities and show good cause for their illegal entry or presence.

Through the Canadian government's specific classification of designated foreign nationals, future asylum seekers arriving on ships like the *Sun Sea* or *Ocean Lady* could be considered security risks by the minister and be declared "irregular." This provision creates uneven access to refugee protection for those who arrive by boat if they are designated as *irregular arrivals*.[49] Even if claimants are found to be asylum seekers who are bona fide refugees, they will be subject to mandatory detention, denied permanent residence for five years, and separated from family members for at least five years, if not more, should they decide to remain in Canada.

In 2010, Canada passed new legislation affecting refugees, specifically the Balanced Refugee Reform Act (BRRA), which granted the government the authority to identify designated countries of origin (DCO). These are defined as "countries that do not normally produce refugees, but do respect human rights and offer state protection."[50] Subsequent legislation passed in 2012, the Protecting Canada's Immigration System Act, allowed the minister of citizenship and immigration the power to choose which countries are safe without the advice of an expert committee, making the system more vulnerable to political interests, and to fast-track the timelines for cases from these designated countries.[51]

Shifting Grounds of Asylum   33

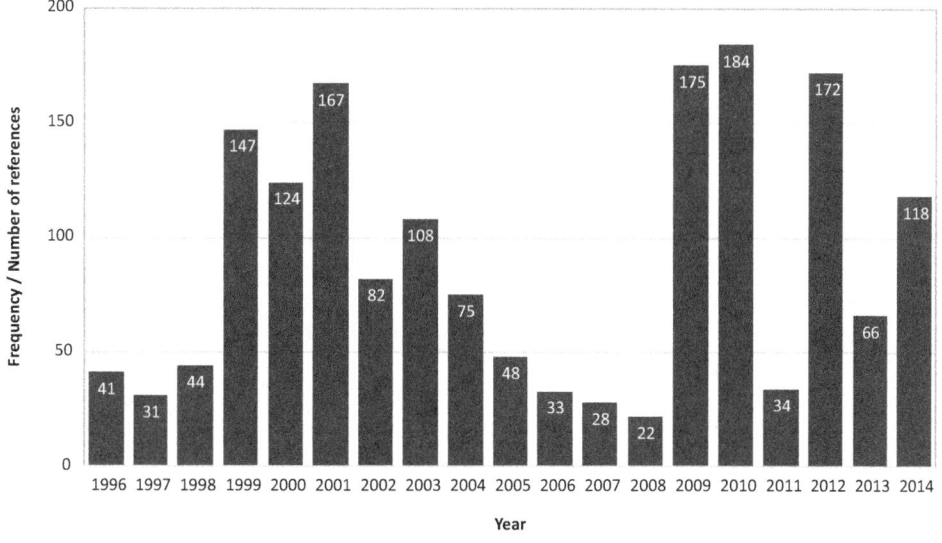

Figure 1.1. Newsprint references to "bogus" and refugee (per year)

In figure 1.1, we outline our findings that illustrate how refugees were represented during this period. Using the Canadian Newsstand database (which comprises all major Canadian newspapers),[52] we searched each category in relation to the word *refugee* and citation of the Immigration and Refugee Protection Act (IRPA). IRPA is the main document and legal framework outlining refugee and immigration policy in Canada; it received royal assent on 1 November 2001 but came into force 28 June 2002, replacing the Immigration Act of 1976. One of the key motivations of this search is to identify patterns of representing refugees as bogus or as queue jumpers ultimately, which may lead to their exclusion. This search used a five-year window to measure any shifts in the usage of these concepts post-IRPA. To this end, the search was limited to the date range of 1996–2014.

For the key words "bogus" and "refugee," there were 1,697 results between 1 January 1996 and 31 December 2014 (see figure 1.1). The terms were searched anywhere in text. Although there are a number of references to bogus refugees between 1999 and 2001, the highest frequency is in 2010 (184 references), with 2009 and 2012 following closely behind (175 and 172 references respectively). A subsequent search of "bogus," "refugee," and "Jason Kenney" during the same time period results in 455, with the largest grouping of references during the same three years: 115 references in 2009; 122 references in 2010; and 133 references in 2012. We included former citizenship and immigration minister Kenney in the search because of his frequent use of these terms, which serve to securitize asylum seekers and refugees.[53]

In order to determine how often the term "bogus" has been referenced and whether this has changed over time, we subsequently searched for the terms "Jason Kenney" and "bogus," this time with *no* date limitations, which yielded 601 results (searched anywhere in text). As it turns out, "bogus" was used extensively by Jason Kenney well before the "bogus refugee" term was coined, just as "bogus refugee" was used before Jason Kenney became minister of citizenship and immigration in 2008.

The first newspaper reference to the term "bogus" by Jason Kenney is 1998, during his time as Calgary Southeast Reform MP and Reform Party tax critic. The first reference to "bogus refugees" appears in 1999, in a discussion of immigration reforms calling for "rapid deportation of bogus refugees, while also urging the government to provide assistance to legitimate refugees."[54] References remain few until almost a decade later, when Kenney became minister of citizenship and immigration. Once again, the "bogus" rhetoric reaches three significant spikes in three separate years, 2009, 2010, and 2012, corresponding to the boat arrivals of the *Ocean Lady* and *Sun Sea* in 2009 and 2010. According to Cynthia Levine-Raskin, "Kenney first used the term 'bogus' in 2009 to describe Roma claimants and has favoured it ever since."[55] Between 2000 and 2008, there are a few dozen references to "bogus," but Kenney's dramatic increase in the use of the term occurs between 2009 and 2012, with 130 results in 2009, 128 in 2010, and 163 in 2012 (there is a drop in 2011 to 27 results). Kenney was elected premier of Alberta in 2019; his discursive strategies should be tracked in order to analyse any new politicized phrases he has adopted.

Perhaps unsurprisingly, each of these spikes in frequency of the term "bogus" corresponds with the introduction of new legislation and significant political shifts in refugee and immigration policy in Canada, which will be discussed in more detail below. We cannot ignore the significance of the increase in frequency in each of these key moments, and their subsequent public repetition by news media. The reiteration of the idea of fraudulent refugees produces a calculated, discursive shift that reinforces a highly problematic binary of the "bad" or "undeserving" refugee in contrast to the passive, resettled "good" or "deserving" refugee. A qualitative analysis examines these moments more closely in order to understand the deep political consequences for the Canadian humanitarian landscape.

What is striking is not only the frequency of the use of the term but also the expansive use of "bogus" in relation to a number of different aspects of refugee and immigration policy. Key references made by Jason Kenney to "bogus" include bogus refugee claimants (2009); bogus asylum seekers (2009); bogus immigration consultants (2009); temporary workers with bogus job offers (2009); bogus certificates (2010); bogus travel documents (2010); bogus marriages (2011); bogus stories about persecution (2011); bogus documents for foreign students (2012); bogus claimants from safe countries (2012); bogus citizenship applications (2012); bogus Roma refugees (2013); bogus travel documents for birth tourists (2013). The frequency of the use of the term "bogus" coincides with the introduction of restrictive policy changes, including the Balanced Refugee Reform Act (2010) and Protecting Canada's Immigration System Act (2012). By tracing the use of discourse in media and as emphasized by the minister of immigration and citizenship, we can clearly see how the discourse of "bogus" was multifaceted, shaping the political valence of people, programs, and places. For example, in 2009, references to "bogus asylum seekers" or "bogus refugee claimants" were made about both Roma and Mexican claimants, at the same time that visa restrictions were placed on these two groups of people. In 2010, a crackdown on human smuggling and "bogus claims" was part of the rationale behind implementing designated countries of origin (DCOs), also known as safe countries, since DCOs are seen to be countries that do not typically produce refugees. In 2012, Canada implemented new policy to crack down on "bogus" or fraudulent marriages, which also led to conditional permanent residence.[56] In short, the coincidence of "bogus" declarations about immigrants and refugee claimants and punitive measures to curb fraudulent behaviour is shown here to be systematic. Whether any proof that an asylum seeker's or refugee's "bogus" status has been verified appears irrelevant. The politicization is in the speech act itself.[57]

The "Queue Jumper" Claim

A similar search for "queue jumper" and "refugee" in the Canadian Newsstand Dailies database reveals fewer references, with a total of 331 results (see figure 1.2). Between 1996 and 2014, references to refugees as queue jumpers remain low until a sudden spike in 1999 with 72 references. A second spike occurs a decade later in 2010, with 68 references. Both spikes correspond to dates of boat arrivals off Canada's West Coast.

Because of Canada's geographically remote location, its "cold ocean geography," boat arrivals have been far less frequent than on the shores

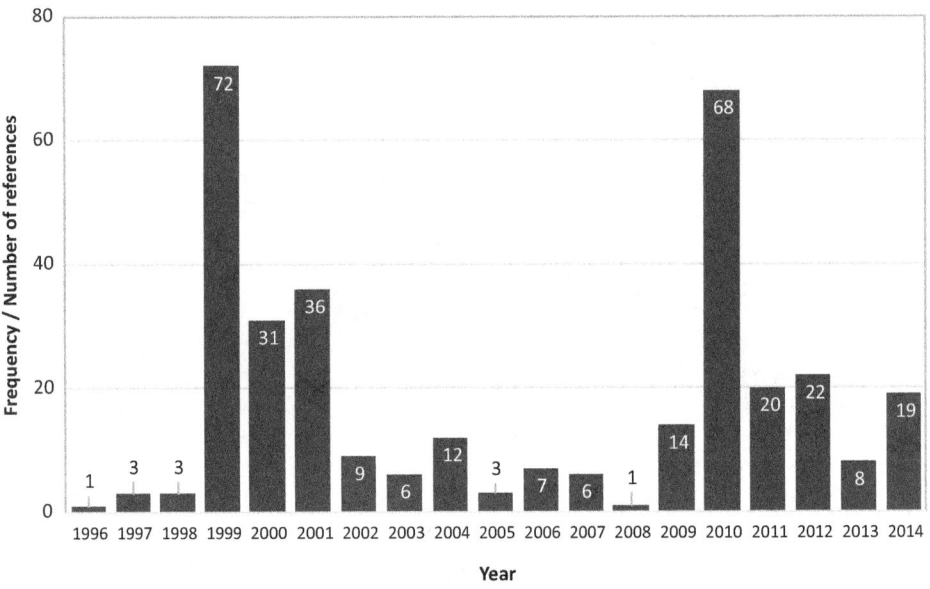

Figure 1.2. Newsprint references to "queue jumper" and "refugee" (per year)

of Europe, for example. But the references to "queue jumpers" coincide with three boat arrivals in 2009 and 2010 at our shores, "irregular arrivals" which caused mass hysteria and anti-immigrant backlash.[58] As noted, in 1999, four ships carrying almost 600 people from Fujian Province in China arrived on the coast of British Columbia. In 2009, 76 Sri Lankans were intercepted on the *Ocean Lady*, and in 2010, 492 Sri Lankan Tamils on the *Sun Sea*, also on the coast of British Columbia. There have been no "irregular arrivals" by ship since the new legislation came into effect. However, if one were to be designated an "irregular arrival" and therefore a Designated Foreign Nationals (DFN) at the discretion of the minister of public safety, one would be put in mandatory detention and denied permanent residence for five years, even if one's refugee claim was granted a positive decision. In 2015, Minister Kenney went on record as saying that "an aggressive posture was needed to prevent future boatloads of asylum seekers from targeting our shores."[59]

Denigrating discourse related to refugees and asylum seekers in public media has coincided with more restrictive policy changes. To what extent has this shift shaped the Canadian context of refugee reception? Our quantitative analysis indicates clear correlations between restrictive policy changes and an increase in the use of negative words describing refugees as "bogus" or "queue jumpers." Negative public opinion of refugees and asylum seekers can create political space and public consent to introduce more draconian laws and regulations to prevent them from arriving, a process called securitization. Some refugee claimants (aka asylum seekers) are produced as "irregular arrivals" with fewer prospects for protection. In contrast, resettled refugees chosen by Canadian visa officers abroad on a discretionary basis are touted as deserving, law-abiding, and orderly, waiting until they are called for settlement in Canada.[60]

Two clusters of boat arrivals under two governments of different political stripes over the last twenty years have led to a litany of legislation and policy initiatives to "crack down" on human smuggling and uninvited asylum seekers. While not direct responses, there are links and correspondences between these events. As far as we could trace, the construction of the "bogus refugee" made its debut in 1999 when four boatloads of asylum seekers arrived in British Columbia from China. The attacks of 11 September 2001 heightened national insecurity everywhere. Tamil asylum seekers arriving by boat in 2009 and 2010 were framed by politicians and media reports as being terrorists before they even landed in Canada. In October 2001, Canada was able to pass the Immigration and Refugee Protection Act (IRPA), which gave smugglers the harshest possible punishment: life imprisonment. At the same time, IRPA generated a stronger emphasis on protection for refugee selection than under previous legislation. This was somewhat miraculous in the shadow of the events of September 11, just a month before, after which the US reduced the number of refugees it would resettle to the lowest since its 1980 Refugee Act was passed.

In 2004, as part of negotiations with the US about the Smart Border Accord in the wake of 9/11, the Canadian Liberal government of Prime Minister Jean Chrétien ushered in the Safe Third Country Agreement, an effective "policy wall" between the US and Canada that prohibited most asylum seekers who first arrived in the US and then came to Canada at a land border port of entry from making a refugee claim. The reverse was also true, but much less common: asylum seekers who arrived in Canada could not cross the land border to the US to make a claim.[61]

In 2006, the government of Prime Minister Stephen Harper was elected, though with minority status; this government was re-elected with a majority, which they held until 2015. During this second window of governance, more restrictive asylum laws and regulations were introduced. Yet the discourse about refugees in Canada and the material protection and hospitality afforded to them had already begun to shift in advance of the legislation, as we have illustrated above. A more draconian system was implemented to *preclude* or prevent the arrival of asylum seekers unless they were *chosen* as resettled refugees.

Below, we place our analysis within a broader historical context by tracing policy and legislative responses to boat arrivals and other unexpected, "spontaneous arrivals," formerly known as asylum seekers, over the last twenty years. The *Sun Sea* and *Ocean Lady* are not the first instances of ships carrying racialized asylum seekers arriving at Canadian shores. Another significant example from more than a century ago is that of the 1914 *Komagata Maru*, carrying Sikhs from British India who were turned away because of the "continuous journey" regulation, which excluded South Asians from entering the country by requiring them to have purchased a single-journey ticket from India to Canada. This was made impossible by cancelling the one continuous route, so few could meet the requirement, as Alia Somani discusses in her chapter for this volume. Though Sikhs on the *Komagata Maru* were considered migrants at the time, they were also British subjects. Their detention and ultimate deportation by the state can be seen as prefiguring subsequent gatekeeping actions.

Mobilizing Post-Colonial, Anti-Racist, Able-ist Critical Tools

The final section of this chapter briefly looks at how Canadian government policy has enacted exclusions that are highly racialized, both in the context of private refugee sponsorship and through the expansion of the Canadian Temporary Resident Biometrics Program (TRBP). Policies and practices put into place under former citizenship and immigration minister Jason Kenney's tenure in relation to private refugee sponsorship reveal themselves as fraught and racialized; strict caps were placed on refugees processed at visa posts in particular world regions and thus from particular countries, and limits were placed on the total number of refugees who could be privately sponsored in a given year. Similarly, the biometric program introduced in 2012 singled out visa applicants from particular countries for reasons of national security, once again targeting twenty-nine nationalities and one territory (Palestine) as "dangerous" regions. By the end of 2018, all visitors requiring visas also required biometrics, eliminating the differential treatment of some visa-listed countries over others. Yet, when the program was first introduced at the end of 2012, most of the thirty territories listed were refugee-producing countries, as we analyse below. We aim to show how structures of inequality and exclusion become visible through these racialized policies introduced during the same time period.

Since the Private Sponsorship Program for refugees began in 1979, Canada has offered protection to more than three hundred thousand people.[62] Until recently, Canada has been unique in a world in which government-assisted resettlement is the norm, and just over two dozen countries provide resettlement. Private sponsorship is remarkable in that groups of citizens finance and volunteer the settlement of refugees to Canada on their own, and this has been going on for more than thirty-five years. The program did, however, undergo notable changes, beginning in 2010, under the Harper government and specifically during the tenure of the then citizenship and immigration minister, Jason Kenney.

Through private sponsorship, sponsors could name the refugees they would support, an arrangement that allowed sponsors to know the family they assisted but also the relatives left behind in refugee camps or countries of first asylum. PSR families in Canada often request that their sponsors consider sponsoring another of their relatives once the twelve-month period is complete, a phenomenon known as the "echo effect."[63] However, the Canadian government suggested that this informal family reunification is a fraudulent use of private sponsorship, and invented a new category, the blended visa office-referred refugee (BVOR).[64] BVORs are jointly funded on an equal basis by government and sponsors; they are screened for eligibility and referred by the UNHCR, and meet its eligibility criteria for "vulnerability." The catch is that sponsors cannot name the refugee family or unit they wish to sponsor. Critics have pointed out that the invention of the BVOR category was an attempt to privatize the costs of government sponsorships, and at the same time wrestle refugee selection away from private sponsors.[65] Furthermore, in 2012 the government introduced new rules that barred Groups of Five and Community Sponsors from sponsoring refugees who have not been individually determined to be refugees by either the UNHCR or the government of the country in which they are staying.[66] In short, who and how many can be sponsored, and from where, has become more restricted, resulting in dramatic changes to the program.[67] In 2015, the Canadian Council for Refugees reported that ministerial priorities decided 60 per cent of private sponsorship allocations instead of sponsors' priorities.[68]

Jennifer Hyndman, William Payne, and Shauna Jimenez point to a federal government practice under Prime Minister Harper of "capping" the numbers of refugees who could be selected by Sponsorship Agreement Holders (SAH) from *particular* Canadian visa posts, not all. This limited refugees of some nationalities, but not others.[69] Upon more careful scrutiny, Hyndman, Payne, and Jimenez unveiled geographic

Table 1.1. Caps and limits on Privately Sponsored Refugees (PSRs) (removed in December 2016)

2016 Sponsorship Agreement Holder (SAH) global cap on PSRs (10,500)	Numbers of refugees to be shared by 102 SAHs
Non-capped missions	8,700
Sub-capped missions	1,650
Nairobi	400
Pretoria	250
Cairo	100
Islamabad	100
Rome	250
Tel Aviv	350
Dar es Salaam	200

Source: Hyndman, Payne, and Jimenez, "The State of Private Sponsorship in Canada"
Note: New SAHs were supposed to share 150 persons. Geographical discrimination in the inequitable distribution of protections spaces by mission is troubling.

prejudice against certain visa posts (those serving sub-Saharan African refugee applicants) at the same time that other visa posts were free of restrictions (see table 1.1). In short, the Harper government created a system of racialized preferences without naming race.[70] The table shows how Nairobi, Pretoria, Cairo, Rome, Tel Aviv, and Dar – all destinations for mostly sub-Saharan refugees – were tightly capped at a few hundred refugees out of an annual total of 10,500 in 2016. This geographical prejudice translated into much longer waiting times for those, mostly Africans, at the "sub-capped" missions.

In 2016, Prime Minister Justin Trudeau eradicated these differential caps on visa posts. Nonetheless, the Syrian Refugee Initiative, which brought more than forty thousand Syrians to Canada between November 2015 and January 2017, also skewed the demographics of who "gets in" as privately sponsored refugees. Those waiting for processing in African locations faced even longer wait times, as Syrian refugees were prioritized in order to meet the campaign promises of 2015. Balibar coins the term "differential racism," which functions within a "framework of 'racism without races.'"[71] Such prejudice is based on race but does not name it. Indeed, Mongia emphasizes this concept in her analysis of the Canadian government's "continuous journey" regulation. As noted, the regulation prohibited Indian, mostly Sikh, passengers on the *Komagata Maru* from landing on Canadian soil if they did not come to Canada directly (without stopping) from their country of birth or citizenship, an impossible feat at the time.[72] This "continuous journey" regulation resulted in excluding Indian immigration to Canada.

In September 2016, one of the authors (Hyndman) documented wait times for applicants to the private sponsorship program, by taking screen shots off the Canadian Immigration, Refugees and Citizenship Canada (IRCC) website that listed wait times. Hyndman found that the waiting time for a privately sponsored refugee who applied and was selected in Kenya was seventy months, while the waiting time for a refugee in Lebanon was eight months and Jordan was ten months, as the latter were prioritized as source countries for the government's Syrian refugee resettlement plan.[73]

Private refugee sponsorship through resettlement is at once laudable as a veritable civil society social movement of sorts and also fraught with racialized politics introduced since 2010. The current government appears to be taking a different approach, both by dismantling the cap system in December 2016 and by initiating the sizeable Syrian refugee resettlement program after its election in November 2015. Representations of refugees and public discourse about asylum seekers and refugees in Canada began to change overnight.[74] To this end, we have shown how public discourse about refugees is made by elected officials and political leaders along with many other civil society actors.

One last notable change introduced in the 2012 Act and accompanying Regulations is the above-mentioned biometric requirement for fingerprints from temporary residents who come to Canada to visit, study, or work, along with a requirement for visas from what we call "designated *dangerous* countries." While not explicitly labelled as such, the twenty-nine countries and one territory (consisting of the West Bank and Gaza) were identified as requiring biometric data to accompany visa applications. At least two-thirds of the entities on this list (see table 1.2) are places affected by acute human displacement related to conflict, war crimes, and human rights violations. In short, they are refugee-producing regions. Instead of adjudicating each visa application on its own merit, all nationals of the countries listed must travel to the nearest biometric lab for approved fingerprinting and submit their prints with visa applications. Geographical discrimination that required biometric visas from people originating in some countries but not others that still require visas is difficult to explain. By the end of 2018, Canada required biometrics of nationals from *all* countries that require visas.

The collection of biometric data is viewed as the most effective way of identifying individuals entering the country in order to reduce identity fraud and "strengthen the integrity of Canada's immigration system."[75] Just as the rhetoric of queue jumpers or bogus refugees is used to justify the implementation of DCO and DFN lists in order to reduce

Table 1.2. Countries for Biometric Screening

Countries for Biometric Screening		
Afghanistan	Haiti	Saudi Arabia
Albania	Iran	Somalia
Algeria	Iraq	South Sudan
Bangladesh	Jamaica	Sri Lanka
Burma	Jordan	Sudan
Cambodia	Laos	Syria
Colombia	Lebanon	Tunisia
Congo, Democratic Republic of	Libya	Vietnam
Egypt	Nigeria	Yemen
Eritrea	Pakistan	
Territory for Biometric Screening		
Palestinian Authority		

Source: *The Canada Gazette* ("Archived – Regulations Amending the Immigration and Refugee Protection Regulations").

risk and enhance security, a similar logic is used to justify the increased use of biometric testing. Through the joint cooperation of Citizenship and Immigration Canada (now IRCC), Canada Border Services Agency, and the Royal Canadian Mounted Police, an enhanced identification system provides a first line of defence against potential security threats or fraudulent applicants, while simultaneously helping to facilitate legitimate travel.[76] Biometric testing is believed to be an effective tool in identity management because of its ability to first establish a person's foundational identity (uniqueness), and consequently to verify a person's authenticity and detect potential identity fraud or identity theft prior to their arrival in Canada. Governments with whom Canada collaborates on intelligence and security data can now ascertain if a person has made a refugee claim in another country in the shared database of the Five Country Conference, whose members include Canada, the US, the United Kingdom, Australia, and New Zealand.[77] In 2014, at least thirteen of the states listed in the *Gazette* were among the top twenty source countries for asylum seekers whose claims were decided, including both new cases since the 2012 legislation was introduced and backlog files from the old caseload. The new legislation aims to deter potential abuse of the system and protect the security and safety of Canadian citizens by preventing asylum seekers from getting to Canada altogether.[78]

After the DCO provisions naming many wealthy countries as "safe" were implemented, and the Temporary Resident Biometric Program (TRBP) introduced in December 2012, the number of asylum applications declined dramatically, by almost half. In 2013, after the implementation of the 2012 Protecting Canada's Immigration System legislation, Canada dropped to sixteenth place as a destination for asylum seekers, from second and third place respectively in 2008 and 2009. Canada's share of asylum applications fell from 10 per cent of the global total in 2008 to 2 per cent in 2013.[79]

Both lists, of DCOs and TRBP regions, make huge generalizations about the entire population. *Safe* and *dangerous* judgments are cast as inherent traits of an entire country rather than contextualized across space and social locations such as race, ethnicity, gender, sexuality, religion, and age. From a "policy-crit" perspective, these lists represent essentialist generalizations, and stereotypes, of who is safe where and who is not. Furthermore, reinforcing negative images of refugees through public discourse helps to make harsher policies more appealing and results in an environment of uncertainty and fear in refugee communities.[80]

Conclusion

From 1999 through 2010, six ships arrived on the West Coast of Canada, stirring fears of invasion and more uninvited asylum seekers to come. Recent shifts in public discourse that denigrate refugees and asylum seekers and subsequent legislation correlate with the arrival of boats in Canada. After the 1999 arrivals, the new Immigration and Refugee Protection Act of 2001 implemented the most punitive penalties for human smugglers: life imprisonment. We have also illustrated the rise in use of the term "bogus" in relation to refugees, claimants, and others, a concept that generates suspicion and undermines the legitimacy of asylum seekers before their claims have been heard; this in turn shapes public opinion. By insinuating that refugees may be fraudulent, the government of former prime minister Harper also created new political space, public consent, and fertile ground for introducing new legislation and policy changes in Canada that have had major implications for asylum seekers.

Despite being a signatory to the 1951 Convention Relating to Refugees and to national legislation in IRPA that ensures refugee protection, Canada actively participates in strategies that push the border out in order to preclude the arrival of asylum seekers, thus making it more difficult to reach Canadian territory. In addition to these policy and legal changes during the Harper government's tenure, a concomitant increase in negative government and media speech acts related to asylum seekers prevailed. While Canada's refugee, immigration, and border policies productively label some as desirable, others are called "queue jumpers" or "bogus refugees," terms that are all part of an alarmist discourse that casts them as threats and, in turn, provides grounds to preclude them. For those fleeing persecution, navigating this discursive and political landscape of the Canadian refugee system is confusing and potentially dangerous to newcomers who might be seen as bringing their conflicts with them. For people whose last resort is getting on a boat destined for Canada, the risk of being a "designated foreign national" – with the mandatory detention and no chance of permanent residence for five years even if granted legitimate refugee status – is too great.

We have provided several analyses of "banal bureaucracy," including government tables showing caps, regulations for visitors on visas that accompany law, and the fine print of policies, to show how the state enacts exclusions in ways that are difficult to see at first glance, but highly racialized, classed, and geographically uneven upon further scrutiny. The designation of *safe* countries and foreign nationals, and the increase in biometric testing for temporary residents coming to Canada, are examples of how the borders are pushed out and the practice of preclusion proceeds. Border practices and enforcement are not only extended beyond the territorial boundaries of the state but are also evident in the caps and limits once placed on selected Canadian visa posts abroad. While this may seem like banal bureaucracy, it risks being a system of racialized preferences masquerading as geography and allocations.

For those interested in critical refugee studies, a critical analysis of government texts, regulations, and "small print" policies can provide important evidence of how policy enacts exclusions that are highly racialized, unearthing what the editors of this volume call in their Introduction "mechanisms of state violence – of exclusion, restriction, policing, and genocide." In this chapter, we have also documented the upward trend in the negative representation of (mostly racialized) refugees before 2015 and explored the relationship and overlap between this trend and the legislation introduced at the time. We contend that such analyses are essential in the contemporary political climate, as countries around the world are closing their doors to those fleeing persecution.

Finally, we make a call to refuse labels and terms that denigrate people on the move in need of protection.[81] Labels like "bogus refugee" and "queue jumper" constitute a form of epistemic violence that is neither accurate nor constructive and only serves to reinforce exclusionary policies framed by unquestioned, de-historicized, and self-serving state logics.[82] Building on the work of Audra Simpson and Jack Halberstam, elaborated and extended by Edward Ou Jin Lee (in this volume), critical refugee studies is an unsettling of the Eurocentric persecution-focused definition and the category of "refugee" itself. "Refugee" in international law is a very narrow definition that excludes more people facing violence and insecurity than it includes. While Canada may be viewed as a global leader at protecting those who fit the definition, it excludes far more people in need of protection than it assists. Rather than patrolling the boundaries of this precious but exclusionary protection space, let us engage beyond the well-worn categories of refugee studies.

NOTES

1. Mongia, "Race, Nationality, Mobility"; Balibar, *We, the People of Europe?*.
2. Truth and Reconciliation Canada. *Honouring the Truth, Reconciling for the Future*.
3. Hyndman, "Second-Class Immigrants or First Class Protection?"
4. Bannerji, *The Dark Side of the Nation*.
5. Hyndman and Giles, "Waiting for What?"
6. UNHCR, "Canada's 2016 Record High Level of Resettlement Praised by UNHCR."
7. For resettlement numbers globally, see UNHCR, *Global Trends*.
8. See Razack, *Race, Space and the Law*.
9. See also Nyers, *Rethinking Refugees*.
10. Jan van Dijk, in Fialho and Mansfield, "Do We Have to Abolish the Victim Narrative to Abolish Immigration Detention?"
11. Betts and Collier, *Refuge*, 30.
12. Zetter, "Labelling Refugees"; Zetter, "More Labels, Fewer Refugees"; Crawley and Skleparis, "Refugees, Migrants, Neither, Both."
13. Al Jazeera, 20 August 2015.
14. Macklin, "Disappearing Refugees," 365.
15. Ibid.
16. See also Bradimore and Bauder, "Mystery Ships and Risky Boat People"; Mann, "Refugees Who Arrive by Boat and Canada's Commitment to the Refugee Convention"; Molnar, "The 'Bogus' Refugee."
17. UNHCR, *Global Trends: Forced Displacement in 2019*.
18. UNHCR's statistics exclude the long-term displacement of Palestinian refugees because they are supported by a different UN organization, the United Nations Relief and Works Agency (UNRWA).
19. UNHCR, "Protracted Refugee Situations," 2.

20 UNHCR, *Global Trends: Forced Displacement in 2018.*
21 "US Slashes Number of Refugees to 30,000." *BBC News*, 18 September 2018.
22 UNHCR, "Protracted Refugee Situations," 2.
23 "Remarks by President Biden on America's Place in the World."
24 Hyndman, "Second-Class Immigrants or First Class Protection?"
25 Crisp, "25 Years of Forced Migration."
26 Girard, "Designated Classes."
27 Government of Canada, Immigration Act, 1976, SC 1976–7, c. 52, s. 6.2.
28 Girard, "Designated Classes," 2–3.
29 For more on designated class and group processing, see Baterseh, "Inside/Outside the Circle."
30 Girard, "Designated Classes," 2–3.
31 Campesi, "Seeking Asylum in Times of Crisis"; Hyndman, "The Securitization of Fear in Post-Tsunami Sri Lanka"; Hyndman, "The Securitisation of Sri Lankan Tourism in the Absence of Peace."
32 Buzan, Waever, and de Wilde, *Security*.
33 "Archived – Admissibility Screening and Supporting Intelligence Activities – Evaluation Study."
34 Ibid.
35 Arbel and Brenner, "Bordering on Failure."
36 Mountz, *Seeking Asylum*, 175.
37 Amnesty International, "Syria."
38 For a more nuanced understanding and critique of the term refugee or migrant "crisis," see Crawley and Skleparis, "Refugees, Migrants, Neither, Both"; Carastathis, Spathopoulou, and Tsilimpounidi, "Crisis, What Crisis?"
39 Government of Canada. "#WelcomeRefugees: Key Figures."
40 Macklin et al., "Preliminary Investigation into Refugee Sponsors."
41 Canadian Council for Refugees, "Call for a Resettlement Plan Reflecting Equity for All Regions."
42 Mountz, *Seeking Asylum*.
43 Tom Fennell, "Canada's Open Door," *Maclean's*, 23 August 1999.
44 Maureen Brosnahan, "Ocean Lady Migrants From Sri Lanka Still Struggling 5 Years Later," *CBC News*, 18 October 2014, http://www.cbc.ca/news/politics/ocean-lady-migrants-from-sri-lanka-still-struggling-5-years-later-1.2804118.
45 Canadian Press, "Tamil *Sun Sea* Refugees' Appeal Reaches Supreme Court."
46 Canadian Press, "Tamil Migrants to Be Investigated: Toews."
47 Ibid.
48 Dhillon, "Canadians 'Hardening' on Refugee Process, Vic Toews Says."

49 Yet the 1985 Singh Decision stipulates that *everyone* physically in Canada has the right to a full oral hearing, including asylum seekers. See Government of Canada, IRPA section 20.1 (1) for definitions of "irregular arrivals."
50 "Backgrounder – Overview."
51 Government of Canada, "Immigration and Refugee Protection Act," Justice Laws Website, http://laws-lois.justice.gc.ca/eng/acts/I-2.5/page-46.html#h-65.
52 The Canadian Newsstand database (now called Canadian Major Dailies) includes the following national newspapers: *Calgary Herald*, *Daily News*, *Edmonton Journal*, *Financial Post*, *Globe and Mail*, *Guardian*, *Kingston Whig-Standard*, Regina *Leader Post*, *Montreal Gazette*, *National Post*, *Ottawa Citizen*, *La Presse Canadienne – Le Fil Radio*, *La Presse Canadienne*, *Province*, Saskatoon *Star-Phoenix*, *Sudbury Star*, St. John's *Telegram*, St. John *Telegraph-Journal*, Victoria *Times-Colonist*, *Toronto Star*, *Tri-Cities Now*, *Vancouver Sun*, *Windsor Star*, *Winnipeg Free Press*.
53 Carlaw, "Authoritarian Populism and Canada's Conservative Decade (2006–2015) in Citizenship and Immigration."
54 Monte, "Reform Immigration Critic Wants National Referendum."
55 Levine-Raskin, "Who Are You Calling Bogus?"
56 "Archived – Backgrounder."
57 Butler, *Excitable Speech*.
58 Neve and Russell, "Hysteria and Discrimination."
59 Quan, "Five Years after the MV *Sun Sea*'s Arrival."
60 Hyndman and Giles, "Waiting for What?"
61 Hyndman and Mountz, "Another Brick in the Wall?"
62 "Why So Many Canadians Privately Sponsor Syrian Refugees."
63 Macklin et al., "Preliminary Investigation into Refugee Sponsors"; for more on the "echo effect," see Chapman, "Private Sponsorship and Public Policy."
64 Black, "Immigration Minister Jason Kenney Announces Tighter Regulation for Family Reunification Refugees."
65 Hyndman, Payne, and Jimenez, "The State of Private Sponsorship in Canada"; McNally, "The Blended Visa Office-Referred Program."
66 Canadian Council for Refugees, "Important Changes in Canada's Private Sponsorship of Refugees Program," January 2013, https://ccrweb.ca/en/changes-private-sponsorship-refugees#FN1.
67 "Why So Many Canadians Privately Sponsor Syrian Refugees." See also Labman, "Private Sponsorship."
68 Canadian Council for Refugees, "Canada's Private Sponsorship of Refugees Program Proud History, Uncertain Future," 2014, 3, http://ccrweb.ca/sites/ccrweb.ca/files/psr-overview-challenges.pdf.

69 Hyndman, Payne, and Jimenez, "The State of Private Sponsorship in Canada."
70 Mongia, "Race, Nationality, Mobility"; Balibar and Wallerstein, ed., *Race, Nation, Class.*
71 Balibar and Wallerstein, ed., *Race, Nation, Class*, 21.
72 Mongia, "Race, Nationality, Mobility."
73 IRCC, 9 September 2016; available at the IRCC processing time webpage at Government of Canada. "Check Processing Times."
74 Canadian Council for Refugees, "Canada's Private Sponsorship of Refugees," n.d., http://ccrweb.ca/en/private-sponsorship-refugees; Hyndman, Payne, and Jimenez, "The State of Private Sponsorship in Canada," 11.
75 "Archived – Harper Government Introduces the Protecting Canada's Immigration System Act."
76 Government of Canada, "Why Use Biometrics?"
77 "About Us."
78 "Archived – Harper Government Introduces the Protecting Canada's Immigration System Act.".
79 These statistics are based on the thirty-eight European and six non-European states that currently provide monthly asylum statistics to UNHCR. For a list of these forty-four countries, see UNHCR, Annex 1, Table 1, in "Asylum Levels and Trends in Industrialized Countries 2013."
80 "Briefing Note – Cessation," 3.
81 Hyndman and Reynolds, "Beyond the Global Compacts."
82 Espiritu, *Body Counts.*

REFERENCES

"About Us." Five Country Conference. https://www.fivecountryconference.org/

Al Jazeera. "Why Al Jazeera Will Not Say Mediterranean 'Migrants.'" 20 August 2015. https://www.aljazeera.com/blogs/editors-blog/2015/08/al-jazeera-mediterranean-migrants-150820082226309.html. Accessed 27 December 2020.

Amnesty International. "Syria: The Biggest Humanitarian Crisis of Our Time." https://www.amnesty.org.nz/take-action/syria-crisis; UNHCR, 15 March 2016, "Syria Conflict at 5 years."

Aradau, Claudia, and Rens van Munster. "Insuring Terrorism, Assuring Subjects, Ensuring Normality: The Politics of Risk After 9/11." *Alternatives: Global, Local, Political* 33, no. 2 (2008): 191–210. https://www.jstor.org/stable/40608534.

Arbel, Efrat, and Alletta Brenner. "Bordering on Failure: Canada-U.S. Border Policy and the Politics of Refugee Exclusion." Harvard Immigration and Refugee Law Clinical Program, Harvard Law School, 2013, 26–7. http://harvardimmigrationclinic.files.wordpress.com/2013/11/bordering-on-failure-harvard-immigration-and-refugee-law-clinical-program1.pdf.

"Archived – Admissibility Screening and Supporting Intelligence Activities – Evaluation Study." Canadian Border Services Agency (CBSA), July 2009. http://www.cbsa-asfc.gc.ca/agency-agence/reports-rapports/ae-ve/2009/assia-aeasr-eng.html.

"Archived – Backgrounder: Conditional Permanent Resident Status." Citizenship and Immigration Canada – Government of Canada, October 2012. http://www.cic.gc.ca/english/department/media/backgrounders/2012/2012-10-26a.asp.

"Archived – Harper Government Introduces the Protecting Canada's Immigration System Act." Citizenship and Immigration Canada – Government of Canada, 16 February 2012. http://news.gc.ca/web/article-en.do?nid=657129.

"Archived – Regulations Amending the Immigration and Refugee Protection Regulations," *Canada Gazette – Government of Canada* 146, no. 49 (8 December 2012). http://www.gazette.gc.ca/rp-pr/p1/2012/2012-12-08/html/reg2-eng.html.

"Backgrounder – Overview: Ending the Abuse of Canada's Immigration System by Human Smugglers." Citizenship and Immigration Canada – Government of Canada, 29 June 2012. http://www.cic.gc.ca/english/department/media/backgrounders/2012/2012-06-29i.asp.

Balibar, Étienne. *We, the People of Europe?: Reflections on Transnational Citizenship*. Princeton: Princeton University Press, 2004.

Balibar, Étienne, and Immanuel Maurice Wallerstein, eds. *Race, Nation, Class: Ambiguous Identities*. London: Verso, 1991.

Bannerji, Himani. *The Dark Side of the Nation: Essays on Multiculturalism, Nationalism, and Gender*. Toronto: Canadian Scholars' Press, 2000.

Baterseh, Robert. "Inside/Outside the Circle: From the Indochinese Designated Class to Contemporary Group Processing." *Refuge: Canada's Journal on Refugees* 32, no. 2 (2016): 54–66. https://refuge.journals.yorku.ca/index.php/refuge/article/view/40254.

Betts, Alexander, and Paul Collier. *Refuge: Transforming a Broken Refugee System*. Oxford: Oxford University Press, 2017.

Black, Debra. "Immigration Minister Jason Kenney Announces Tighter Regulation for Family Reunification Refugees." *Toronto Star*, 10 May 2013. https://www.thestar.com/news/canada/2013/05/10/immigration_minister_jason_kenney_announces_tighter_regulations_for_family_reunification_program.html. Accessed 4 September 2018.

Bradimore, Ashley, and Harald Bauder. "Mystery Ships and Risky Boat People: Tamil Refugee Migration in the Newsprint Media." *Canadian Journal of Communication* 36, no. 4. (2011): 637–61.

"Briefing Note – Cessation." Canadian Association of Refugee Lawyers. 19 April 2016. http://www.carl-acaadr.ca/sites/default/files/CARL%20%20Cessation%20Briefing%20Note%20for%20Minister%20McCallum%2019%2004.pdf.

Butler, Judith. *Excitable Speech: A Politics of the Performative*. London/New York: Routledge, 1997.

Buzan, Barry, Ole Waever, and Jaap de Wilde. *Security: A New Framework for Analysis*. Boulder, CO: Lynne Rienner, 1998.

Campesi, Giuseppe. "Seeking Asylum in Times of Crisis: Reception, Confinement, and Detention at Europe's Southern Border." *Refugee Survey Quarterly* 37, no. 1 (March 2018): 44–70. https://doi.org/10.1093/rsq/hdx016.

"Canada's Private Sponsorship of Refugees Program Proud History, Uncertain Future." Canadian Council for Refugees. December 2014. http://ccrweb.ca/sites/ccrweb.ca/files/psr-overview-challenges.pdf.

Canadian Council for Refugees. "Call for a Resettlement Plan Reflecting Equity for All Regions." May 2016. http://ccrweb.ca/en/call-resettlement-plan-reflecting-equity-all-regions.

– "Canada's Private Sponsorship of Refugees Program Proud History, Uncertain Future." December 2014. http://ccrweb.ca/sites/ccrweb.ca/files/psr-overview-challenges.pdf

Canadian Press. "Tamil Migrants to Be Investigated: Toews." *CBC News*, 13 August 2010. http://www.cbc.ca/news/canada/british-columbia/tamil-migrants-to-be-investigated-toews-1.898421.

– "Tamil *Sun Sea* Refugees' Appeal Reaches Supreme Court." *Globe and Mail*, 18 April 2014. http://www.theglobeandmail.com/news/british-columbia/tamil-sun-sea-refugees-appeal-reaches-supreme-court/article18068813/.

Carastathis, Anna, Aila Spathopoulou, and Myrto Tsilimpounidi. "Crisis, What Crisis? Immigrants, Refugees, and Invisible Struggles." *Refuge: Canada's Journal on Refugees* 34, no. 1 (2018): 29–38. https://refuge.journals.yorku.ca/index.php/refuge/article/view/40482/0.

Carlaw, John. "Authoritarian Populism and Canada's Conservative Decade (2006–2015) in Citizenship and Immigration: The Politics and Practices of Kenneyism and Neo-Conservative Multiculturalism." *Journal of Canadian Studies* 51, no. 3 (2017): 782–816.

Chapman, Ashley. "Private Sponsorship and Public Policy: Political Barriers to Church-Connected Refugee Resettlement in Canada." Citizens for Public Justice. 2014. https://www.cpj.ca/private-sponsorship-and-public-policy.

Crawley, Heaven, and Dimitris Skleparis. "Refugees, Migrants, Neither, Both: Categorical Fetishism and the Politics of Bounding in Europe's 'Migration Crisis.'" *Journal of Ethnic and Migration Studies* 44, no. 1 (2018): 48–64. https://www.tandfonline.com/doi/full/10.1080/1369183X.2017.1348224.

Crisp, Jeff. "25 Years of Forced Migration." *Forced Migration Review*, November 2012, 4–8. http://www.fmreview.org/en/FMR%2025th%20anniversary%20full%20issue%20web.pdf.

Dhillon, Sunny. "Canadians 'Hardening' on Refugee Process, Vic Toews Says." *Globe and Mail*, 20 January 2011. http://www.theglobeandmail.com/news/british-columbia/canadians-hardening-on-refugee-process-vic-toews-says/article4267824/.

Espiritu, Yen Le. *Body Counts: The Vietnam War and Militarized Refugees*. Oakland, CA: University of California Press, 2014.

Fialho, Christine, and Christina Mansfield. "Do We Have to Abolish the Victim Narrative to Abolish Immigration Detention?" *HuffPost*, 12 September 2017. https://www.huffpost.com/entry/do-we-have-to-abolish-the-victim-narrative-to abolish_b_59c53e36e4b08d6615504213?fbclid=IwAR2kcaDFeVRqGKz6HkTFH6WM1q2uhfZYd5gQIhcCb-fo0IHK5iHPV3_nqwY.

Girard, Raphael. "Designated Classes: A Regulatory Device to Target Humanitarian Resettlement Programs." Canadian Immigration Historical Society (CIHS), 1 January 2005. http://cihs-shic.ca/2005/01/designated-classes/.

Gonzalez-Barrera, Ana, and Phillip Connor. "Around the World, More Say Immigrants Are a Strength Than a Burden," Pew Research Center, 14 March 2019. https://www.pewresearch.org/global/2019/03/14/around-the-world-more-say-immigrants-are-a-strength-than-a-burden/

Government of Canada. "Check Processing Times." https://www.canada.ca/en/immigration-refugees-citizenship/services/application/check-processing-times.html. Accessed 9 September 2016.

– Immigration Act, 1976, SC 1976–7, c. 52, s. 6.2.

– Immigration and Refugee Protection Act, SC 2001, c. 27. https://laws.justice.gc.ca/eng/acts/i-2.5/.

– "#WelcomeRefugees: Key Figures." Immigration, Refugees and Citizenship Canada, last modified 27 February 2017. http://www.cic.gc.ca/english/refugees/welcome/milestones.asp.

– "Why Use Biometrics?" Citizenship and Immigration Canada, 19 October 2012. http://www.cic.gc.ca/english/department/biometrics-why.asp.

Huysmans, Jef. *The Politics of Insecurity: Fear, Migration and Asylum in the EU*. New International Relations Series. London: Routledge, 2006.

Hyndman, Jennifer. "Second-Class Immigrants or First-Class Protection? Resettling Refugees to Canada." In *Resettled and Included? Employment*

Integration of Refugees, edited by Pieter Bevelander, Mirjam Hagstrom, and Sofia Ronnqvist, 247–65. Malmö: Malmö University, 2009.
– "The Securitisation of Sri Lankan Tourism in the Absence of Peace." *Stability: International Journal of Security and Development* 4, no. 1 (2015): 1–16. http://dx.doi.org/10.5334/sta.fa.
– "The Securitization of Fear in Post-Tsunami Sri Lanka." *Annals of the Association of American Geographers* 97, no. 2 (2007): 361–72.
Hyndman, Jennifer, and Wenona Giles. "Waiting for What? The Feminization of Asylum in Protracted Situations." *Gender, Place & Culture* 18, no. 3 (2011): 361–79.
Hyndman, Jennifer, and Alison Mountz. "Another Brick in the Wall? Neo-Refoulement and the Externalization of Asylum by Australia and Europe (PDF)." *Government & Opposition* 43, no. 2 (2008): 249–69.
Hyndman, Jennifer, William Payne, and Shauna Jimenez. "The State of Private Sponsorship in Canada: Trends, Issues and Impacts." RRN/CRS Policy Brief, 2017.
Hyndman, Jennifer, and Johanna Reynolds. "Beyond the Global Compacts: Re-imagining Protection." *Refuge: Canada's Journal on Refugees* 3, no. 1 (2020): 66–74.
Labman, Shauna. "Private Sponsorship: Complementary or Conflicting Interests?" *Refuge: Canada's Journal on Refugees* 32, no. 2 (2016): 67–80. http://refuge.journals.yorku.ca/index.php/refuge/article/view/40266.
Levine-Raskin, Cynthia. "Who Are You Calling Bogus? Saying No to Roma Refugees." *Canadian Dimension* 46, no. 5 (September/October 2012). https://canadiandimension.com/articles/view/who-are-you-calling-bogus.
Macklin, Audrey. "Disappearing Refugees: Reflections on the Canada-U.S. Safe Third Country Agreement." *Columbia Human Rights Law Review* 36, no. 2 (2005): 365–426.
Macklin, Audrey, Kathryn Barber, Luin Goldring, Jennifer Hyndman, Anna Korteweg, Shauna Labman, and Jonna Zfyi. "Preliminary Investigation into Refugee Sponsors." *Canadian Ethnic Studies* 50, no. 2 (2018): 35–58.
Mann, Alexandra. "Refugees Who Arrive by Boat and Canada's Commitment to the Refugee Convention: A Discursive Analysis." *Refuge: Canada's Journal on Refugees* 26, no. 2 (2009): 191–206.
McNally, Rachel. "The Blended Visa Office-Referred Program: Perspectives and Experiences from Rural Nova Scotia." In *Strangers to Neighbours*, edited by Shauna Labman and Geoff Cameron, 134–51. Montreal and Kingston: McGill-Queen's University Press, 2020.
Molnar, Petra. "The 'Bogus' Refugee: Roma Asylum Claimants and Discourses of Fraud in Canada's Bill C-31." *Refuge: Canada's Journal on Refugees* 30, no. 1 (2014): 67–80.

Mongia, Radhika. "Race, Nationality, Mobility: A History of the Passport." *Public Culture* 11, no. 3 (1999): 527–55.
Monte, Stewart. "Reform Immigration Critic Wants National Referendum." *Calgary Herald*, 6 October 1999. Accessed 1 February 2018.
Mountz, Alison. *Seeking Asylum: Human Smuggling and Bureaucracy at the Border*. Minneapolis: University of Minnesota Press, 2010.
Neve, Alex, and Tiisetso Russell. "Hysteria and Discrimination: Canada's Harsh Response to Refugees and Migrants Who Arrive by Sea." *University of New Brunswick Law Journal* 62, no. 1 (2011): 37–46.
Nyers, Peter. "Dueling Designs: The Politics of Rescuing Dual Citizens." *Citizenship Studies* 14, no. 1 (2010): 47–60. 10.1080/13621020903466324.
– *Rethinking Refugees: Beyond States of Emergency*. New York: Routledge, 2006.
La Presse Canadienne. "Hausse fulgurante des demandes de visas temporaires depuis 2015 au Canada." 23 May 2019. Radio Canada. https://ici.radio-canada.ca/nouvelle/1171522/immigration-hausse-fulgurante-demandes-visas-temporaires-canada?depuisRecherche=true.
"Private Sponsorship of Refugees." Canadian Council for Refugees. n.d. http://ccrweb.ca/en/private-sponsorship-refugees.
Quan, Douglas. "Five Years after the MV *Sun Sea*'s Arrival, Crackdown on 'Irregular Arrivals' Draws Praise, Scorn," *National Post*, 6 August 2015.
Razack, Sherene. *Race, Space and the Law: Unmapping a White Settler Society*. Toronto: Between the Lines, 2002.
"Remarks by President Biden on America's Place in the World." White House Briefing, 4 February 2021. https://www.whitehouse.gov/briefing-room/speeches-remarks/2021/02/04/remarks-by-president-biden-on-americas-place-in-the-world/.
Shire, Warsan. "Home." https://www.facinghistory.org/standing-up-hatred-intolerance/warsan-shire-home.
Truth and Reconciliation Canada. *Honouring the Truth, Reconciling for the Future: Summary of the Final Report of the Truth and Reconciliation Commission of Canada*. Winnipeg: Truth and Reconciliation Commission of Canada, 2015. http://www.trc.ca/assets/pdf/Honouring_the_Truth_Reconciling_for_the_Future_July_23_2015.pdf.
UN General Assembly. Convention Relating to the Status of Refugees, 28 July 1951, United Nations, Treaty Series 189, 137, available at: https://www.refworld.org/docid/3be01b964.html. Accessed 26 June 2018.
UN High Commissioner for Refugees (UNHCR). "Asylum Levels and Trends in Industrialized Countries 2013." United Nations High Commissioner for Refugees (UNHCR), 26 March 2014. http://www.unhcr.org/5329b15a9.html.

- "Canada's 2016 Record High Level of Resettlement Praised by UNHCR." 24 April 2017. http://www.unhcr.org/news/press/2017/4/58fe15464/canadas-2016-record-high-level-resettlement-praised-unhcr.html.
- *Global Trends: Forced Displacement in 2017*, 22 June 2018. available at: http://www.unhcr.org/5b27be547.pdf.
- *Global Trends: Forced Displacement in 2018*, 19 June 2019. https://www.unhcr.org/statistics/unhcrstats/5d08d7ee7/unhcr-global-trends-2018.html.

UNHCR, *Global Trends: Forced Displacement in 2019*. 2020. https://www.unhcr.org/statistics/unhcrstats/5ee200e37/unhcr-global-trends-2019.html

- "Protracted Refugee Situations." Executive Committee of the High Commissioner's Program, Standing Committee, 30th Meeting, EC/54/SC/CRP.14. Geneva, 10 June 2004.
- "Syria Conflict at 5 Years: The Biggest Refugee and Displacement Crisis of Our Time Demands a Huge Surge in Solidarity." 15 March 2016. http://www.unhcr.org/afr/news/press/2016/3/56e6e3249/syria-conflict-5-years-biggest-refugee-displacement-crisis-time-demands.html.

"US Slashes Number of Refugees to 30,000." *BBC News*. 18 September 2018. https://www.bbc.com/news/world-us-canada-45555357.

"Why So Many Canadians Privately Sponsor Syrian Refugees." *Economist*, 3 March 2016. https://www.economist.com/the-economist-explains/2016/03/03/why-so-many-canadians-privately-sponsor-syrian-refugees.

"Why Use Biometrics?" Citizenship and Immigration Canada – Government of Canada, 19 October 2012. http://www.cic.gc.ca/english/department/biometrics-why.asp.

Zamore, Leah, and Alex Aleinikoff. "The Arc of Protection: Toward a New International Refugee Regime." Center on International Cooperation, 22 May 2018. https://cic.nyu.edu/news/arc-of-protection-refugees-zamore.

Zetter, Roger. "Labelling Refugees: Forming and Transforming a Bureaucratic Identity." *Journal of Refugee Studies* 4, no. 1 (1991): 39–62. https://doi.org/10.1093/jrs/4.1.39.

- "More Labels, Fewer Refugees: Remaking the Refugee Label in an Era of Globalization." *Journal of Refugee Studies* 20, no 2 (June 2007): 172–92. https://doi.org/10.1093/jrs/fem011.

2 Untangling the Strands of Memory: Historicizing the 1914 *Komagata Maru* Incident and the Concept of Refugeeness

ALIA SOMANI

Introduction

On 23 May 1914, the *Komagata Maru* arrived in Vancouver. Nearly two months earlier, the ship had departed from Hong Kong, carrying 376 Punjabi migrants who had journeyed from the Far East where most of them had held low-paying, menial jobs. Though the voyage was difficult, the migrants were optimistic that they could make a better life in Canada. As British subjects, they had the right to settle anywhere in the Empire, including the British Dominion of Canada. While the passengers felt assured of their rights as British subjects and, as such, subscribed to a notion of imperial citizenship that was based on the ideas of universality and cosmopolitanism, the same notion was mobilized by Canadian officials to exclude certain groups from Canada.[1] For the latter, imperial citizenship manifested in a number of racist immigration policies, one of which was the "continuous journey regulation," stipulating that all immigrants had to come to Canada via a continuous journey from the country of their birth. Another policy was that immigrants of Asiatic origin had to possess two hundred dollars to gain entry into Canada. In drafting these policies, Canadian officials were careful not to expose the paradoxical ways in which imperial citizenship was being used. They were also responding to British imperial officials who sanctioned exclusionary policies but warned Canadian officials that these policies should not further fuel anti-colonial nationalist sentiment among Indians in North America. Therefore, the policies referenced neither race nor Indians specifically, even though they were intended to prevent Indians from settling in Canada. As Hugh Johnston explains, "there was no direct steamship from Canada to India at the time, and 200 dollars was an exorbitant sum of money, even for wealthy Indians."[2]

For Gurdit Singh, the Sikh businessman who chartered the ship, the journey of the *Komagata Maru* was both a commercial venture and a chance to test the Canadian legal system by challenging restrictive immigration policies.[3] However, as has been well documented, the passengers were prohibited from disembarking in Vancouver. At the time of the ship's arrival, Canadian officials fought hard to detain and prevent the passengers from going to the courts and testing the law. As part of their stalling tactics, they ordered the passengers to undergo extensive medical exams, limited their food and water, and denied them direct contact with their lawyer and supporters. When the passengers were finally granted a chance to present their claims before a Board of Inquiry, they were defeated.[4] In the end, only twenty who could prove that they were returning migrants were allowed entry. The rest were turned away and forced to return to India, where they were greeted by British officials who saw them as threats to the Empire and suspected that they had become aligned with the Ghadarites, a group based in North America that was committed to the overthrow of the British Raj in India. In the ensuing violent confrontation at Budge Budge, some of the passengers were arrested, many injured, some forced into hiding, and twenty even killed.

The story of the *Komagata Maru* invokes what we tend to associate with a refugee experience: persecution, lives at risk, statelessness, and ships arriving in Western countries with people in search of refuge. It is important to note, however, that when the passengers of the *Komagata Maru* arrived in Canada, the term "refugee" did not exist as a legal category, and as such, they were labelled migrants rather than refugees. As Alexandra Mann explains, "it was not until the signing of the *Refugee Convention* in 1951 that states undertook a legal obligation to offer refuge to those fleeing persecution,"[5] and, as the Introduction to this volume notes, Canada defined refugees for the first time in 1976 with the passage of the Immigration Act. This case therefore reminds us not only that the experience of refugeeness predates legal categories, but also that these legal categories themselves have limitations. In her chapter, Laura Madokoro makes precisely this point, explaining for example that the 1951 definition focuses narrowly on individual persecution, and that many of the legal definitions have in fact been used to exclude people from the refugee process. Looking beyond legal discourse, therefore, I take my cue from scholars like Mann who have argued that, in spite of the context, we can read the experience of the *Komagata Maru* passengers as exemplifying refugeeness. As she points out, the fact that the passengers aboard the *Komagata* could not return home to India without risking their lives, that they were rendered stateless, is reminiscent of many of the cases involving refugees today. Even more significant is that this case alerts us to the fact that Canada has a record of turning away people in need. Instead of receiving protection upon their arrival in Canada, the passengers were publicly demonized and left "imprisoned" on their ship for two months, until they were finally deported back to India, a place where their lives would be at risk.[6]

The *Komagata Maru* Incident, as a symbol of Canada's racist treatment of "refugees," is at odds with the dominant narrative of Canadian humanitarian exceptionalism that the editors discuss in their Introduction. In order to discursively produce and maintain its image of hospitality, Canada has had to actively suppress or "forget" events involving racial exclusion as well as the dispossession of Indigenous people. In light of this forgetting, I argue that cultural texts that memorialize the 1914 trauma can rupture hegemonic narratives of timeless Canadian generosity and renarrativize Canada as a nation built on a history of violent exclusion and rejection. Analysing these texts is significant because it will help to put in perspective the contemporary Canadian narrative of humanitarian exceptionalism, which has actually been used to shore up an image of the nation's vulnerability and to recast refugees as criminals intent on exploiting Canadian generosity. As Audrey Macklin notes, the rejection of asylum seekers today hinges on as much on "interdiction and non-entrée policies" as it does on the discursive "demonization" of asylum seekers as "criminals" taking advantage of a Canada that is *just* too nice.[7] Thus, certain cultural texts, to the extent that they recover the memory of the *Komagata Maru* Incident and draw attention to the nation's history of exclusionary immigration policies, can construct a counternarrative of the nation, one that may be used to advocate for refugees in the current era – which I will show with the case of the MV *Sun Sea*.

The MV *Sun Sea*

In 2010, memories of the *Komagata Maru* surfaced when the MV *Sun Sea* arrived in British Columbia carrying 492 Tamil migrants fleeing Sri Lanka in the aftermath of its civil war and seeking refuge in Canada. One year earlier, 76 Tamil migrants had arrived aboard the MV *Ocean Lady*, also seeking refugee status. The case of the Tamil refugees is worth paying attention to here for two reasons. First, this contemporary case and the similarities it bears to the 1914 *Komagata Maru* Incident, as I will show, remind us of the limits of official rhetoric in defining a refugee experience. Second, the case of the *Sun Sea* sheds light on some of the central concerns in this chapter regarding the intersections between memory and trauma in the context of critical refugee studies.

In 1914, the passengers aboard the *Komagata Maru* were detained at Vancouver's harbour and denied access to food, legal counsel, and their advocates; similarly, the Sri Lankan migrants aboard the *Sun Sea* were treated with hostility upon their arrival in Canada.[8] According to one report, the *Sun Sea* passengers "were subjected by the government to prolonged detention, intensive interrogation and energetic efforts to exclude them from the refugee process, or to contest their claim if they succeeded in entering the refugee process."[9] In fact, even before the *Sun Sea* docked in British Columbia, the passengers were publicly vilified as "queue jumpers," and even "criminals" "and "terrorists," who sought to exploit Canada's generosity, as Johanna Reynolds and Jennifer Hyndman discuss in their chapter.[10] Canadian officials such as Public Safety Minister Vic Toews made deliberate attempts to reinforce Canada's reputation as a nation open to refugees, even as they rejected the passengers aboard the *Sun Sea*. In an official statement, for example, Toews stated that the arrival of the *Sun Sea* was an "unacceptable abuse of international law and Canadian generosity."[11] Toews's statement cast the Tamils as criminals taking advantage of Canada rather than refugees in need of state protection, thereby justifying their detention. At the same time, Toews not only invoked a narrative about Canada's record of generosity but also emphasized it as a source of the nation's vulnerability.

In response to the official discourse, scholars and activists have pointed out that the hostile treatment of the Tamil migrants is a reminder of the *Komagata Maru* Incident. In "Tamil, Tiger, Terrorist?" for example, lawyer and activist Fathima Cader compares the treatment of the Tamil asylum seekers to a series of exclusions in Canada that she traces back to the 1914 *Komagata Maru* Incident, thereby suggesting that the *Sun Sea* case marks just the latest moment in a long history of denying asylum to migrants aboard ships.[12] By invoking the *Komagata Maru* Incident and suggesting parallels between these two cases, Cader asserts that Canada's callous response to the Tamil refugees is not a unique and isolated occurrence; it is part of a pattern and reflects a long history of exclusionary racial politics and immigration policies in Canada. To further emphasize this historical continuity, Cader explicitly describes the passengers of the *Komagata Maru* as refugees. "Most of the refugees were Sikhs," she writes of the *Komagata Maru* passengers.[13] Here, Cader's invocation of the category of "refugees" does not denote misunderstanding of the distinction between migrant and refugee, nor is she unaware of history. Instead, this invocation is a strategic political move: that is, Cader invokes the *Komagata Maru* Incident as a cautionary narrative, a reminder that, like their 1914 predecessors, the Tamil asylum seekers aboard the *Sun Sea* would face persecution and perhaps even death if they were denied refugee status and deported back to their homeland.

The case of the *Sun Sea* and responses to it, in explicitly evoking the *Komagata Maru* Incident as a precedent, draw attention to two competing strands of memory. On the one hand, there is the dominant group's self-congratulatory narrative about the nation's benevolence and hospitality. This is a narrative that hinges on "forgetting" events like the *Komagata Maru* Incident, which symbolize racial exclusion and the rejection of asylum seekers at Canada's border. On the other hand, there is the activist's subversive narrative about the nation's histories of rejecting those who come to Canada seeking refuge. This is a narrative that hinges on the very opposite process of "remembering" and resurrecting cases such as the *Komagata Maru* Incident and mapping them onto the public record.

The conflict over memorializing the *Komagata Maru* Incident reminds us that memories are not neutral recollections of the past. In her study on Cambodian genocide and remembrance practice, Cathy Schlund-Vials suggests that memories are resources that can be used strategically by different groups for different political purposes.[14] Building on this claim, this chapter considers two historical accounts of the *Komagata Maru* Incident, which constitute acts of memory: Gurdit Singh's *Voyage of the Komagata Maru, or India's Slavery Abroad* (1928) and Ali Kazimi's *Undesirables: White Canada and the Komagata Maru* (2011). At first glance, these texts appear to be very different. Whereas Singh's text was published in 1928 and is an account of the trauma by someone who was directly involved, Kazimi's text was published almost a century later and is an illustrated account of 1914 trauma. Despite their differences, I argue that both these texts, because they resurrect the story of the *Komagata Maru*, help to subvert hegemonic narratives about timeless Canadian generosity. In addition, these texts, though they do not use the term "refugee," also draw attention to and complicate our understanding of refugeeness, reminding us that the current "refugee crisis" in Canada is not a new phenomenon, but has roots in histories that predate even the use of the term refugee as a legal concept.

Gurdit Singh's *Voyage of the Komagata Maru*

Gurdit Singh's *Voyage of the Komagata Maru, or India's Slavery Abroad* offers us the unique perspective of someone who experienced the Incident first-hand. Indeed, he is a key figure in the *Komagata Maru* Incident, having chartered the journey from the Far East to Canada and back to India, which he documented in his memoir. This memoir, moreover, was written and published in Punjabi while he was on the run from British authorities in India.[15] Singh was among those passengers who managed to escape during the massacre at Budge Budge. For seven years, he went into hiding until he turned himself in to the police and was convicted on charges of sedition.[16] The revised English translation – the text that I examine in this chapter – was published in Kolkata in 1928, after Singh was released from a five-year prison sentence.[17] Singh's personal history attests to the refugeeness of this case, to the fact that the passengers faced persecution upon their return to India and were treated as enemies of the British Raj.

The publication history of Singh's account speaks to the complicated politics of remembering and forgetting. When I began my research in 2006, Singh's manuscript was difficult to access; as primary archival material, I could only locate it at the Nehru Memorial Library and Museum in New Delhi, India, where, as I discovered, the book could not be taken out (most likely because only one copy of it existed) and could only be photocopied. It was not until 2007 that the book was published as a second edition in India, making it more widely accessible. These details, although seemingly trivial, are worth noting because they speak to official attempts to suppress the trauma. In India, the *Komagata Maru* Incident threatened to expose the British Raj's promise of equality as false; in Canada, it threatened to expose the racism underlying the continuous journey policy and to undermine the image of civility that Canadians sought to cultivate as early as the 1900s. In both contexts, therefore, there was a deliberate effort to bury the *Komagata Maru* Incident, that is, to excise it from the public record.

In his account, Gurdit Singh draws attention to the "forgetting" that took place in official accounts of the Incident. According to Singh, British officials sought "to 'whitewash' the doings of the Canadian Authorities and the officials at Budge Budge."[18] Historian Hugh Johnston echoes Singh's claim, explaining that the report published by the Inquiry Committee in 1915 in India offered a sanitized version of the tragedy: in the report, "Canada and the Canadian authorities escaped censure, and the police at Budge Budge were criticized only for searching the ship less carefully than circumstances required."[19] Singh reminds us (as does Johnston) that in the official discourses, the refugeeness of the case – the fact that the passengers were in danger for their lives, that they faced persecution – was being strategically and systematically erased from the public record. Instead, the passengers were being constructed in official records as "criminals" who tried to "evade" the law. The discursive criminalization of the passengers aboard the *Komagata Maru* resonates with cases today in which refugees are labelled "criminals" or "bogus migrants" and framed as breaking the law.

The tone of Singh's account is angry rather than composed and careful; the language is ungrammatical; and there is evidence to suggest that it was not written by Singh himself. For one thing, Gurdit Singh admits that he narrated the story in Gurmukhi, "and some good friends gave it the present shape in English."[20] Second, the style of writing shifts slightly from the beginning to the end, rendering the text polyphonic and suggesting that it was written by more than one writer or translator. The text also includes endless repetition of trivial information, including transcripts of letters and interviews, detailed descriptions of squabbles, a charter contract, excerpts from the Canadian Immigration Act, a list of provisions, and more. Although Singh's account is easily dismissible for these stylistic shortcomings, such "weaknesses" can be construed as strengths, however. Singh's ungrammatical style, his use of inconsequential details, and his affect-laden tone contribute to a disorderliness that reflects the event as it was experienced, and in doing so, directly challenges official efforts to deny the seriousness of the trauma. Singh, then, not only engages in the process of remembering and recovering the story of the *Komagata Maru* but actually dramatizes the experience of uncertainty and fear, or the affective dimensions of the refugee experience. As Vinh Nguyen argues, "refugeeness" is not a temporary condition that is resolved when the subject is granted asylum; rather, it is a "psychic quality or condition of embodiment that results from seeking refuge."[21] In Singh's case, the refugeeness of his experience emerges in the writing of the text itself and the very messiness of his prose.

In his account, Singh asks us to remember that racism at the Canadian border was masked by a performance of legality. He explains that "[t]he Government of Canada wanted to make the whole thing appear like a farce to the outside world after having defrauded our rights and having debarred me from entering Canada."[22] Canadians, he explains, "could have said that they were not harsh to the Indians but [that they] could pay our liabilities for which we were dispossessed of the ship by the owners."[23] Canadians, Gurdit Singh seems to agree, represented themselves not as racist but rather as very judicious and sober, as belonging to a nation that went by the letter of the law. Singh's narrative highlights what Daniel Coleman calls "white civility," a term that denotes how Canada has historically produced itself as a "civil" nation, as good, polite, and law-abiding, but in a manner that conflates civility with English Canadian whiteness.[24] For Coleman, "white civility" manages and excludes "non-white" individuals who are unable to conform to the white racial norm at the same time as it distinguishes Canada from its "uncivil" American neighbour.[25] Singh exposes the fact that in 1914 Canadians were using their "civilized laws," notably the continuous journey regulation, to actually conceal an otherwise clear racial hostility towards Indians and an unwritten policy in support of white dominance. In his account, Singh evokes Canada's image of benevolence only to sardonically question it. For example, he documents the Shore Committee's demands for provisions and then concludes that "the 'benevolent' government consented to the committee and brought rations for us who had had no proper feed for the last six days."[26] Singh's sarcastic tone, indicated most notably by his use of quotation marks around the word "benevolent," signals his suspicion of Canada's claims of goodness.

Although Singh does not employ the term "refugee" to describe the passengers, refugeeness nevertheless is discernible in their experiences of deprivation and precarity – and their subsequent persecution when they were sent back to India, which culminated in the violence at Budge Budge. For Singh, the injustice begins in the Far East. He uses the metaphor of "sucked oranges,"[27] eaten and discarded, to describe the treatment of Indians in British territories outside India and suggests that there is an "utter hollowness of the equality-cult of Western democracies," where, he says, "[c]olour-prejudice is almost a disease."[28] For Singh, the violence at Budge Budge is worse for the passengers than the denial of entry at the Canadian border, though clearly the former followed from the latter. The injustice of Budge Budge and the harm done to the passengers there directly resulted from Canada's refusal to allow them to settle in Vancouver. Singh suggests that "[w]hat happened at Budge Budge cannot be described"[29] and that the experience of trauma has left him speechless. He goes on to explain that, "[t]hough we were unarmed and like sheep in a pin [sic], yet the wolves in authority used most condemnable deception and cruelty in their dealings and bungled the whole affair."[30] Evoking the image of a helpless animal being attacked by a pack of ferocious wolves, Gurdit Singh attempts to express the intensity of his rage and his sadness at the Incident. His account shows how, for him, the experience at Canada's border was a source of mental stress as well as physical suffering, which could be compared to that of refugees who are stateless or in between borders today.

Singh's account draws attention to the fact that refugeeness is often produced by transnational networks of power and injustice. The very structure of his narrative – the fact that it begins in the Far East and ends in India – reminds us of the transnational dimensions of the tragedy. In her analysis of Singh's memoir, Renisa Mawani suggests that "Singh viewed the ship's detention in Vancouver, its deportation to India, and the subsequent massacre at Budge Budge to be part of a much longer history of racial and legal violence."[31] Singh repeatedly points out that the passengers were subjects of a British-controlled India, rather than subjects of an independent nation. Their "homeland" was occupied by the British. In the Far East, where many escaped to survive, Singh says that they were treated like "coolies" and calls their condition "slavery abroad." In Canada, their statelessness was produced as a result of immigration policies that prevented them from landing – policies that, as Singh mentions, were drafted with the help of the British. Singh refers here to the 1908 Orders in Council that were drafted to prevent Indians from entering Canada. According to historical accounts, the British Raj sanctioned these orders, in part because of growing concern with the increasing power of the Ghadar movement and the threat it posed to the Empire. By drawing attention to the transnational dimensions of the tragedy, Singh challenges hegemonic attempts to construct the event as a small local case at Vancouver's border and shows us how the refugeeness of the passengers is produced by multiple geopolitical forces.

Ali Kazimi's *Undesirables: White Canada and the Komagata Maru*

Whereas Gurdit Singh's account dramatizes the experience of refugeeness in terms of both form and content, Kazimi's account, which emerges many decades after the trauma and thus has the advantage of hindsight, offers us a more interpretive account of the *Komagata Maru* Incident by historicizing the statelessness of the passengers and framing their deportation within a longer history of exclusionary immigration policies. Structured chronologically, *Undesirables* traces the passengers' journey from the Far East to Canada and back to India. The combination of texts and images (photographs, archival images, official documents) highlights the refugeeness of the passengers and situates their experience within a history of exclusionary politics in Canada. Kazimi himself notes in his Introduction, "Although most Canadians descend from people who arrive by ship, these new migrants are often referred to as 'boat people.' All of the recent ships have carried non-European migrants; their passengers have been [of] South Asian (Sikh and Tamil) and Chinese (Fujian) origin. The history of the *Komagata Maru* resonates with each new arrival."[32] Kazimi's text draws our attention to the significance of the *Komagata Maru* Incident for understanding refugee cases today, even though it does not use the term "refugee" explicitly to describe the *Komagata Maru* passengers.

Kazimi's text was funded by the Community Historical Recognition Program of Citizenship and Immigration Canada (CHRP), which was established by the Canadian government in 2008. As the Government of Canada's website suggests, the purpose of this program was to fund community organizations and associations "to undertake projects aimed at recognizing and commemorating the experience of certain ethno-cultural communities that underwent hardships as a result of federal immigration restrictions and wartime measures." The description of the grant is worth noting here, for it erases the violence of events like the *Komagata Maru* Incident by reducing them to "hardships," and relegates them to the past, distinct from the present. Thus, I argue that Kazimi, like his predecessor Gurdit Singh, also responds to a kind of state forgetting, although one that takes a very different form. In Singh's account, official forgetting constitutes a straightforward denial that an injustice has taken place. For Kazimi, official forgetting is premised on a subtle and paradoxical form of remembering in order to forget. In the book, Kazimi recognizes this paradoxical form of state forgetting. He notes that the *Komagata Maru* Incident has been framed as "Incidental" in the popular imagination, as an isolated event in Canada's past, one that is distinct from its multicultural present. Kazimi's goal seems to be to push back against this national narrative, to challenge it, and to show that "the *Komagata Maru* 'Incident' was not incidental in the context of Canada's desire to be a 'white man's country.'"[33] He takes up this task, moreover, by employing the very resources meant to predicate acts of historical forgetting.

Like Gurdit Singh, Kazimi highlights the fact that the passengers aboard the *Komagata Maru* were treated as criminals rather than asylum seekers, although he does so in a very different way: by using a combination of images and text. For example, he presents us with a newspaper clipping from the period which has as its headline: "Hindu Invaders Now in the City Harbour on *Komagata Maru*." In the caption, Kazimi writes, "Vancouver papers were filled with sensational reports and rumours days before the *Komagata Maru* finally arrived in Vancouver."[34] He wants us to see that the public's fear of foreign "invasion" was unfounded in 1914. As such, he juxtaposes the newspaper headline with another image: one that captures the passengers when they first arrived in Canada. In this image, the passengers are on the deck of the ship; Gurdit Singh is at the centre and has his arms outstretched in a kind of celebratory gesture. Perhaps even more interesting are the facial expressions of the passengers – they are smiling. The image frames the passengers as non-threatening and presents their arrival as *anything but* an invasion. Instead, it draws our attention to their hopeful attitudes and their innocent optimism that Canada would honour their rights as British subjects and allow them to land. Kazimi's strategic placement of images not only challenges the representation of the passengers as "Hindu Invaders" but also reminds us that the public demonization of refugees today (as Johanna Reynolds and Jennifer Hyndman discuss in detail) is tied to a longer history dating back to the *Komagata Maru*.

In the book, the juxtaposition of photos, together with Kazimi's narrative, prompts readers to remember that Canada was built upon racist immigration policies and the deliberate exclusion of racialized subjects. For example, Kazimi presents not only images of the exclusion of the *Komagata Maru*'s passengers but also images that draw attention to the fact that, while Canada excluded racialized others, it celebrated the arrival of white subjects. One image in the book, for instance, depicts an advertisement, presumably from the late 1800s, that reads: "Free Farms for the Million: Dominion of Canada." Below is an image of a Canadian landscape with large plots of land. The land, the poster says, is "[g]iven to every Male Adult of 18 years and over, in the great fertile best of Manitoba, Canadian North-West, and British Columbia."[35] Another image is of "the Canadian Emigration office" in London in 1911. Here, Kazimi tells us that "[t]he Canadian government launched an aggressive campaign to recruit British immigrants."[36] While these advertisements seem to bolster Canada's national image as a "nation of immigrants," Kazimi emphasizes that Canada offered free land only to certain "desirable" immigrants, and that desirability was linked with whiteness. In doing so, he challenges the myth of "humanitarian exceptionalism" and shows us how Canada sought to deny entry to migrants that it saw as undesirable.

Against the ads targeting white Europeans, Kazimi draws our attention to photographs of populations that were excluded from Canada through a series of restrictive immigration policies. For example, he presents us with an image of Chinese immigrant men who came to Canada during the gold rushes and another image shows us a Head Tax certificate used to curb Chinese immigration to Canada. That Kazimi points out that the image of the Chinese men is a "rare early photograph"[37] suggests that such images and stories, including the story of the *Komagata Maru* Incident, have been elided from the nation's consciousness, while the arrival of British immigrants has been well documented and remembered. In addition to the Chinese Head Tax, Kazimi also refers to the continuous journey policy; in fact, he links both of these exclusionary measures to Canada's unwritten policy of maintaining the hegemony of whiteness.

66   Alia Somani

One of the most haunting images in the book is a picture of a group of white settlers in Saskatoon standing behind an Indigenous man. The photograph is obviously staged: the white settlers are staring at the camera while the Indigenous man sits on the dirt road before them. The Indigenous man is wrapped in a dirty blanket, and his eyes are slightly closed and his hair dishevelled. The black-and-white image draws attention to the manner in which Indigenous people were treated as curious spectacles and regularly dehumanized by the white settler subject. In a number of ways, the image encapsulates the politics of memory. The image itself has been forgotten. As Kazimi tells us, "No details are available about this image from 1905."[38] Thus, to see this image is, first, to *remember* Canada's history of genocide against Indigenous people and, second, to be alerted to the history of inequality upon which the nation rests. By emphasizing this image, Kazimi underscores the fact that, whereas white men were given free land, the Indigenous people to whom the land actually belonged were treated as inhuman and subject to unspeakable atrocities. In the text, Kazimi explains:

> Canada's aboriginal peoples were kept strictly on the margins. Residential schools that sought to "civilize" aboriginal children, legal restrictions on traditional aboriginal practices, externally applied rules that defined who was an Indian, and the encroachment on and confiscation of traditional lands were deliberate policies designed to destroy aboriginal culture and ways of living.[39]

Although the history of residential schools may seem out of place in a narrative about the *Komagata Maru* Incident, Kazimi draws attention to a pattern of exclusionary policies that marked certain bodies as undesirable and others as desirable.

Kazimi, whose book was published many decades after Gurdit Singh's, suggests that the *Komagata Maru* reverberates in new forms in the present. He refuses to see the *Komagata Maru* Incident as part of a past separate from the multicultural present, and instead connects it and the experiences of refugees in the present day, especially those who arrive by boat. For one thing, Kazimi compares the continuous journey policy and the present-day Safe Third Country Agreement, which regulates and (excludes) refugees from seeking asylum in Canada. He notes that the Safe Third Country Agreement, which was "signed in 2002 between Canada and the United States," "echoes the continuous journey regulation in its requirement that people seeking asylum must arrive directly from their country of citizenship."[40] The Safe Third Country Agreement, Kazimi points out, has reduced the number of refugees entering Canada by "more than 43 per cent."[41] While the agreement is framed in seemingly neutral ways, Kazimi's linkage of the current policy towards refugees and the continuous journey policy lays bare the discriminatory policies that undergird nation-building.

While Kazimi insists on drawing attention to the racial hypocrisies underlying the nation and its immigration policies – both then and now – he also understands the refugeeness of the passengers aboard the *Komagata Maru* as produced by transnational forces. In this way, Kazimi's efforts parallel Gurdit Singh's 1928 attempt to consider the broader context for the Incident. Kazimi's account resists the confines of the nation as a methodological frame of understanding the tragedy and looks at it through the lens of global complexity. For Kazimi, racism at the Canadian border had "global ramifications."[42] Most notably, it exposed the British Empire's promise of equality towards its subjects as false. Kazimi draws attention to this promise from the very outset of the book with a photograph of a military procession in London. We are told that on 22 June 1897, soldiers of the British army, many of whom were from British India, marched in support of Queen Victoria and celebrated her Diamond Jubilee.[43] The full-page photograph figures as a powerful symbol of that promise of equality – a promise that Kazimi challenges throughout his account. Thus, he draws attention to the treatment of indentured labourers in the British colonies, documents the famine in India that led many to migrate elsewhere, and traces the journey of the *Komagata Maru* to Budge Budge and the massacre that follows. While the centre of the story is the *Komagata Maru* Incident or the racist turning away of the passengers at Canada's border, Kazimi suggests that we can only understand this turning away by looking at it within a larger historical framework that demonstrates how the injustice of the Incident is tied to unjust treatment of asylum seekers.

Conclusion

While Canada tends to be understood as a site of humanitarian goodness, as a global citizen on the world's stage, numerous scholars have noted that it is not as welcoming as its public image suggests. Kazimi's and Gurdit Singh's attempts to resurrect the *Komagata Maru* Incident and to inscribe it into the national consciousness have the potential to alter the way we perceive Canada. Both these texts not only draw attention to one of the nation's early treatments of migrants who arrived in Canada seeking "refuge" but also remind us of the ways in which the turning away of the 1914 passengers was tied to the politics of imperial citizenship, to the fact that the Canadian government acted in conjunction with the British Empire. In so doing, these texts ask us to rethink Canada's response to "refugees," whether or not they define themselves as such, to understand the way in which refugeeness is produced within global systems, and above and beyond that, to question the very principles of benevolence and generosity that the nation claims to cherish.

NOTES

1. Daniel Gorman argues in his account of imperial citizenship that there was a "division between those who advocated a parochial, nationalist, imperial citizenship and those who supported a nascent, cosmopolitan, imperial citizenship," 5.
2. Johnston, *The Voyage of the "Komagata Maru"*, 4–5.
3. A boatload of Indian migrants who arrived in Canada one year earlier had successfully challenged the immigration barriers in the courts. Singh was influenced by the outcome of this case.
4. Johnston, *The Voyage of the "Komagata Maru"*, 57.
5. Mann, "Refugees Who Arrive by Boat," 193.
6. Ibid., 192.
7. Macklin, "New Directions for Refugee Policy," 1.
8. Krishnamurti, "Queue-Jumpers, Terrorists, Breeders," 139.
9. Canadian Council for Refugees, "*Sun Sea*: Five Years Later," 1.
10. Krishnamurti notes that "in popular and populist discourse, Tamil and Tiger are inextricable," but in the case of neither the *Sun Sea* nor the *Ocean Lady* "has it been conclusively proven that such ties [to the Tamil Tigers] exist" ("Queue-Jumpers, Terrorists, Breeders," 149).
11. Quoted in Canadian Council for Refugees, "*Sun Sea*: Five Years Later," 16.
12. Cader, "Tamil, Tiger, Terrorist?"
13. Ibid.
14. Schlund-Vials argues in *War, Genocide, and Justice* that Cambodian officials use the genocide to shore up a narrative of national triumph, while American officials misremember America's complicity in the violence; both groups are thus engaging in a kind of "forgetting" or selective remembering of the past. Against this selective memory, she focuses on the work of Cambodian American refugee artists and writers who, she argues, resuscitate the past as sites of healing and alternative justice.
15. Johnston, *The Voyage of the "Komagata Maru"*.
16. Mawani, "Criminal Accusation as Colonial Rule," 217.
17. Johnston, *The Voyage of the "Komagata Maru"*, 185.
18. Singh, foreword to *Voyage of the Komagata Maru*, 126.

19 Johnston, *The Voyage of the "Komagata Maru"*, 168.
20 Singh, foreword to *Voyage of the Komagata Maru*.
21 Nguyen, "Refugeetude," 111.
22 Singh, *The Voyage of the Komagata Maru*, Part I, 55.
23 Ibid.
24 Coleman, *White Civility*, 5.
25 Ibid.
26 Singh, *Voyage of the Komagata Maru*, Part I, 112.
27 Ibid., 1.
28 Ibid., 5.
29 Singh, *Voyage of the Komagata Maru*, Part II, 34.
30 Singh, *Voyage of the Komagata Maru*, Part I, 35.
31 Mawani, "Criminal Accusation as Colonial Rule," 89.
32 Kazimi, *Undesirables*, 9.
33 Ibid., xvii.
34 Ibid., 94.
35 Ibid., 44.
36 Ibid., 45.
37 Ibid.
38 Ibid., 70.
39 Ibid.
40 Ibid., 11.
41 Ibid.
42 Ibid., 52.
43 Ibid., 13.

REFERENCES

Cader, Fathima. "Tamil, Tiger, Terrorist? Anti-Migrant Hysteria and the Criminalization of Asylum Seekers." *Briarpatch*, 7 July 2011. https://briarpatchmagazine.com/articles/view/tamil-tiger-terrorist.

Canadian Council for Refugees. "*Sun Sea*: Five Years Later." ccrweb.ca, August 2015. http://ccrweb.ca/sites/ccrweb.ca/files/sun-sea-five-years-later.pdf. Accessed 10 April 2017.

Coleman, Daniel. *White Civility: The Literary Project of English Canada*. Toronto: University of Toronto Press, 2006.

"Community Historical Recognition Program." Government of Canada. https://www.canada.ca/en/immigration-refugees-citizenship/corporate/reports-statistics/evaluations/historical-recognition-programs.html#profile. Accessed 10 May 2019.

Gorman, Daniel. *Imperial Citizenship: Empire and the Question of Belonging*. Vancouver: University of British Columbia Press, 2006.

Johnston, Hugh. *The Voyage of the "Komagata Maru": The Sikh Challenge to Canada's Colour Bar*. 2nd ed. Vancouver: University of British Columbia Press, 2014.

Kazimi, Ali. *Undesirables: White Canada and the Komagata Maru*. Vancouver: Douglas and McIntyre, 2011.

"Komagata Maru", A Challenge to Colonialism: Key Documents. Edited by Malwinderjit Singh Waraich and Gurdev Singh Sidhu. Chandigarh: Unistar Books, 2005.

Krishnamurti, Sailaja. "Queue-Jumpers, Terrorists, Breeders: Representations of Tamil Migrants in Canadian Popular Media." *South Asian Diaspora* 5, no.1 (2013): 139–57.

Macklin, Audrey. "New Directions for Refugee Policy: Of Curtains, Doors, and Locks." *Refugee* 19, no. 4 (2001): 1–4.

Mann, Alexandra. "Refugees Who Arrive by Boat and Canada's Commitment to the Refugee Convention: A Discursive Analysis." *Refugee* 26, no.2 (2009): 191–206.

Mawani, Renisa. "Criminal Accusation as Colonial Rule: The Case of Gurdit Singh (1859–1954)." In *Accusation: Creating Criminals*. Edited by George Pavlich and Matthew P. Unger, 73–99. Vancouver: University of British Columbia Press, 2016.

Nguyen, Vinh. "Refugeetude: When Does a Refugee Stop Being a Refugee?" *Social Text* 37, no. 2 (2019): 109–31.

Price, John. *Orienting Canada: Race, Empire and the Transpacific*. Vancouver: University of British Columbia Press, 2011.

Rae, Bob. "Lessons to Be Learned." Ottawa: Her Majesty the Queen in Right of Canada, 2005. 1–42. https://www.publicsafety.gc.ca/cnt/rsrcs/pblctns/lssns-lrnd/lssns-lrnd-eng.pdf.

Schlund-Vials, Cathy J. *War, Genocide, and Justice: Cambodian American Memory Work*. Minneapolis: University of Minnesota Press, 2012.

Singh, Gurdit. Foreword to *Voyage of the Komagata Maru: or India's Slavery Abroad*. Part I. Calcutta: n.p. (1928).

– *Voyage of the Komagata Maru: or India's Slavery Abroad*. Part I. Calcutta: n.p. (1928): 1–128.

– *Voyage of the Komagata Maru: or India's Slavery Abroad*. Part II. Calcutta: n.p. (1928): 1–200.

3 Erasing Exclusion: Adrienne Clarkson and the Promise of the Refugee Experience

LAURA MADOKORO

Introduction

In October 2015, the former governor general of Canada, the Right Honourable Adrienne Clarkson, née Poy, penned an op-ed for the *New York Times* in which she wrote about three-year-old Aylan Kurdi. Almost a month earlier, on 2 September 2015, his body had washed up on a Turkish beach after a boat in which he and his family were fleeing the civil war in Syria capsized in the Mediterranean Sea. Images of his prone body provoked an international outcry and mobilized previously apathetic publics to do something on behalf of Syrian refugees. As part of Clarkson's insistence that governments in the United States and Canada needed to act, she declared, "at the same age as that toddler, I came to Canada as a Chinese refugee soon after Hong Kong fell to the Japanese in late December 1941."[1]

Though Clarkson's public claiming of a refugee identity was not new, the tone of her intervention was far more insistent than in previous incarnations. In the decade that followed her departure as Canada's twenty-sixth governor general, Clarkson shaped the public's understanding of her life, as well as refugee experiences more generally, through numerous publications ranging from *Heart Matters* (her 2007 memoirs), to an edited collection of refugee, migrant, and citizen experiences titled *Room for All of Us: Surprising Stories of Loss and Transformation* (2011), to reflections on the nature of citizenship in Canada in *Belonging: The Paradox of Citizenship* (2014) (the print version of her 2014 Massey Lectures), and finally to her opinion piece on the politics of refugee protection in the face of the Syrian refugee crisis in 2015. Throughout these works, Clarkson provided a narrative account of her family's flight from wartime Hong Kong and their eventual settlement in Canada in 1942. It is a story of promise and, in some ways, redemption – one that evokes a rags-to-riches narrative that has become important in recent years as activists have sought to encourage public support for refugees.[2] It is also one that normalizes the opportunities of refuge, suggesting – as Clarkson does – that such experiences are "remarkable" yet also typical of life in Canada.[3]

Critically, it is not a story of racialized exclusion or a story of the 1923 Chinese Immigration Act, which prohibited the permanent settlement of most Chinese migrants – with the exception of diplomats, merchants (and their wives), and students – until it was repealed in 1947. The Chinese Immigration Act was in effect when the Poys arrived in Canada. The very existence of this exclusionary legislation should have made the idea of Chinese refugees in Canada unfathomable. Yet it did not, for the Poys overcame structural barriers in order to settle in Canada beyond all that they overcame in fleeing war-torn Hong Kong. In ignoring this history of racism, Clarkson's narrative privileges gratitude and a sense of hopeful optimism about the future over all else.

Scholar Mimi Nguyen charges that narratives of refugee gratitude have done critical recuperative work in the wake of US imperial projects.[4] Although Nguyen focuses solely on the American context, many of her ideas translate to the Canadian context as well. Narratives of refugee gratitude celebrate the generosity of states while at the same time shaping generalized understandings of refugee experiences in which displacement, passive vulnerability, and eternal gratitude are key. Such narratives assume a particular register in the context of the ongoing history of settler colonialism in Canada and the related practice of colonial denial, in which the continued violence against, and dispossession of, Indigenous peoples is rendered implausible by a self-proclaimed liberal, progressive identity.[5]

Indeed, there is a great deal that is rendered invisible in the production of refugee narratives of gratitude. Such narratives are implicitly ahistorical, erasing particular contingencies in the face of universal tropes. In the process, the complexities that attend on any experience of displacement and search for refuge disappear. Instead, the refugee subject becomes a "speechless emissary," a universal subject in need of rescue and an entirely ahistorical entity whose lived experience is meant to address expectations of struggle and liberation.[6] In this totalizing fashion, the particular historical contingencies that shape the nature of someone's flight and the character of their refuge disappear.

Intrigued by the structure and substance of Clarkson's narrative, as well as the manner in which it has thickened over almost a decade of literary output, in this chapter I reconsider the historical context in which the Poy family left Hong Kong and settled in Canada. The chapter focuses in particular on the fact that the Poys moved at a time when there was no legal category for refugee admissions in Canada and underscores that this absence does not determine understandings of Clarkson's refugee identity: even without legal sanction, Clarkson nevertheless considers her family's experience to be one of refugees in search of protection and security. By exploring the tensions between legally defined categories of migration and lived experiences, this chapter draws attention to the myriad ways that refugee experiences manifested themselves historically – beyond the legal categories of refugeehood in the League of Nations era and the international refugee regime that emerged after the Second World War, with the 1951 United Nations Convention Relating to the Status of Refugees as its cornerstone.

The federal government Canada signed the UN convention and associated protocol in 1969, though it engaged with refugee protection prior to then, most prominently for displaced persons in Europe after the Second World War. It also engaged in discrete refugee resettlement schemes, including those for refugees from the Hungarian Revolution in 1956, for one hundred refugees affected by tuberculosis (who normally would have been excluded on medical admissibility grounds) in 1960, and for the first Chinese refugees officially resettled from Hong Kong to Canada in 1962. All of these discrete initiatives – and most particularly the resettlement of Chinese refugees given Clarkson's own story – are important because they suggest the entangled and somewhat strained relationship between legal categories of migration, lived experiences, and contests over refugee identities.

The idea of contested refugee identities also informs the second thread of analysis in this chapter, which is a close reading of Clarkson's interventions on the subject of refugeehood, including passages from her memoir, as well as from *Room for All of Us*, *Belonging*, and her 2015 op-ed piece in the *New York Times*. A focused examination of these texts shows the deep tensions in Clarkson's writing as she perpetuates stereotypes of the desirable, accomplished refugee subject who thrives in a new homeland by insisting that her family's experience was ordinary, simply one variety of "remarkable," even though it was far from this. In fact, the experience was exceptional both in the manner in which the Poy family arrived in Canada and in the platform Clarkson now has as a prominent public figure to give weight to ideas about refugee experiences and identities. Crucially, over her decade of public interventions, Clarkson's writings have perpetuated universalized notions of refugeehood. This construction results in large part from her reluctance to detail the history of racism in Canada. The result is a refugee narrative that promotes a one-dimensional refugee identity and suppresses the historically contingent, the exceptional, and the unsavoury.

Historicizing the Narrative

Adrienne Clarkson's personal refugee story is one that pre-dates the web of legal definitions that have defined refugee movements since the Second World War. Although the idea of a refugee dates to biblical times and the stories of Exodus, the legally defined notion of a refugee as a category of migrant, with implied responsibility for state protection, is an entirely twentieth-century phenomenon beginning with the work of the League of Nations in the 1920s. After the Second World War, in the wake of massive displacement in Europe, Asia, Africa, and, later, Latin America, states developed the 1951 UN Convention Relating to the Status of Refugees, the 1969 OAU Refugee Convention, and the 1984 Cartagena Declaration of Refugees, the cornerstones of what is now described as the international refugee regime – a web of laws, policies, and state and non-state actors largely focused on issues around protection.[7] This timeline does not mean that there were no refugees beyond the categories of statelessness developed over the course of the twentieth century. Rather, as Clarkson's story makes clear, legal definitions have only ever captured some of the ways that people move as refugees. Many others experience fear and displacement without having legal recognition of these processes. Clarkson's prominence as a public figure, means that she can claim an identity that is not necessarily available to those in more vulnerable positions, particularly contemporary refugees who must convince states and publics of their legal status by conforming to strict, and legally bounded, ideas of refugeehood in order to obtain the benefits of protection.

Adrienne Clarkson was born in Hong Kong in 1940 to William Poy (Ng Ying Choi) and Ethel Lam (Lam May Ngo). William was born in Australia but eventually moved to China and then Hong Kong, where he met Ethel. They were married at St. John's Anglican Cathedral in 1934. As will be detailed in this chapter, the Poy family moved to Canada in 1942 from Japanese-occupied Hong Kong. They were part of a civilian exchange negotiated between the American and Japanese governments, in which US authorities also negotiated the exchange of Canadian citizens. While all of the civilians involved fled the military occupation of Hong Kong, the Poys were unusual in that they participated in the exchange in order to seek refuge in a new land (as opposed to most others, who were returning home). And they alone, as a result of Adrienne Clarkson's literary outputs, have been memorialized as refugees.

Crucially, the Poys moved at a time when legal categories of refugeehood and attendant state responsibilities to provide protection or humanitarian relief were still in their nascent form. Previous efforts, most notably under the League of Nations, had been limited to specific groups, including stateless Armenians and Russians following the fall of the Ottoman Empire and the Russian Revolution. The Poys moved in somewhat of a legal vacuum and were therefore never legally identified, or assisted, as refugees. Instead, they seem to have benefited in part from the idea of imperial citizenship, since both William and Ethel May were British subjects.[8] William's status as Australian-born may have furthered their case for assistance, as there is some suggestion that they initially hoped to go to his birth country, but the proximity of the Japanese forces convinced them to remain on board the SS *Gripsholm* all the way to New York. They were ultimately permitted to land in Canada based on exemption criteria in the 1923 Chinese Immigration Act, which allowed for the entry of students, as well as diplomats, merchants, and their wives. All other Chinese migrants were banned, reflecting a deep-seated animosity to permanent migration from Asia that shaped Canadian immigration policy from the late nineteenth century.

After arriving in Canada, the family settled in Ottawa. Clarkson was a star student throughout her time in high school and university and rose to prominence as a journalist for the CBC, where she worked for almost thirty years. From 1999 to 2005, Clarkson served as governor general of Canada, during which time she radically raised the profile of the position, in particular promoting the Canadian North and the country's arts and culture. Since leaving the office of governor general in 2005, Clarkson has remained a prominent public figure, co-founding the Institute for Canadian Citizenship to promote opportunities for "active citizenship" and publishing a memoir and other works. Over the course of her public engagement with questions of citizenship and inclusion, Clarkson has become increasingly outspoken about her own family's refugee experiences.

Chinese Exclusion and Civilian Exchange

To fully understand the implications of Clarkson's evolving narrative about her family's history and their reception by the Canadian state and Canadian society more broadly, it is important to underscore the long history of exclusion that shaped Canada's evolution as a white settler society. As a result of the large number of labourers who made their way to Canada in pursuit of economic opportunity in newly discovered gold mines and on the construction of transcontinental railroads, Chinese migrants were subject to punitive immigration restrictions.[9] Fears of economic competition twinned with racial discrimination led the federal government to impose increasingly stiff capitation taxes from 1885 to 1923 in order to deter Chinese migrants from permanent settlement. Beginning with a fifty-dollar head tax in 1885, the fee grew in size over the years, reaching the sum of five hundred dollars in 1904. When the tax failed to sufficiently deter migration from China, the federal government introduced the Chinese Immigration Act in 1923, a law that banned Chinese migration almost completely. This ban was still in place when the Poy family arrived in Canada from war-torn Hong Kong in 1942. The legislation was repealed five years later, following the considerable pro-Chinese sentiment that manifested itself during the Second World War as allied China was subject to a brutal Japanese occupation.

War broke out between China and Japan in 1937 in what some historians identify as a prelude to the Second World War. Japanese attacks on Pearl Harbor in December 1941 brought formal declarations of war from the United States, Canada, and other allies. On Christmas Day 1941, governing British authorities in Hong Kong surrendered to the Japanese Imperial Army. Canadian soldiers from the Winnipeg Grenadiers and Royal Rifles had formed part of the defence of Hong Kong, and many were wounded or killed in the attack; 1,685 Canadian soldiers were taken as prisoners of war (POWs).[10] The term "prisoner of war" refers to "a person who has been captured or who has surrendered to an opponent in war; a captive."[11] The term generally refers to soldiers and other military personnel rather than civilians, though there are numerous contemporary and historical exceptions.[12]

Over the course of the twentieth century, an elaborate international legal framework emerged around the rights of POWs and the responsibilities of their keepers, with some attention to the treatment of civilians as well. Many of these rights were first elaborated in 1907, revised in 1929, and further refined in 1949 under the Third Geneva Convention. The 1929 Convention Relative to the Treatment of Prisoners of War contained some key provisions that shaped the work of the International Committee of the Red Cross (ICRC) during the Second World War. In particular, Articles 77 and 79 provided for the establishment of a Central Agency of Information in a neutral country to facilitate the exchange of information about prisoners of war, and ultimately the exchange of prisoners themselves.

The Imperial Government of Japan was not a signatory to the 1929 Convention, although it had agreed to the terms regarding the work of the ICRC. As a result, the degree to which the Japanese Imperial Government and Army were willing to comply with the terms of the Convention was always a point of concern.[13] Within a few days of the attack on Pearl Harbor, US officials contacted their counterparts in Japan to seek guarantees about the treatment of American prisoners of war.[14] The Japanese Imperial Government provided assurances with some delay. As these were less than convincing, throughout the war allied nations and the ICRC (charged with monitoring the situation in Hong Kong) expressed reservations about the extent to which Japanese imperial forces were in fact respecting the Convention.[15]

Worries about the fate of military personnel in Japanese-occupied Hong Kong extended to that of the civilian population. Canadian government files from the period are rife with rumoured and documented atrocities committed by Japanese soldiers. Reports indicated that British and American civilians (as well as civilians from other countries, including Canada) were "marched off to third-rate Chinese hotels where the accommodations were very poor, and where those who had failed to bring sufficient personal effects and bedding found life rather miserable. Only rice and hot water were supplied."[16] In her memoir, *Heart Matters*, Clarkson recalls, "The conditions had been hideous in Hong Kong – there was little food and many rumours that people had become cannibals. I know that my parents were very worried from day to day about where our food would come from."[17]

By May 1942, Canadian reports underscored that "life for the civilian population both Chinese and foreign is daily becoming less tolerable. Foodstuffs and commodities in common use have risen to seven times their pre-war price."[18] As a result, the Canadian government was very anxious that ICRC representatives visit Hong Kong to document what was taking place.[19] Vincent Massey, then Canadian high commissioner to London, argued in February 1942 that it was "essential that [an] ICRC delegate should proceed to Hong Kong and Kowloon [as early as] possible to report on conditions and exercise restraining influence." Massey was particularly vexed about obtaining details related to "a) location of prisoners of war and internees, b) treatment with special reference to food and medical attention c) lists of names of prisoners of war and internees and d) lists of killed or missing."[20] However, attempts by the ICRC to document what was happening were regularly rebuffed, as were efforts by governments to send ships with humanitarian relief supplies.[21] There was therefore both an implicit and explicit sense among concerned observers that the Japanese Imperial Government was not cooperating on the issue of POWs, and these suspicions carried over, to some extent, to the situation of civilians caught up in the hostilities.

To address the plight of civilians engulfed by conflict, exchanges were negotiated between Axis and Allied powers throughout the

Second World War. These exchanges involved diplomats, journalists, missionaries, businesspeople, and students. As historian Rowena Ward notes, reciprocity was central to the character of these exchanges.[22] For every individual exchanged on one side, another was to be returned. Significantly, these individuals had to be of equal value (in terms of status): a diplomat for a diplomat and a non-official for a non-official. This equality of exchange was difficult to execute in practice, however. Moreover, limited ship capacity meant that not everyone could be exchanged, and so the story of wartime exchanges is as much about who was included as who was not.[23]

To facilitate the exchanges, the Japanese government relied on the Swiss government, as a Protective Power, to negotiate with Allied nations for the exchange of prisoners of war, while the United States worked through the government of Argentina. Negotiations were highly complex, and it took months for the Red Cross to orchestrate the first of the exchanges between the United States and Japan, which occurred in the summer of 1942.[24] To be included in an exchange, one had to fall within a privileged category. For the Japanese Imperial Government, this meant government officials as well as merchants, scholars, and students, while the US government focused on officials, businessmen, missionaries, and educators.

Ensuring reciprocity proved one of the most difficult aspect of negotiations. The uneven number of nationals in the United States and in Japan meant that, as negotiations progressed, nationals of other countries and other geographic regions were brought within the scope of the agreements. The American government ultimately negotiated the exchange of its own citizens as well as Canadian and Latin American nationals in order to facilitate the return of Americans from Manchukuo and occupied China. As historian Bruce Elleman observes, this broad approach meant that, over the course of two exchanges, the US government successfully negotiated the return of "virtually all American government officials, as well as thousands of ordinary American citizens."[25] Yet not everyone was included, and thousands of Americans, including many civilians, remained in the Pacific Theatre until 1945, when the war ended.[26]

The hierarchy of civilians was evident from the outset of the first exchange. Among the Canadians included in the initial party were E. D'arcy McGreer, Canadian chargé d'affaires in Tokyo, Paul McLane, trade commissioner at Hong Kong, and Mrs. McLane, Col. E. Doughty, Canadian immigration officer at Hong Kong, and V.E. Duclos, trade commissioner at Shanghai, his wife, and their two children, and members of the Women's Missionary Society and Board of Foreign

Missionaries. Journalist Jack Sullivan described the returning Canadians as individuals "who first tasted the bitter fruits of war in the Pacific, the hardy missionaries, newspapermen, business men and diplomats for whom the months since Dec. 7 have been difficult and in some cases painful."[27]

William Poy, who had worked for the Canadian trade commissioner for twelve years, and his family, including three-year-old Adrienne, were among the almost 1,500 passengers who arrived aboard the SS *Gripsholm* in New York in August 1942. Clarkson describes the circumstances of her family's departure from Hong Kong as follows:

> We did not have the kind of vast fortunes and property that enabled some Chinese families in Hong Kong to escape to their estates on mainland China. Not for us the beautiful fish ponds and rice fields of the Chinese interior, or the quantity of jade bracelets that were broken off women's arms and either sold or traded. To stay alive, my father occasionally was able to do a deal on watches or selling rice. But he knew we had to get out, and preferably to Australia, where his family – eight brothers and sisters and his mother and her new husband – still lived. But the war in the Pacific made that impossible.
>
> So my father wrote to Canadian trade commissioners with whom he had worked and become friends ... No one answered the letters. But one night in June there was a loud knocking at the door. It was the Kempitei, the Japanese equivalent of the Gestapo. My parents, terrified, opened the door and, when asked who they were, identified themselves. The officer in charge said, "You are on a list to be exchanged by the Red Cross. Be down at Stanley dock with one suitcase for each member of your family at dawn."[28]

This development is astonishing, given the historical circumstances in which refuge was secured. As noted above, none of the Poys were Canadian-born, though all were British subjects. And they were Chinese at a time when the 1923 Chinese Immigration Act continued to be enforced, meaning that they had to fit into one of the specific categories of exemption in order to be permitted entry. William Poy was likely admitted to the country as a diplomat or merchant, with his family as dependents. There is no way the Poys could have been legally admitted otherwise.

No doubt William Poy was the central figure in securing this admission. It seems he was able to get a position on the boat because of his station and good words from his employer. Aboard the *Gripsholm*, Poy (like many other passengers) was interviewed about his past and his experiences in Hong Kong.[29] Compared to the information provided by others aboard the ship, Poy's answers were rather cursory. He indicated that he was born on 17 May 1907 in Australia and that he was a British national, and he listed his occupation as "Clerk." He explained that he had lived in Hong Kong since 1926 and identified English, Cantonese, and Toyshan (Taishanese) as his spoken languages. He named the Department of Trade and Commerce in Ottawa as his destination in Canada.[30] His wife, Ethel May, identified as being Hong Kong born and a British national. Her occupation was recorded as "Housewife" and she identified the same destination as her husband.

Once this personal information was confirmed, Department of National Defence officials interrogated the passengers for any intelligence information they could provide.[31] Poy (identified as the "Chief Clerk, Canadian Trade Commissioner's Office") offered details about territory controlled by Japanese naval forces as well as the number of military police located in the central police station. He explained further that "Indian troops act as street guards, armed with wood batons. In many cases, these were prisoners of war, who were released because of their willingness to cooperate with the Japanese. These troops are treated particularly well." Government officials noted his example of a "Japanese officer who takes his Indian chauffeur to eat lunch with him."[32]

Supplementary archival records point to the fear that animated the Poys' desire to leave Hong Kong, concerns that are well documented in Clarkson's account of their departure.[33] They also point to a sense of loss. This sentiment is palatable in both emotional and financial terms from the records documenting William Poy's postwar claim to the Custodian of Enemy Property, which he submitted in the hopes that he could obtain financial compensation for the material goods he lost in Hong Kong.[34] According to Poy, the total loss of his personal and household effects, destroyed at 5 Broome Road, Hong Kong, amounted to $12,073.00 (approximately $159,263.22 in today's money). This included losses in the drawing room, dining room, bedroom, library, and nursery.[35] Included in the itemized list of losses, Poy highlighted:

> ... a fur coat, pair [of] silk riding breeches, morning suit and silk hat, Jaeger dressing gown, four racing saddles, eight racehorse blankets, four sets racing silks, 2 sets of children's furniture, teak desk, iron safe, bearskin rug, seventeen silver cigarette cases, miniature cocktail bar, 1 GE 5 Tube radio, 1 chrome mosquito net attachment and net, gold plated manicure set.[36]

Although Poy argued that he should be compensated because he was working for the Canadian government at the time of the Japanese invasion, his claim was rejected because he was not a Canadian citizen when the losses occurred. Indeed, the adjudicators made a point of noting in the margins that Poy was Australian-born to British parents.[37]

The Poys' citizenship status was complicated in 1942. As residents of Hong Kong, they were British subjects, not citizens. As historian Daniel Gorman has observed, "the term 'citizen' was an ambiguous concept in the British empire" and an unofficial one, meaning that it was defined and redefined in localized contexts and under varying conditions.[38] As Chinese living in Hong Kong, the Poys were subjects of the British Crown, but they were not citizens, and although theoretically there was freedom of movement within the British empire, national restrictions limited this possibility.[39]

Clarkson herself has claimed "statelessness" as the descriptor for the Poys' status and understands it as the reason they were chosen for the exchange.[40] In fact, Clarkson considers this status a blessing. As she observed in *Heart Matters*, "The British were left in internment camps in places like Hong Kong ... In a way, being stateless was a help to us. After all, we were Chinese, and although we were British subjects, we were not British."[41] The question of citizenship is central to the substance and reach of Clarkson's refugee narrative. In many ways, the passengers aboard the *Gripsholm* that arrived in New York in the summer of 1942 could be described as refugees, since they were all desperate to get out of Japanese-occupied Hong Kong. And yet, because most were citizens returning to their place of citizenship (with the striking exception of the Poys), they were referred to as refugees only in the context of fleeing a violent military occupation. Adrienne Clarkson alone has claimed a refugee identity based on the conditions upon which her family left Hong Kong and the uncertainty about where they might end up.

Evolving Refugee Definitions

Statelessness has long been the defining aspect of the refugee experience, and especially in the early twentieth century when relief efforts were undertaken by the League of Nations.[42] After the Second World War, and with the dawn of the Cold War, the legal definition of this aspect of a refugee's situation evolved to incorporate individual persecution. The 1951 Convention Relating to the Status of Refugees defined a refugee as someone who,

> owing to well-founded fear of being persecuted for reasons of race, religion, nationality, membership of a particular social group or political opinion, is outside the country of his nationality and is unable or, owing to

such fear, is unwilling to avail himself of the protection of that country; or who, not having a nationality and being outside the country of his former habitual residence as a result of such events, is unable or, owing to such fear, is unwilling to return to it.

The 1951 UN Convention is the cornerstone of the international refugee regime as we know it today. However, as numerous critics have pointed out, the 1951 definition of a refugee is also a very narrow one, contingent on rigid and frugal notions of individual persecution.[43] It is, moreover, a definition born of the particular historical circumstances that existed at the end of the Second World War: the massive displacement and uprooting of individuals in Europe and Asia, the tragic suffering among persecuted groups at the hands of Nazi Germany, and the onset of the Cold War that pitted Western democracies against a Communist world view. The purpose of the 1951 Convention was to address the outstanding issue of displaced persons in Europe, not to perpetuate a permanent refugee situation. The Convention was thus narrow in focus and approach when it emphasized individual persecution above all else.[44]

Despite the drafters' intentions, since the introduction of the 1951 Convention, a permanent, international refugee regime has emerged. Over the decades it has grown in size and complexity, evidenced by myriad administrative, regulatory, and legal processes by which someone might now be identified as a refugee and assisted as such. States have developed refugee determination processes that align with their responsibilities outlined in Article 33 of the Convention to ensure that refugees are not returned to danger. At the same time, the United Nations High Commissioner for Refugees (UNHCR) has expanded its operations by moving beyond its mandated focus on individuals outside their country of origin to consider the plight of internally displaced people or IDPs. The labels, categories, and definitions of refugeehood have multiplied in tandem.

Canada signed the 1951 Convention and the associated 1967 Protocol (which removed original geographical and temporal limitations) in 1969. From that date, the federal government began to develop mechanisms to determine whether or not individuals presenting themselves in Canada for protection met the definition of a Convention refugee. In 1978, the term "refugee" was defined in Canadian law for the first time, and adjudication measures were further enhanced, providing individuals who met the Convention's definition of a refugee with the possibility of state-proffered refuge, including pathways to permanent residency and citizenship akin to those of other migrants.

At the same time, the 1951 Convention also became a tool to refuse migrants who did not fit its narrow definition of refugeehood. In Canada, and elsewhere, governments have deployed the language of the Convention to reject responsibilities for migrants who fail to meet the restrictive terms of individual persecution.[45] Moreover, in response to pressure on governments to abide by the terms of the Convention, in resistant states there has also been a growth in the language of "economic migrants" and "bogus refugees" (as discussed in the chapter by Jennifer Hyndman and Johanna Reynolds). The use of such vocabulary makes it more challenging for people to explain their claims to refugee status in ways that are believable, understood, and palatable. Unless one can convince the Canadian state to admit people on the basis of humanitarian and compassionate grounds, persecution remains the threshold for refugee status and admission.[46]

The evolving contexts in which refugee definitions have been contested make Adrienne Clarkson's interventions all the more significant. In publicly claiming a refugee identity, Clarkson offers a reminder of the variety of refugee experiences that existed historically and the many ways that they continue to manifest themselves in the present. Her interventions undermine the uniform narratives of individual persecution that the state demands of supplicants seeking protection under the terms and conditions of the 1951 Convention while at the same time feeding certain expectations of refugees, including public expressions of gratitude.

Clarkson began to discuss her family's refugee experiences publicly in *Heart Matters*, the memoir she published two years after stepping away from her role as the Queen's representative in Canada. In the Introduction, she detailed the terrible conditions in wartime Hong Kong and her parents' life-changing decisions about the future. While she described her parents' efforts in warm terms, Clarkson also underscored the element of chance in her family's experience. In particular, she alluded to the racism that still governed Canadian immigration policy in the period by recalling their close encounter with a Canadian official who did not think they belonged in Canada:

> As we stood there on the dock, in what my mother always remembered as being unrelenting sun, we were lined up alphabetically. A Canadian official who was part of the group of five hundred that had come from Tokyo looked at us and turned to one of his colleagues and said, "What are *these* people doing here? They're not white!" ... the colleague said, "Well, they're on the list. Why don't we just leave them there? They're okay." It was a busy morning, and the man who had spotted us had other things

to do, so he turned away. And by his turning away, we were destined for Canada, even though we were Chinese, even though we were Oriental, even though we were not wanted.[47]

Significantly, Clarkson did not detail the powerful impact of the 1923 Chinese Immigration Act, attributing the possibility of exclusion in this instance to personal discretion. In this first public accounting of her family's history she emphasized good fortune and chance, rather than grappling with the structural exclusion that shaped the experiences of many Chinese migrants in Canada. The Canadian official who nearly turned the Poy family away was not acting in isolation, but had an entire legal regime to support and explain his view.

In *Room for All of Us: Surprising Stories of Loss and Transformation*, published four years later in 2011 and on the sixtieth anniversary of the 1951 UN Convention, Clarkson assembled the stories of refugees and migrants from all parts of the world who now live in Canada to give a human face to the experiences of people that media and policy often render as distant and foreign. Crucially, the experiences of the people profiled did not necessarily meet the strict definition of refugeehood advanced by the 1951 Convention. Rather, Clarkson underscored the fact that "the idea of Canada as refuge *is an undercurrent* in all these stories" (emphasis added).[48] Such statements privilege lived experience as the basis for refugeeness above and beyond any legal parameters.

Clarkson introduced the volume by explaining, "This book is about people like me."[49] She then downplayed the exceptional qualities of her own experience:

> All of my life, I've met people who have lived trajectories not exactly like mine but in their own way, just as remarkable. Like me, the people in this book came out of cataclysm and catastrophe not of their own making and found themselves almost thrown into Canada.[50]

The Introduction stressed luck and resilience. Although she mentioned the presence of racism in Canada in passing, her emphasis was on the country's capacity for change as evidenced by the trajectories described in the volume. In this way, *Room for All of Us* echoed the approach Clarkson adopted in her memoirs, where the focus was on the possibility of refuge, rather than on structures of exclusion that might render refuge impossible.

Three years later, in her 2014 Massey Lectures on citizenship and belonging, Clarkson continued to refine her presentation of her family's refugee experience while also making increasingly pointed references to the racism that governed the outlook on immigration from Asia or the "Orient" in Canada from the late nineteenth century.[51] On her refugee experience, Clarkson nuanced the idea that her family was destined for Canada, or that Canada was destined to be a place of refuge, elaborating that "I came to this country as a refugee. I didn't willingly choose this destination. But once it became our destination, my family and I determined that it would be fully ours. And I don't think I'm alone in this."[52] Weaving a tale that moves from refugees with nothing to people who flourish and, importantly for Clarkson, achieve a sense of belonging, she later explained:

> As someone who came to this country with one suitcase, I have never lost the sense that I came from that minimal place where everything had been taken away. It is part of my recognition that I am human and that I belong to every experience that human beings undergo.[53]

She then concluded:

> I have made belonging the interest of my life. I was, and am, a child of diaspora. I am someone who, for a while, did not belong anywhere. And I will always be someone who understands the ever-lasting anguish of not belonging. We arrived in this country under the shield of the Red Cross, stateless, as refugees. Then Canada took us in.[54]

Clarkson's powerful narrative has proven compelling because she emphasized the country's generosity and her own sense of belonging instead of engaging with the question of why she didn't feel she belonged in any detailed way.[55] In doing so, she has played the part of the grateful refugee, in a manner characteristic of the politics identified by Mimi Nguyen in *The Gift of Freedom*, where refugee gratitude works to absolve the state of its own complicity in a refugee's displacement and sometimes unhappy resettlement. Clarkson's early expressions of gratitude erased the structural discrimination that necessitated a sense of relief and gratitude in the first instance. It is therefore striking that, in *Belonging: The Paradox of Citizenship* (based on her 2014 Massey Lectures), Clarkson focused explicitly on her encounter with tangible evidence of the discriminatory structures that characterize modern immigration systems. Significantly, she wrote:

> Imagine the shock I felt when I looked at a document that was sent to me this year: a photocopy from a register in British Columbia's archives

listing Adrienne Louise Poy, age nine, female, together with the rest of my family – my father, William; my mother, Ethel; and my brother, Neville – on the Chinese head tax registry. Having grown up and lived in this country since my family arrived on these shores as refugees in 1942, I always reviled the head tax and thought it was a part of history. While I always felt implicated by this law because of its innate racism, somehow I never thought it really applied to me. My identity was first and foremost tied to my family. I somehow never felt that what was written about Chinese in Canada, and about the head tax, applied to me and my brother – the cherished children of two people who had lost everything and invested their hearts, their souls, and anything they could earn in our present and in our future. I belonged to them first of all ... Had I known then what I know now, I wonder if it would have made me feel that I belonged less to Canada, that I was less committed to being Canadian. I was part of a despised and rejected group, but I did not feel, nor did my family ever feel, personally despised and rejected. We were popular in school and at church. No one ever said, "You shouldn't be here." No one ever told us that we did not belong.[56]

I quote this passage at length because of its importance in illuminating the stakes of Clarkson's interventions. Specifically, by emphasizing her family's, and her own, capacity to overcome, she minimized the devastating impact of decades of racist legislation. Even while acknowledging that her family was touched by exclusionary legislation, she neutralizes the impact of the capitation tax and the 1923 Chinese Immigration Act by focusing instead on her family's positive experiences.

The evolution in Clarkson's narrative – from one where racism appeared almost accidentally in the character of the Canadian official at the dock to one where it was rooted in exclusionary legislation – reveals an emergent inclination to acknowledge the profound and systemic racism that informed the immigration laws and regulations governing Chinese migration to Canada after 1885. The tensions inherent in this evolution strain below the surface of the original story of the search for refuge. On the one hand, Clarkson carefully narrates her family's story to ensure that it meets expectations of worth, merit, and gratitude held by state authorities and citizens alike. We see this in Clarkson's narrative as she details her parents' difficult decisions, and describes a palatable sense of loss with repeated mention of travelling with only "four suitcases" (one each).[57] At the same time, she is careful about minimizing the larger structures of exclusion that made her family's story so extraordinary.

Conclusions

Adrienne Clarkson embraces a refugee identity on her own terms. This claiming is in and of itself important, speaking as it does to myriad refugee experiences that go beyond historical and contemporary legal definitions of refugeehood, both conceptually and temporally. Yet Clarkson's narrative trajectory is also significant on many other levels: for one, it reveals the limitations of legal categorizations of refugeehood, which flatten the highly contingent nature of refugee experiences and dehistoricize refugee subjects. At the same time, it also shows us how personal narratives can similarly mute historical contingencies in favour of a more universal narrative. With its emphasis on opportunity, and only peripheral engagement with histories of racism and exclusion in Canada, Clarkson's narrative also alerts us to the power dynamics involved in laying claim to a refugee identity. People in vulnerable positions who seek relief or protection are rarely able to challenge notions of what it means to be a refugee. Clarkson has the benefit of being an established and accomplished individual, whose narrative of refuge, however exceptional, nonetheless presents as a viable possibility for all.

Very few public individuals have felt as comfortable or have been as intent as Clarkson about narrating their family's history as one of displacement, statelessness, and a search for refuge.[58] On occasion however, other prominent public figures have also mobilized their personal stories to raise awareness and spark empathy among the general public. Much as Clarkson did in 2015, former US secretary of state Madeleine Albright (1997–2001) referenced, in 2017, her own family's history to address concerns about the Trump administration's refugee policies. Albright is a self-described refugee whose Jewish family escaped persecution and likely death in the Czech Republic in 1937. However, in contrast to Clarkson, her embrace of a refugee identity has been episodic. For many years, particularly in the early stages of her career, she expressed disinterest in embracing a refugee identity and professed ignorance about her family's Jewish background.[59] In 2012, however, she wrote a memoir about her family's wartime experiences (*Prague Winter: A Personal Story of Remembrance and War, 1937–1948*). In January 2017, she was quick to describe herself as a refugee in order to severely critique the Trump administration's travel ban that targeted migrants from several majority-Muslim countries and also placed limits on refugee admissions. In response to the ban, Albright wrote:

> Refugees should not be viewed as a certain burden or potential terrorists ... They have already made great contributions to our national life. Syrian

refugees are learning English, getting good jobs, buying homes, and starting businesses. In other words, they are doing what other generations of refugees – including my own – did.[60]

In this passage, Albright draws on her family's refugee experience to lend credibility to her scathing condemnation of the Trump administration's refugee policies.

Similarly, Clarkson's refugee narrative took on new significance in the face of the emerging refugee crisis in Syria over the course of 2015. As this chapter has explored, her earliest writing imagined Canada as a land of possibilities, as evidenced in her memoir and *Room for All of Us* in particular. This framing required that the history of racism in Canada be minimized, including the legislative impediments that made it very difficult for Chinese migrants to settle permanently in Canada until after 1947 (and even then, restrictions remained). Although she has occasionally alluded to the racism that shaped Canadian society at the time of her family's arrival, Clarkson has largely downplayed this facet of her family's story in public commentary on the subject. Instead, her emphasis has been on aspirational possibilities, without considering how her family's settlement in Canada is rendered all the more extraordinary precisely because of the race-based exclusions that existed in Canadian immigration law at the time of their arrival. In her 2015 op-ed, Clarkson explicitly advanced her own family's refugee experience to press the federal government to resettle refugees from Syria. In doing so, she offered a narrative of Canada as a country where refuge was the historical norm – tracing responses to Ugandan and Indochinese refugees in the 1970s to humanitarian challenges in the present. Nowhere did she mention the structures of exclusion that her family and others had to overcome.

Under the headline "Canada Knows How to Respond to Refugees," Clarkson wrote of seeing the photo of three-year old Aylan Kurdi, washed up dead on a Turkish beach, and feeling "an electrifying stillness." Clarkson noted that she too had been a toddler when the Japanese Imperial Army took over Hong Kong.[61] In making the connection between the tragic death of Aylan Kurdi and her own fortunate experience, Clarkson used her family's story to pressure then Prime Minister Stephen Harper to do more. Her appeal was devastating:

What would he have done if he had grown up in Canada as I did? What if he had been taken to a small Canadian city where the Jewish drugstore owner gave him free cough drops along with his prescription, and told his own son to walk him home through the snow? What if his family had found housing in a little apartment in a French-Canadian neighborhood where the neighbors taught his mother how to cook stew and beans?

Like all refugees, I am imprinted with the nature of loss and the necessity for reinvention. By surviving, you gain the chance, like Tennyson's Ulysses, "to strive, to seek, to find and not to yield."

I went to neighborhood public elementary and high schools and a public university. My brother went to McGill to become a surgeon, and I went to the University of Toronto and became a TV broadcaster and then Canada's governor-general. Little Aylan Kurdi will never have an opportunity to aspire to any of this.[62]

Stephen Harper's government lost in the federal election held in November 2015, and the elected government, under Prime Minister Justin Trudeau, promptly announced plans to resettle twenty-five thousand refugees within a few short months.[63]

Appeals such as Clarkson's op-ed in the *New York Times* contributed to the confidence and determination with which the new Liberal government pursued resettlement plans. Clarkson's message was one of reassurance and promise. By tracing the contours of her own family's history, she pointed to the possibilities inherent in welcoming refugees to Canadian soil. Yet the Poys' arrival in Canada was much more precarious than a conventional rags-to-riches story might suggest. Immigration regulations and contemporary laws made the idea of Chinese refugees arriving in Canada in 1942 almost unfathomable. The Poys arrived in Canada at a time when there was no legal category of admissions for refugees. Instead, they were admitted based on an exemption provided for in the 1923 Chinese Immigration Act, which otherwise would have made their legal entry impossible. Their admission was exceptional, not typical. Indeed the very structure of Canadian society and the continued preference for white settlers meant that the Poys' story of triumph was not just about their escape from war-torn Hong Kong but also about overcoming structural exclusion in Canadian society. The very premise of Clarkson's narrative is therefore fragile, as it relies on emphasizing individual triumphs and generosity over structural and systemic issues of racism and discrimination.[64]

Perhaps not surprisingly, recent refugee "success stories" have perpetuated this narrative device. In the wake of the Syrian refugee resettlement program in 2015–16, there has been considerable public enthusiasm for other exceptional stories in Canada. The story of Tareq Hadhad's successful Peace by Chocolate business, a case that Gada Mahrouse takes up more extensively in this volume, has been celebrated as exemplifying refugee resilience and Canadian values.[65] The increase in Islamophobia and hate speech acts since 2001 rarely appears in the same frame.[66] The production and circulation of such stories, which mingle gratitude with opportunity and success, facilitate the erasure of settler colonialism, racism, and discrimination from the national imaginary. They render inclusion and belonging the normative experience for refugees and migrants, an enterprise that promises future possibilities while marginalizing the historical contingencies and unsavoury realities that are a vital part of refugee histories. To normalize refuge is to lose sight of the very fragile and precarious grounds upon which any claims to refuge are made and received, whether they are made according to evolving legal frameworks or reside in the realm of public sentiment. To normalize refuge is to raise false expectations about a future that may be even more precarious than the historical past.

NOTES

1 Clarkson, "Canada Knows How to Respond to Refugees."
2 For a recent example, see the UNHCR's description of Habso Mohamud and her work, https://www.unhcr.org/news/stories/2019/4/5cbe18694/former-somali-refugee-inspires-children-illustrated-book.html, accessed 19 June 2019.
3 Clarkson, *Room for All of Us*, 1.
4 In *The Gift of Freedom*, Mimi Thi Nguyen writes critically of the empire of "liberal benevolence" in the United States and the power contests at play in the rescue of refugees and their subsequent displays of public gratitude, as well as the "labor that the gift of freedom performs on behalf of liberal empire." As Nguyen demonstrates in her careful analysis, there is a large and complicated afterlife to the relationship between refugees and the states where they find physical refuge. Of the enduring effect of state interventions in the life of refugees, Nguyen observes, "To give a blow, to give life, to give death – the gift is itself a surface on which power operates as a form of subjection – and its magnitude might indeed be profound" (8, 24, 195).
5 Wherry, "What He Was Talking about When He Talked about Colonialism." There was further evidence of colonial denial in the summer of 2017 when heated debates erupted over the commemoration of Sir John A. Macdonald in public life, given the role he played in orchestrating the residential school system, among other policies, that had a devastating impact on the life of Indigenous peoples in Canada (Csanady, "Teachers Union Missed the Mark with Call to Rename John A Macdonald Schools"). These battles became even more pitched in June 2019 with the release of the final

reports of the Inquiry into Missing and Murdered Indigenous Women in Canada, in which the authors concluded that the violence against Indigenous girls, women, and 2SLGBTQQIA (Two-Spirit, lesbian, gay, bisexual, transgender, queer, questioning, intersex, and asexual) was part of a larger history of genocide against Indigenous peoples. Use of the term "genocide" created a media storm of protest and revealed a great deal about how Canadians understand their own history (Elliott, "Canada Grapples with the Charge of Genocide").
6 On the ahistorical refugee subject, see Malkki, "Speechless Emissaries."
7 Betts, *Protection by Persuasion*.
8 William was born in Australia. Ethel May was born in Hong Kong. They were included in the exchange at a time when British subjecthood and Canadianness were fluid and ambivalent. It is not until the 1947 Canadian Citizenship Act that one can talk about a legal definition of Canadian citizenship rather than one of imperial citizenship. For a further discussion on the ambivalence of citizenship and subjecthood in the evolving British world, see Buckner, ed., *Canada and the British World*.
9 For recent scholarship on the subject of Chinese labour migration, Indigenous dispossession, and US imperialism, see Maruka, *Empire's Tracks*.
10 Hong Kong veterans fought for decades to obtain adequate compensation for their experience. On the POW experience in Hong Kong, see Palmer, *Dark Side of the Sun*; Greenfield, *The Damned*; and Flanagan, *The Endless Battle*.
11 *Oxford English Dictionary*, www.oed.com, accessed 24 May 2017.
12 See Brooke, "Civilian Prisoners of War Recall Their Ordeals."
13 Holmes, *Guests of the Emperor*, 68.
14 Ward, "The Asia-Pacific War and the Failed Second Anglo-Japanese Civilian Exchange, 1942–45." The Canadian Committee of the Red Cross also picked up on the issue of Japan's non-signature very quickly and sought guidance from the Canadian government on how best to meet the needs of the POWs in Hong Kong. P.H. Gordon, chairman of the Executive Committee of the Canadian Red Cross Society, wrote the Department of External Affairs five days after the attack on Pearl Harbor and simultaneous attacks in Asia: "you are no doubt fully aware of the fact that the Japanese were not parties to the Convention of 1929. Have you any idea as to whether Japan will act as though she were a party to that Convention? Will it be the policy of the Government to supply names of the International Committee of Japanese who may be captured? ... Another question that is worrying me is how we are to get parcels to POWs in the Far East. I can imagine that they will not be over fed. The rations given to a Japanese would hardly be sufficient for a North American. Have you considered this feature at all?" See "Arrangements with Japan re: Treatment of Prisoners of War – General File.".

15 For instance, only in April 1942 did the ICRC obtain details about American soldiers and civilians captured during the battles on Wake and Guam Islands (*Report of the International Committee of the Red Cross on Its Activities during the Second World War*, 261).
16 See correspondence in "Canadian High Commissioner to Great Britain to Secretary of State for External Affairs, Canada." For details on the treatment of civilians, see Kong, "'Clearing the Decks'"; Archer and Fedorowich, "The Women of Stanley."
17 Clarkson, *Heart Matters*, 9.
18 "Excerpts from the Chinese Press." According to historian Bruce Elleman, "anywhere from one-third to one-half of the Americans in some Japanese camps died of mistreatment and starvation" (*Japanese-American Civilian Prisoner Exchanges and Detention Camps, 1941–1945*, 4).
19 One report that appeared in duplicate in numerous files was an account by Lois Fearon, who worked with St. John's Ambulance, RG25-G-2, Vol. 2920, File 2670-D-40, Treatment of Prisoners of War and Civilians by Japanese at Hong Kong.
20 "Canadian High Commissioner to Great Britain to Secretary of State for External Affairs, Canada."
21 As documented in "Canadian Minister to the Argentine, BA to SSEA, 22.2.42." See also Forsythe, *The Humanitarians*, 43–4.
22 Ward, "The Asia-Pacific War," 1. Ward notes that reciprocity evolved from "Reciprocity in funding" to "the right of each state to nominate those to be repatriated" and to ensure that repatriation was voluntary (4). See also Elleman, *Japanese-American Civilian Prisoner Exchanges and Detention Camps, 1941–1945*, 2, 11, and 22.
23 Stories of exclusion include that of a Dutch-born veteran of the Canadian Expeditionary Force who was interned in the Philippines but not put on the SS *Gripsholm*, despite the fact that his wife was ailing and they were with their four children. See Roy et al., *Mutual Hostages*, 199. Clarkson emphasizes how fortunate her family was to be included in the exchange, noting that one of the boats she travelled on in the transfer "carried 30 per cent more passengers than it legally should have." See "In Making Room for Others, We Make Room for Ourselves – and for Canada."
24 In the end, there were only two exchanges negotiated between the United States and Japan, but they involved far more people than American-German exchanges. The Canadian government, as well as the American one, was disappointed that there were not future exchanges. Canadian officials had hoped to return Japanese nationals interned at the POW camp in Angler, Ontario. The Japanese Imperial Government ceased negotiating exchanges after the second voyage of the *Gripsholm* in 1943, after Australia declared pearl divers to be security risks and therefore not

eligible, and allegedly out of concern about conditions at the internment camp at Tule Lake. See Roy et al., 208.
25 Elleman, *Japanese-American Civilian Prisoner Exchanges*, 2.
26 Negotiations were most complicated around individuals who both sides suspected might be of strategic benefit to the other. Bruce Elleman observes, "The very nature of these categories in late 1941 meant that they would be mainly, if not completely, educated males, and probably from the samurai – or formerly noble – class. A high proportion of these would be qualified either to bear arms on behalf of Japan, or to work in the civilian sectors of the Japanese war effort" (*Japanese-American Civilian Prisoner Exchanges*, 23). Elleman's overall thesis is that the forced relocation of Japanese Americans during the Second World War facilitated the orchestration and conduct of civilian exchanges. According to Elleman, "Once the first official exchange was concluded, then virtually all Japanese and American government officials had been successfully repatriated to their home countries. As might be expected, Japan's interest in the exchange program diminished once it had regained its top officials. This was not the case with the United States, since there were still many more thousands of American non-officials detained in Japanese camps in Manchukuo, occupied China, and in the Japanese home islands. In order to trade for these American citizens, the US government would have to locate thousands of Japanese-Americans willing to repatriate to Japan." Elleman believes that such individuals were identified through the internment process (*Japanese-American Civilian Prisoner Exchanges*, 54).
27 Sullivan, "69 Canadians from Orient Arrive," 3.
28 Clarkson, *Heart Matters*, 9.
29 Civilians and military personnel being repatriated as part of prisoner of war exchanges were excellent sources of information for contemporary observers. Prior to disembarking, all passengers completed questionnaires that included questions about conditions in Hong Kong. Some, such as nurse Kathleen G. Christie, provided full accounts of the conditions that led to their arrival, internment, and release in Hong Kong. See Christie, "Report by Miss Kathleen G. Christie, Nurse with the Canadian Forces at HONG KONG, as given on board the *SS Gripsholm* November 1943." See also Roy et al., *Mutual Hostages*, 199. Newspaper stories about the ship's voyage were a source of great information and impressions for the general public ("Only Way to Stop the Japs Is to Kill, Says Refugee," 3). Allied governments sought to use stories from the passengers for propaganda advantage, but they also recognized that, if the stories were too negative, it would jeopardize the possibility of future exchanges with the Japanese Imperial Government.

30 "Department of External Affairs, questionnaires for Canadians repatriated from Japan on S.S. 'GRIPSHOLM.'"
31 "Interrogation of Canadian Repatriates from the Orient aboard GRIPSHOLM."
32 Ibid.
33 See Chapter 1, "Towards Canada," in Clarkson, *Heart Matters*.
34 "Claim of W.G. Poy to Property in Hong Kong."
35 "Claim of W.G. Poy to Property in Hong Kong."
36 "W.G. Poy, Claims Files."
37 Ibid.
38 Gorman, "Wider and Wider Still?"
39 Dhamoon et al., eds. *Unmooring the "Komagata Maru"*.
40 Clarkson, *Heart Matters*, 10.
41 Ibid.
42 See Skran, *Refugees in Inter-war Europe*; Kaprielian-Churchill, "'Misfits.'"
43 See work by B.S. Chimni, most notably "The Geopolitics of Refugee Studies."
44 On the refugee and displaced person situation in Europe, see Cohen, *In War's Wake*.
45 See discussion in Dauvergne, *Humanitarianism, Identity, and Nation*.
46 https://www.canada.ca/en/immigration-refugees-citizenship/services/refugees/claim-protection-inside-canada/after-apply-next-steps/refusal-options/humanitarian-compassionate-grounds.html, accessed 19 June 2019.
47 Clarkson, *Heart Matters*, 11.
48 Ibid.
49 Ibid., 1.
50 Ibid.
51 Somewhat ironically, the annual Massey Lecture series is named after Vincent Massey, a former governor general and also, as noted previously in this chapter, the high commissioner to London during the Japanese occupation of Hong Kong.
52 Clarkson, *Belonging*, 111.
53 Ibid., 135.
54 Ibid., 179.
55 Madokoro, "Family Reunification as International History."
56 Clarkson, *Belonging*, 75.
57 Clarkson, *Heart Matters*, 9.
58 Here I am making a distinction between personal stories where people self-identify as refugees and publicity campaigns such as those undertaken by the International Rescue Committee, which highlight the extraordinary qualities of refugees such as Albert Einstein, Freddie Mercury, and Elie

Wiesel, https://www.rescue.org/article/watch-three-stars-special-video-letter-famous-refugees, accessed 19 June 2019.
59 Friedberg, "Family Politics," 45. My thanks to Gogbokoru S. Tanyildiz for drawing my attention to the parallels between Madeleine Albright's and Adrienne Clarkson's stories.
60 Greenwood, "Madeleine Albright Slams Trump's Proposed Action on Refugee Crackdown." Albright has intervened in other public policy discussions, using her family's story to make a compelling case. See "Email from Madeleine Albright."
61 Clarkson, "Canada Knows How to Respond to Refugees."
62 Ibid.
63 Statistics from Immigration, Refugees and Citizenship Canada show that 25,555 Syrian refugees arrived in Canada between 1 December 2015 and the end of February 2016 (Immigration, Refugees and Citizenship Canada).
64 Nguyen, *The Gift of Freedom*, 31.
65 Bresge, "Syrian Refugee Says Family's Chocolate Business Shows Value of Canadian 'Openness.'"
66 Minsky, "Hate Crimes against Muslims in Canada Increase 253% over Four Years."

REFERENCES

Archer, Bernice, and Kent Fedorowich. "The Women of Stanley: Internment in Hong Kong 1942–45." *Women's History Review* 5, no. 3 (1996): 373–99.
"Arrangements with Japan re: Treatment of Prisoners of War – General File." RG25-A-3-b, Vol. 2939, File 2998-40, LAC.
Betts, Alexander. *Protection by Persuasion: International Cooperation in the Refugee Regime*. Ithaca: Cornell University Press, 2011.
Bresge, Adina. "Syrian Refugee Says Family's Chocolate Business Shows Value of Canadian 'Openness.'" *Toronto Star*, 13 March 2017. https://www.thestar.com/news/canada/2017/03/13/syrian-refugee-says-familys-chocolate-business-shows-value-of-canadian-openness.html. Accessed 25 August 2017.
Brooke, James. "Civilian Prisoners of War Recall Their Ordeals." *New York Times*, 9 September 1995. http://www.nytimes.com/1995/09/09/us/civilian-prisoners-of-war-recall-their-ordeals.html?mcubz=3. Accessed 31 August 2017.
Buckner, Philip, ed. *Canada and the British World: Culture, Migration and Identity*. Vancouver: University of British Columbia Press, 2005.
"Canadian High Commissioner to Great Britain to Secretary of State for External Affairs, Canada." RG25-G-2, Vol. 2920, File 2670-D-40, Treatment

of Prisoners of War and Civilians by Japanese at Hong Kong, Library and Archives Canada (LAC).

"Canadian Minister to the Argentine, BA to SSEA, 22.2.42." RG25-G-2, Vol. 2920, File 2670-D-40, Treatment of Prisoners of War and Civilians by Japanese at Hong Kong, LAC.

Chimni, B.S. "The Geopolitics of Refugee Studies: A View from the South." *Journal of Refugee Studies* 11, no. 4 (1998): 350–75.

Christie, Kathleen. "Report by Miss Kathleen G. Christie, Nurse with the Canadian Forces at HONG KONG, as Given on Board the *SS Gripsholm* November 1943." *Canadian Military History* 10, no. 4 (2001): 27–34.

"Claim of W.G. Poy to Property in Hong Kong." RG 25, Vol. 3920, File 9445-X-40, LAC.

Clarkson, Adrienne. *Belonging: The Paradox of Citizenship*. Toronto: House of Anansi Press, 2014.

– "Canada Knows How to Respond to Refugees." *New York Times*, 7 October 2015.

– *Heart Matters*. Toronto: Penguin Canada, 2007.

– "In Making Room for Others, We Make Room for Ourselves – and for Canada." *Globe and Mail*, 19 August 2016. https://beta.theglobeandmail.com/news/national/in-making-room-for-others-we-make-room-for-ourselves-and-for-canada/article31464060. Accessed 31 August 2017.

– *Room for All of Us: Surprising Stories of Loss and Transformation*. Toronto: Allen Lane, 2011.

Cohen, Daniel. *In War's Wake: Europe's Displaced Persons in the Postwar Order*. Oxford: Oxford University Press, 2011.

Csanady, Ashley. "Teachers Union Missed the Mark with Call to Rename John A. Macdonald Schools: Kathleen Wynne." *National Post*, 25 August 2017. http://nationalpost.com/news/canada/teachers-union-missed-the-mark-with-call-to-rename-john-a-macdonald-schools-kathleen-wynne. Accessed 31 August 2017.

Dauvergne, Catherine. *Humanitarianism, Identity, and Nation: Migration Laws of Australia and Canada*. Vancouver: University of British Columbia Press, 2005.

"Department of External Affairs, Questionnaires for Canadians Repatriated from Japan on S.S. 'GRIPSHOLM' (Names Only – Dappen to Fairbairn) 1942/08–1944." RG25-G-2, Vol. 2932, File 2864-B-40, LAC.

Dhamoon, Rita, Davina Bhandar, Renisa Mawani, and Satwinder Kaur Bains, eds. *Unmooring the "Komagata Maru": Charting Colonial Trajectories*. Vancouver: University of British Columbia Press, 2019.

Elleman, Bruce. *Japanese-American Civilian Prisoner Exchanges and Detention Camps, 1941–1945*. London: Routledge, 2006.

Elliott, Alicia. "Canada Grapples with the Charge of Genocide. For Indigenous Peoples, There's No Debate." *Washington Post*, 11 June 2019. https://www.washingtonpost.com/opinions/2019/06/11/canada-grapples-with-charge-genocide-indigenous-people-theres-no-debate/?noredirect=on&utm_term=.e49bf3831293. Accessed 19 June 2019.

"Email from Madeleine Albright: When I Was Welcomed as a Refugee." https://obamawhitehouse.archives.gov/blog/2016/09/20/email-madeleine-albright-when-i-was-welcomed-refugee. Accessed 31 August 2017.

"Excerpts from the Chinese Press." Chungking to General Intelligence Section, RG25-G-2, Vol. 2920, File 2670-D-40, Treatment of Prisoners of War and Civilians by Japanese at Hong Kong, LAC. 31 May 1942.

Flanagan, Andy. *The Endless Battle: The Fall of Hong Kong and Canadian POWs in Imperial Japan*. Fredericton: Goose Lane Editions, 2017.

Forsythe, David P. *The Humanitarians: The ICRC*. Cambridge: Cambridge University Press, 2005.

Friedberg, Aaron. "Family Politics." *New York Times Book Review*, 9 May 1999.

Gorman, Daniel. "Wider and Wider Still?: Racial Politics, Intra-Imperial Immigration and the Absence of an Imperial Citizenship in the British Empire." *Journal of Colonialism and Colonial History* 3, no. 3 (Winter 2002). Published online: 10.1353/cch.2002.0066. Accessed 31 August 2017.

Greenfield, Nathan. *The Damned: The Canadians at the Battle of Hong Kong and the POW Experience, 1941–45*. Toronto: HarperCollins, 2010.

Greenwood, Max. "Madeleine Albright Slams Trump's Proposed Action on Refugee Crackdown." *The Hill*, 27 January 2017.

Holmes, Linda. *Guests of the Emperor: The Secret History of Japan's Mukden POW Camp*. Annapolis, MD: Naval Institute Press, 2010.

Immigration, Refugees and Citizenship Canada. https://www150.statcan.gc.ca/n1/pub/75-006-x/2019001/article/00001-eng.htm. Accessed 19 June 2019.

"Interrogation of Canadian Repatriates from the Orient aboard GRIPSHOLM." RG 24, Vol. 11966, File 168-3, LAC.

Kaprielian-Churchill, Isabel. "'Misfits': Canada and the Nansen Passport." *International Migration Review* 28, no. 2 (Summer 1994): 281–306.

Kong, W.V. "'Clearing the Decks': The Evacuation of British Women and Children from Hong Kong to Australia in 1940." Thesis. University of Hong Kong, Pokfulam, Hong Kong SAR, 2015. Retrieved from http://dx.doi.org/10.5353/th_b5760966. Accessed 8 June 2017.

Madokoro, Laura. "Family Reunification as International History: Rethinking Sino-Canadian Relations after 1970." *International Journal* 68 (2013): 591–608.

Malkki, Lisa. "Speechless Emissaries: Refugees, Humanitarianism, and Dehistoricization." *Cultural Anthropology* 11, no. 3 (1996): 377–404.

Maruka, Kanu. *Empire's Tracks: Indigenous Nations, Chinese Workers, and the Transcontinental Railroad*. Berkeley: University of California Press, 2019.

Minsky, Amy. "Hate Crimes against Muslims in Canada Increase 253% over Four Years." Global News, 13 June 2017. https://globalnews.ca/news/3523535/hate-crimes-canada-muslim. Accessed 19 June 2019.

Nguyen, Mimi Thi. *The Gift of Freedom: War, Debt and Other Refugee Passages*. Durham, NC: Duke University Press, 2012.

"Only Way to Stop the Japs Is to Kill, Says Refugee." *Globe and Mail*, 8 August 1942.

Oxford English Dictionary. www.oed.com. Accessed 24 May 2017.

Palmer, Michael. *Dark Side of the Sun: George Palmer and Canadian POWs in Hong Kong and the Omine Camp*. Ottawa: Borealis Press, 2009.

Report of the International Committee of the Red Cross on Its Activities during the Second World War, September 1, 1939–June 30, 1947, Volume II, The Central Agency for Prisoners of War. Seventeenth International Red Cross Conference. Geneva: May 1948.

Roy, Patricia E., J.L. Granatstein, Masako Iino, and Hiroko Takamura. *Mutual Hostages: Canadians and Japanese during the Second World War*. Toronto: University of Toronto Press, 1990.

Skran, Claudena. *Refugees in Inter-war Europe: The Emergence of a Regime*. New York: Oxford University Press, 1995.

Sullivan, Jack. "69 Canadians from Orient Arrive." *Globe and Mail*, 26 August 1942.

Ward, Rowena G. "The Asia-Pacific War and the Failed Second Anglo-Japanese Civilian Exchange, 1942–45." *Asia-Pacific Journal: Japan Focus* 13, no. 11 (2015).

"W.G. Poy, Claims Files." RG 117, Vol. 510, File BEW 434, LAC.

Wherry, Aaron. "What He Was Talking about When He Talked about Colonialism." *Maclean's*. http://www.macleans.ca/uncategorized/what-he-was-talking-about-when-he-talked-about-colonialism. Accessed 31 August 2017.

4 Petitions and Protest: Refugees and the Haunting of Canadian Citizenship

PETER NYERS

Introduction

Refugees have a paradoxical relationship with the Canadian citizenship regime. According to the received traditions of politics, it is the citizen who possesses all the qualities and capabilities of "being political."[1] A refugee, by contrast, is the mirror image of the citizen. Not only are refugees legally non-citizens, but they are also typically defined in terms of what they *lack*: that is, they lack the qualities of citizens. The voicelessness, dislocation, and dependency that is associated with refugeeness is typically contrasted to the vocal political speech, belongingness, and autonomy that is the story of citizenship. Moreover, while refugees are expected to be grateful, dutiful, and productive subjects, they are at the same time often forced to advocate and mobilize for their own political, social, and human rights. The refugee experience, therefore, involves a tension between deference to sovereign authorities and institutions, and democratic acts of political engagement that potentially subvert dominant power relations.

This chapter investigates the tensions and paradoxes that emerge when refugees engage in politics, make rights claims, and enact themselves as political beings. These tensions and paradoxes are explored with reference to activities of the Non-Status Women's Collective of Montreal, a group whose members include many refugees who do not have formal status in Canada. The Collective was formed in 2015 in order to create a space for non-status refugee women to share their experiences, engage in consciousness raising about their circumstances, and develop a community of mutual care and support. Non-status refugees and migrants face significant constraints on their social rights and are often ineligible for services and entitlements such as social housing, rent supplements, child care supports, legal employment, and so on.[2]

Confronted by the precariousness of their situation, the Collective quickly moved beyond consciousness-raising activities and entered the public realm. Of course it is risky for non-status refugees to come out in public in order to express their political views and make rights claims. However, as Bonnie Honig notes, "political action comes to us"[3] – it can be thrust upon individuals and communities because of the urgency to rectify their social exclusion. This became the case for the Collective in November 2015, when it delivered a petition to the newly elected Canadian prime minister, Justin Trudeau – who also happened to be their local member of Parliament. Despite repeated efforts to connect with the prime minister, their letter went unanswered and unacknowledged, seemingly confirming their claim that they live "in the shadows, invisible and excluded."[4] Convinced that the government's view was that they "did not exist," the Collective began "haunting" Trudeau's constituency office in Montreal. Members of the Collective dressed up as ghosts to underscore their simultaneous presence and invisibility in Canadian society.

Both the petitioning and the ghostly political actions of the Collective suggest that there is an "irregular" or "haunted" form of citizenship that refugees enact in relation to "regular" citizenship.[5] I will say more about the ways that refugees haunt citizenship in a moment, but first let us consider the significance of the petitioning efforts by the Collective. One of the principal aims of this chapter is to shed light onto some of the practices, techniques, and technologies that characterize the political struggles of refugees, rejected asylum applicants, undocumented workers, and non-status migrants in Canada.[6] Much of the literature on refugee political activism focuses on dramatic acts of non-compliance, contestation, and claims-making, such as hunger strikes, public demonstrations and marches, delegate visits and sit-ins at bureaucratic offices, and so on.[7] Here, I focus on an understudied and comparatively more mundane practice that nonetheless runs throughout the history on refugee political activism: that is, the utilization of petitions and petitioning as a means of securing political voice among non-citizen subjects. The reliance on petitions produces a complex history of non-citizen activism. This is because the petitioner is invariably caught in a struggle between reinforcing *and* subverting state authority. On the one hand, petitions concerning immigration matters inevitably appeal to already established political authorities and institutions, thus reaffirming the state's dominant role within the political imagination. At the same time, however, the history of petitioning shows that it has been a key means through which marginalized citizens and non-citizens have made claims, mobilized a community of support, and, in so doing, enacted themselves as social and political beings. This latter element is crucial to remember when confronted with the criticisms of petitioning, which often dismiss petitions as too embedded in the status quo of what counts as proper political authority, space, and subjectivity. In this view, petitioning has become so routinized and institutionalized, so embedded in existing political frameworks, that it has lost its critical edge as a transformative act. For example, the explosion of online petitioning has been criticized as being just another form of "thin" political activism, or "clicktivism." While there is certainly some validity to these criticisms, I want to emphasize the various ways petitioning by refugees and non-status migrants can also introduce a rupture, a break in the routines, self-understandings, and practices of citizenship. In the case of the irregular petition of Montreal's Non-Status Women's Collective, I argue that a haunted form of citizenship was enacted.

Haunted citizenship links up with other interventions on refugee political subjectivity found within critical refugee studies. Refugees haunt the category of citizenship in at least two ways. As non-citizens, the members of the Women's Collective engaged in political acts normally associated with citizenship: petitioning, protesting, social mobilization, etc. Their political acts establish them as political actors despite the lack of the formal status of citizenship. In this way, haunted citizenship is a particular manifestation of what Vinh Nguyen calls "refugeetude." Nguyen affixes the suffix -*tude* to the word *refugee*. He does so in order to signal a connection to, and alliance with, other critical projects such as negritude, coolitude, and migritude – all of which aim to "create new historical consciousness, wherein negative experiences become sources for constructing integral subjectivities and modes of aesthetic and social projection."[8] Refugeetude, from this perspective, is a "mode of relationality" that seeks to comprehend the refugee "not as an irregularity or disruption of political subjecthood – a crisis to be resolved – but as an experiential resource for developing significant and durable ways of being in and moving through the world."[9]

The experience of being a refugee can haunt citizenship in other ways as well, including long after people have legally ceased to be refugees and have formally obtained citizenship. The experience of being a refugee – of feeling unrooted, dispossessed, discriminated against – can extend well beyond the expiration of that formal status and its replacement by citizenship. This speaks to a fundamental paradox in labelling refugees: that is, the conditions and self-consciousness of being a refugee often far outlast the legal expiration of the status.[10]

Drafting petitions, signing petitions, and mobilizing public support for petitions is a means of narrating "refugeetude" that is not typically considered within critical refugee studies, with its ethnographic focus on personal narratives, on the one hand, and more spectacular public demonstrations, on the other. The chapter will begin by providing a history of the forms, techniques, and subjects of petitioning in order to understand how political subjectivities (of citizens *and* non-citizens) are enacted through the act of petitioning. The chapter will then turn to analyse the petition efforts of the Non-Status Women's Collective of Montreal. Their petition can be described as a "irregular petition" because it did not conform to the received norms and institutional expectations of what a petition should look like. Irregular or not, the petitioning campaign nonetheless constituted the members of the Collective as political subjects, thereby challenging the received expectations placed upon refugee subjectivity.

Refugees and the Politics of Petitioning

Petitioning is interesting to investigate from the perspective of refugee protests because it involves acts of political subjectification. The refugee enacts himself or herself as a political being through the act of petitioning. It is worthwhile to provide a brief history of petitioning in order to understand how this works. As we shall see, petitioning straddles the borderline between challenging and reproducing the political status quo. Petitioners have the potential to act as a rupture in the established order, or to constitute an act of refounding and smoothing out of the inconsistencies of this order. The struggle that animates these dialectics of refounding and rupture, supplication and subversion, can be seen in a series of controversies about the forms of petitions, the tone and language in which they are written, the manner in which they are delivered to authorities, and the conduct of the petitioners. How each of these elements is enacted, by both petitioners and authorities alike, has important consequences for the kind of political subjectivities that emerge out of acts of petitioning. Providing an account of how these norms and practices have emerged historically is important for what is at stake, politically, when non-citizen subjects (i.e., non-status refugees) engage in petitioning activities.

Petitions are commonly understood as tools used in movements and campaigns aimed at changing public opinion, pressuring governmental officials, and provoking debate. Petitions are a well-known and frequently deployed means to influence public policy and legislative agendas. From the politician's or government's perspective, petitions can act as a barometer of public opinion, with the number of signatures showing which issues matter to the most citizens. However, the history of petitioning has been far from unified and is "notably discontinuous": "Different people at different times have exploited the petition for different sorts of ends, and the only feature remaining unchanged is the *formula* in which petitions continue to be couched."[11] Identifying some of the key features of the formula, or form, in which petitions are constructed is helpful for understanding the politics that are enacted in, through, and against petitioning. These features, as we shall see in the discussion below, are caught up in a complex and paradoxical politics of reaffirmation and resistance. On the one hand, acts of petitioning have the potential to be a subversive political force that can shake up established authorities and institutions. On the other hand, they can be an act of refounding and relegitimization for these same authorities and institutions.

In her book *Signatures of Citizenship*, Susan Zaeske notes that there is a distinct narrative style to early forms of petitioning: petitioners would supplicate the sovereigns they addressed. This obsequiousness is reinforced by some elements of the etymology of the word "petition" – although, as we shall see below, there is a deep tension that runs through this etymology, since the meaning of the term contains multiple elements that can be variously reinforcing, ambiguous, and contradictory. The English word "petition" began to be used in the early fourteenth century with the meaning of "a supplication or prayer." It was a word borrowed and adapted from the French word *peticion*, meaning "request." These words have several Latin origins, including *petitionem*, which when used in a legal context means "a claim, suit," and the verb *petere*, meaning "ask for, beseech." The meaning "request" implies that there must be an authority figure that is in a position to hear the petition. To petition is, therefore, to immediately establish a relationship between the petitioner and the petitioned. The association of the word "petition" with the meaning "supplication or prayer" implies that this relationship is unequal and hierarchical, with the petitioned holding the greater power and authority. It also makes demands on the conduct of the petitioner, who must be humble and respectful in all their interactions with the authority figure. During the Middle Ages, for example, petitioners would use words such as "sage," "haut," and "puissant" when addressing authority figures. By contrast, when referring to him- or herself, the petitioner would use words such as "humble," "*pover*," and "obeisant." Humility, supplication, modesty – this was a deferential mode of politics, with aristocratic orders expecting deference from commoners.

Despite its hierarchical nature, petitioning is never a unidirectional power relationship. The petitioner, through the very act of petitioning, also exerts power. As Zaeske explains, "The people's right of petition, after all, imposed a responsibility on the part of the ruler to hear their grievances and, whether it be positive or negative, give some response."[12] The language of supplication began to shift by the seventeenth century when activists brought petitions to English Parliament as a means to provoke debate and publicize their cause – as opposed to seeking immediate redress or resolution to a grievance. There began a shift in the performativity of petitions, from a way to articulate individual grievances to a tool for collective political action. As a result of protest movements, including the storming of Parliament by petitioners, in 1669 the House of Commons acknowledged that all commoners possessed the right to petition. Moreover, the House acknowledged its obligation to receive these petitions. New rights were met with new obligations.

A deep tension runs throughout these demands on proper forms of citizen conduct. Acts of petitioning, after all, emerge out of a context of injustice or wrongdoing. Petitions articulate a grievance and a demand for its remedy. While conducting themselves in an obsequious manner has been a challenge for many petitioners, the tension here is not limited to the idiosyncrasies of individual personalities. At stake here are broader questions about the dynamism of acts of citizenship. Petitions, in the very rules and convention of their form, demand an active citizen. This is because petitions that lack an active component are not petitions. For petitions to be recognized as such, they must make a clearly worded request for the relevant authorities to do something (or refrain from doing something). Petitions that do not have this active component – e.g., petitions that only articulate a grievance – are normally rejected out of hand.

A pervasive paradox or tension runs through the history of petitioning – what Zaeske calls its "deeply subversive potential" to transform established political authorities and institutions.[13] In this way, petitioning animates the dialectic of submission and subversion that is a crucial part of the historical story of citizenship. The citizen's political agency can be found in the "gap between the capacity to submit to authority and yet the ability to act in dissent."[14] Petitioning is a practice of citizenship that performatively negotiates this line between the submissive and subversive. The demand for obsequious conduct is in tension with other dimensions in the etymology. The Latin verb *petere* not only means "ask for, beg, beseech, request"; it also has the more politically assertive meaning of "demand" and "require" and, more dramatically, "attack" and "assail." We can further see this struggle between supplication and protest in the Latin *petitionem*. We have seen already that, when used in a legal context, this word means "a claim, suit." But it has the additional meaning of "a blow, thrust, attack." This latter element can be found in examples when the failure of a sovereign or Parliament to respond to repeated petition became seen, according to Zaeske, as "acceptable grounds for revolution."[15] For example, the increase in the number of failed petitions served as part of the precipitous backdrop to the American Revolution. As stated in the Declaration of Independence: "In every stage of these oppressions we have petitioned for redress in the most humble terms: our repeated petitions have been answered only by repeated injuries."[16] The right to petition was, therefore, enshrined in the First Amendment of the new American state. However, even in the immediate aftermath of the Revolution, the uprisings and rebellions in Massachusetts (1786) and Pennsylvania (1794) emerged after many failed attempts at petitioning. A petitioning movement among artisans in Connecticut (1792) was distinctive for its bold and non-supplicant discourse and language. As Zaeske further explains, "These collective petitions reflected the notion that a democratized government should be responsive to the demands of the common people and that petitioning was an important mechanism to convey the peoples' opinions to their representatives."[17] Petitioning not only brings justice and rights to marginalized individuals and groups. It can also be a means of enacting these rights. In this way, petitioning can be understood as an act of citizenship. Placing one's signature on a petition transforms that piece of paper into something with political force. As Giorgio Agamben explains, "the signature decisively changes our relation to the object as well as its function in society."[18] But the signature does more. The act of signing a petition signals political subjectivity for three key reasons. First, petitioning is an enactment of a basic democratic right: the freedom of expression and opinion. Moreover, this expression articulates a grievance, a wrong, and asks for an action to remedy the situation. So, petitioning is central to democratic values of equality, political voice, and the achievement of social justice within the political community.

Petitions are political acts in another way: they are formative of the very political subjects that write or sign the petition. In other words, we can say, with Jacques Derrida, that the "signature invents the signer."[19] In making this claim, Derrida is drawing on J.L. Austin's distinction between constative and performative speech acts. Constative acts are statements that signify a meaning; performative acts are utterances that are accomplished through force. Derrida argues that signatures are interesting precisely because of their duality: they are both constative and performative. The signature is constative because it signifies the intent of the person signing, and it can be verified as a true or false representation of this person. However, the signature is also performative in that it retroactively creates the very subject it is meant to represent. So, the formulation – the "signature invents the signer" – only appears tautological if it is taken to mean that before the signature the signer did not exist. The point, rather, is that the signature on a petition signifies the name, and thereby the namer, as a political subject. The signature is constative and performative, involving representation and creativity. Signing a petition enacts political subjectivity through its appeal for justice to a grievance.

Haunting Citizenship through Irregular Petitioning

When a petition takes an irregular form, is it no longer a petition? What about people who cannot petition because they have no official status within political society? As we shall see in the discussion below, citizenship can erupt in moments when it is not following the rules, prompting the emergence of political subjectivities that are waging struggles against already established norms, authorities, dominations, and power relations.

Petitioning is not the exclusive domain of citizens. Non-citizens – including deportees and non-status refugees and migrants – have also been active in this mode of political expression and mobilization. In France, for example, the Réseau Education Sans Frontières (RESF) movement has mobilized against the deportation of schoolchildren whose parents are *sans-papiers*, and petitioning has been prominent, though not determinate, in that struggle. The petitioning efforts by the RESF resulted in impressive numbers: "A first national petition released in April 2006 and entitled 'Nous les prenons sous notre protection' (We are taking them under our protection) received over 130,000 signatures. A second national petition, accompanying the film 'Laissez les grandir ici' (Let them grow up here) released in March 2007 has so far amassed nearly 100,000 signatures."[20] While these petitions followed the regular form, tone, and process demanded by national authorities, there are examples of irregular forms of petitioning by non-status migrants as well. For example, in 2005, a group of three thousand non-status Sudanese refugees mobilized a three-month sit-in outside the Cairo offices of the UNHCR. A petition was a central part of their campaign, listing thirteen "requests" – not demands, as per the history of deferential language – to the UN officials.[21]

In the remainder of this chapter, I will focus on an irregular petition produced by the Non-Status Women's Collective of Montreal. On 27 November 2015, the Collective delivered a petition to the recently elected Canadian prime minister, Justin Trudeau. Many of the women resided in the Montreal constituency of Papineau that Trudeau represents as a member of Parliament. They are, in their words of their petition,

> women and mothers who live and work in the shadows, invisible and excluded. We live in precarity because of our immigration status. Our precarious status threatens our security, our liberty as women, our rights as workers, our families. We live here; we will remain here. This is our home and our children's home. We want to live in dignity, peace and stability; we want an end to the fear that constantly tortures us.[22]

In order to address these issues, the petition asks the prime minister to "take a position on the regularization of non-status people in Canada." In addition, it makes a specific request for a meeting with Trudeau. As there was no immediate response to the petition – not even an acknowledgment of receipt – the Collective emailed a copy of the petition to Trudeau and to the minister of immigration on 7 December 2015. Another copy was sent on 3 January 2016, but it was also unanswered. The government's lack of acknowledgment and response seemed only to confirm the claims made in the original petition – that these women live "in the shadows, invisible and excluded." On 18 January 2016, four of the women who had originally drafted the petition held a press conference at Concordia University's Simone de Beauvoir Institute to speak about the petition and to share their experiences as non-status people. They wore white masks to cover their faces for fear of being recognized, reported, and deported – but also to emphasize their invisibility within Canadian society. Later that spring, convinced that the government's view was that they "did not exist," the Collective began a series of "hauntings" of Trudeau's constituency office in Montreal. They dressed up as ghosts to underscore their invisible presence in Canadian society, a paradoxical and precarious status that was summed up by one of the speakers: "You don't see us, you don't hear our voices, but we are here: we will stay here, we live here, it's a fact!" With Trudeau still absent and no response from any government agency or representative, the Collective member was nonetheless gracious when ending her speech: "Thank you for listening to this message from ghosts."[23]

The petition written by the Non-Status Women's Collective poses some unique challenges. In the first place, the Collective's petition violates the form, tone, and substance of regular petitions. It is written in a vernacular and dramatic style. While it does make a specific request about regularization of status, many of its demands are too broadly stated to fit within the narrow parameters of petitions for government action. Second, the petition does not follow a format expected of official petitions, nor does it follow the normal procedures for submitting a petition. It was not submitted to the government's online e-petitioning platform, nor did it follow very many of the official rules outlined on the site. Third, it is unclear if the petition is addressed to the proper authority figure. For example, the petition was sent to Trudeau as a representative member of Parliament, and not as the prime minister of Canada. Fourth, the signatures on the petition are irregular in form. As we have seen, petitions usually require the provision of the petitioner's full name and often an address, telephone number, or email address. For people without official immigration status, this poses some serious challenges. To reveal oneself to authorities as being without legal status is to risk exposure to the deportation apparatus of the state. The Collective's petition prefaces the signature section by saying: "We who sign this letter are among tens or even hundreds of thousands of non-status people in Canada. Mr. Trudeau was elected in a Montreal riding where thousands of non-status people live. But, officially, we don't exist."[24]

How, then, can someone who does not exist sign a petition? If the signature makes the signer, what subjects emerge in the context of the Collective's petition? Some of the women who signed the petition used only their first names: "Anne-Marie" and "Lucinda" are examples. Others included details such as their age, the number of children they have, and other descriptions of their life: "Fatma, mother of four children, part-time restaurant worker, afraid for the future of her children" and "Fatima, 30 *ans*, single, cashier, physically and mentally exhausted after 9 years of struggle." Other signatories took the opportunity to articulate longer narratives about their struggles as women living in Canada without legal status. When "Sofia" signed her name, she added:

> I have been here 5 years, the government rejected my case because I am Mexican, that is what my lawyer said because I did everything to be accepted. I am a responsible and honest woman, I work to support myself, and my mother who is elderly and sick in Mexico. In my last job I faced discrimination, shouting, and exploitation because they knew my situation, and they did the same to other people in the same situation. For 11 months I had a hand injury, because of the heavy work, and there was no compensation, and I could not stop working. My sisters and I face many injustices and stress. Now I am looking for work, and above all hope for us, to have a dignified life, and stop living in isolation and fear. I call on your human side, because we all have daughters and sisters and mothers who we do not want to suffer the same, thank you!![25]

What Sofia brings into being with her description is the complex reality of living without status. These complexities cannot be reduced to a signature. The exploitation, injuries, and indignities described by Sofia are unique to her as an individual, but also shared among a wider population of migrants with precarious status.[26] If the signature makes the signer, what we see here is a *relational subject*, one who refuses to be cut off from the wider struggle of which she is a part.

Finally, the Collective's use of public action and protest is by no means unique in the history of petitioning. However, it has more often been the case for collective action to take place during the delivery of petitions to authority figures. In the case of the Collective, their actions came after the repeated delivery of their petition. If petitioning is usually the culmination of mobilization efforts to bring an issue or cause to the political stage, in this case it was only the beginning. The government's refusal to acknowledge the petition meant that other forms of political action were required to force a response. These actions included organizing a press conference and, later, public protests and pickets outside of Trudeau's Montreal constituency offices. In both cases, the petitioners wore disguises – blank theatrical facemasks – in order to conceal their identities. In doing so, they engaged in what Jenny Edkins calls "face politics."[27] Such a politics is dominated by the calculations and surveillance made by dominant authorities and institutions, and this politics of control is well reflected in the Collective's strategy. As already noted, members of the Collective donned masks as part of a strategy of self-protection – i.e., revealing their "true" identities could potentially expose themselves to immigration authorities and, therefore, to increased surveillance, apprehension, detention, and deportation. However, there is another dimension to face politics, one that Edkins calls "dismantling the face" and that is linked to Deleuze and Guattari's invitation to "escape the face ... to become imperceptible, to become clandestine."[28] As a group of women who are forced into a life of being imperceptible and clandestine, the Collective nonetheless starts from this position in order to articulate their demands and enact themselves as political beings. The use of masks, therefore, makes the pressing point that, despite their invisible status within mainstream Canadian society, they are nonetheless an enduring political presence.

The strategy of "haunting" the prime minister's office is notable in this regard. This is because haunting, as Avery Gordon explains, describes "those singular yet repetitive instances when home becomes unfamiliar, when your bearings on the world lose direction, when the over-and-done-with comes alive, when what's been in your blind spot comes into view."[29] Anthropologist Ann Laura Stoler also recognizes the deep paradoxes that run throughout acts of haunting; they are both "familiar and strange," at once a "threatening presence" and an "invisible occupation."[30] She further explains that haunting "wrestles with elusive, nontransparent power and, not least, with attunement to the unexpected sites and lineaments that such knowledge requires."[31] In their hauntings, members of the Collective shrouded themselves in white sheets, the common apparel of ghosts. They carried protest signs, but no words were printed on them. Haunting offers a way of understanding the politics of presence even when the subject or words appear to be absent. As non-citizens, the identity of non-status refugees is expected to be marked by silence and concealment. Hauntings paradoxically allow for both while still being vocal and public.

Finally, the hauntings by the Collective were notable for being public events, and so they raise the issue of the kind of relationships that are enacted. Esther Peeren reminds us that the relationships between ghosts and the people and places they haunt are always symbiotic and defined by a mutuality: "ghosts haunt because they need something from the living (revenge, justice, reparation, assistance) and, conversely, the living conjure ghosts because they want them to provide access to the past or to other worlds."[32]

In their irregular petitioning and spectral demonstrations, the members of the Collective similarly articulated demands to Canadian authorities (legal status, regularization, social assistance) and to Canadian citizens (recognition, respect, solidarity). At the same time, hauntings provide citizens access, in Peeren's words, to "other worlds." In political terms, this could be a world held in common that does not rely on the strict inside/outside logic of modern state sovereignty and citizenship.[33]

Conclusion

When the refugee determination system results in an asylum claim being denied, petitioning emerges as a tactic to articulate grievances, demand action, make claims, and mobilize broader public support. This chapter has argued that, far from being a basic and unremarkable element in any activist's toolkit – refugee or otherwise – the petition is central for understanding the performative elements of citizenship. Crucially, these elements are often enacted by people who are not formally recognized as citizens, such as refugees and non-status migrants.

The petitioner negotiates the complex politics of supplication and protest, refounding authorities and creating a rupture in the political scene. These tensions make the petition something much more than just a piece of paper or an online form. The tensions are enacted through the collective embodiment of petitioning in the form of delivery and presentation. As we saw with the petitioning efforts of the Non-Status Women's Collective, this embodiment can include the embodied spectres of non-status people forced to haunt authorities in order to be recognized as legitimate petitioners. Indeed, if there is a hauntology to petitioning, this act is haunted by the presence of that which should be absent. That is to say, the forms of behaviour, utterances, and codes of conduct that regulate the norms of petitioning are often exceeded and defied by the petitioners. In this understanding of haunting, we find resonance with Derrida's call to resist the urge to exorcize or assimilate the ghosts we encounter and, instead, learn to live with spectres, knowing full well that the results of such a relationship can be unpredictable and full of risks, but also politically transformative and the beginning of new modes of relating to one another in common.[34]

NOTES

1 Isin, *Being Political*.
2 Goldring and Landolt, eds., *Producing and Negotiating Non-Citizenship*.
3 Honig, "Toward an Agonistic Feminism," 223.
4 Open Letter.
5 Nyers, *Irregular Citizenship, Immigration, and Deportation*.
6 For a discussion of the various terms used to describe non-citizens, see Nyers, "No One Is Illegal between City and Nation"; and Bauder, "Why We Should Use the Term 'Illegalized' Refugee or Immigrant."
7 See Nyers and Rygiel, eds., *Citizenship, Migrant Activism, and the Politics of Movement*; and Ataç, Rygiel, and Stierl, "Introduction."
8 Nguyen, "Refugeetude," 110.
9 Ibid., 110–11.
10 Um, *From the Land of Shadows*; and Tang, *Unsettled*.
11 Leys, "Petitioning in the Nineteenth and Twentieth Centuries," 45, emphasis added.
12 Zaeske, *Signatures of Citizenship*, 13.
13 Ibid., 12.
14 Isin and Ruppert, *Being Digital Citizens*, 23.
15 Zaeske, *Signatures of Citizenship*, 15.
16 Cited in ibid., 16.
17 Ibid., 18.
18 Agamben, *The Signature of All Things*, 40.

19 Derrida, "Declarations of Independence," 10.
20 Freedman, "The Réseau Education Sans Frontières," 615.
21 Moulin and Nyers, "'We Live in a Country of UNHCR.'"
22 Open Letter.
23 Ertekin, "Non-Status Women of Montreal Demand Justice." See also Open Letter; and "Non Status Women to Prime Minister."
24 Open Letter.
25 Ibid.
26 Goldring, Berinstein, and Bernhard, "Institutionalizing Precarious Migratory Status in Canada."
27 Edkins, *Face Politics*.
28 Deleuze and Guattari, *A Thousand Plateaus*, 171.
29 Gordon, *Ghostly Matters*, cited in Mountz, "The Enforcement Archipelago."
30 Stoler, *Haunted by Empire*, 1.
31 Ibid., xiii.
32 Peeren, "Specters," 168.
33 Jones, ed., *Open Borders*.
34 Derrida, *Specters of Marx*.

REFERENCES

Agamben, Giorgio. *The Signature of All Things: On Method*. New York: Zone Books, 2009.

Ataç, Ilker, Kim Rygiel, and Maurice Stierl. "Introduction: The Contentious Politics of Refugee and Migrant Protests and Solidarity Movements: Remaking Citizenship from the Margins." *Citizenship Studies* 20, no. 5 (2016): 527–44.

Bauder, Harald. "Why We Should Use the Term 'Illegalized' Refugee or Immigrant: A Commentary." *International Journal of Refugee Law* 26, no. 3 (2014): 327–32.

Deleuze, Gilles, and Felix Guattari. *A Thousand Plateaus: Capitalism and Schizophrenia*. Minneapolis: University of Minnesota Press, 1987.

Derrida, Jacques. "Declarations of Independence." *New Political Science* 15, no. 1 (1986): 7–15.

– *Specters of Marx*. New York: Routledge, 1994.

Edkins, Jenny. *Face Politics*. London: Routledge, 2015.

Ertekin, Cem. "Non-Status Women of Montreal Demand Justice." *McGill Daily*, 18 January 2016. http://www.mcgilldaily.com/2016/01/non-status-women-of-montreal-demand-regularization/. Accessed 3 June 2016.

Freedman, Jane. "The Réseau Education Sans Frontières: Reframing the Campaign against the Deportation of Migrants." *Citizenship Studies* 15, no. 5 (2011): 613–26.

Goldring, Luin, Carolina Berinstein, and Judith K. Bernhard. "Institutionalizing Precarious Migratory Status in Canada." *Citizenship Studies* 13, no. 3 (2009): 239–65.

Goldring, Luin, and Patricia Landolt, eds. *Producing and Negotiating Non-Citizenship: Precarious Legal Status in Canada*. Toronto: University of Toronto Press, 2013.

Gordon, Avery. *Ghostly Matters: Haunting and the Sociological Imagination*. Minneapolis: University of Minnesota Press, 2008.

Honig, Bonnie. "Toward an Agonistic Feminism: Hannah Arendt and the Politics of Identity." In *Feminists Theorize the Political*. Edited by Judith Butler and Joan Scott, 215–35. London: Routledge, 1992.

Isin, Engin F. *Being Political: Genealogies of Citizenship*. Minneapolis: University of Minnesota Press, 2002.

Isin, Engin F., and Evelyn Ruppert. *Being Digital Citizens*. London: Rowman and Littlefield, 2015.

Jones, Reece, ed. *Open Borders: In Defense of Free Movement*. Athens: University of Georgia Press, 2019.

Leys, Colin. "Petitioning in the Nineteenth and Twentieth Centuries." *Political Studies* 31 (1955): 45–64.

Moulin, Carolina, and Peter Nyers. "'We Live in a Country of UNHCR': Refugee Protests and Global Political Society." *International Political Sociology* 1, no. 4 (2007): 356–72.

Mountz, Alison. "The Enforcement Archipelago: Detention, Haunting, and Asylum on Islands." *Political Geography* 30 (2011): 118–28.

Nguyen, Vinh. "Refugeetude: When Does a Refugee Stop Being a Refugee?" *Social Text 139* 37, no. 2 (2019).

"Non Status Women to Prime Minister: 'Continue to Ignore Us, We Don't Exist.'" Press release, *Montreal Newswire*, 19 March 2016. http://newswiremtl.info/non-status-women-to-prime-minister-continue-to-ignore-us-we-dont-exist/. Accessed 3 June 2016.

Nyers, Peter. *Irregular Citizenship, Immigration, and Deportation*. London: Routledge, 2019.

– "No One is Illegal between City and Nation." *Studies in Social Justice* 4, no. 2 (2010): 127–43.

Nyers, Peter, and Kim Rygiel, eds. *Citizenship, Migrant Activism, and the Politics of Movement*. New York: Routledge, 2012.

Open Letter from the Non-Status Women's Collective of Montreal, 10 January 2016. http://www.solidarityacrossborders.org/en/open-letter-from-the-non-status-womens-collective-of-montreal.

Peeren, Esther. "Specters." In *Symptoms of the Planetary Condition: A Critical Vocabulary*. Edited by Mercedes Bunz, Birgit Mara Kaiser, and Kathrin Thiele, 167–71. Lüneburg: Meson Press, 2017.

Stoler, Ann Laura. *Haunted by Empire: Geographies of Intimacy in North American History*. Durham, NC: Duke University Press, 2006.

Tang, Eric. *Unsettled: Cambodian Refugees in the NYC Hyperghetto*. Philadelphia: Temple University Press, 2015.

Um, Khatharya. *From the Land of Shadows: War, Revolution, and the Making of the Cambodian Diaspora*. New York: New York University Press, 2015.

Zaeske, Susan. *Signatures of Citizenship: Petitioning, Antislavery, and Women's Political Identity*. Chapel Hill: University of North Carolina Press, 2003.

PART TWO

CONJUNCTIONS

5 Where Are We From? Decolonizing Indigenous and Refugee Relations

JENNIFER ADESE AND MALISSA PHUNG

Introduction

In Indigenous Studies there is growing acknowledgment that "Canada" no longer looks as it did at the outset of colonization and Canadian nation-building. There has been a substantial shift from when Canada invoked its manufactured authority over Indigenous lands and lives to declare nationhood in 1867. No longer a "white settler society," if it ever truly was, Canada has become a country comprised of a multitude of peoples representing a vast array of ethnicities and nationalities. The population of people living in what is often currently referred to as Canada has become increasingly diverse – people from around the world, and their descendants, now call these lands home. While there are substantive differences between Indigenous peoples and "arrivants,"[1] the colonial phenomenon of enforced migrants, which in our view includes refugees, to these lands, there is much that Indigenous peoples and refugees share.

Indeed, it would appear that Indigenous and refugee populations occupy "opposite vectors on the continuum of displacement: Indigenous peoples, who may still live on their ancestral lands but whose relationship to that land has been abrogated[,] and refugee-ed people,

---

Throughout the essay, we have prioritized the Indigenous in our relational theorizing to make a political statement. By placing the Indigenous in front of the refugee relation not only in our terminology but also in the way we have ordered each section of this chapter, we make claim to the priority of Indigenous experiences, epistemologies, and ontologies. While this tactic respects the autochthonous connections and responsibilities that tie Indigenous peoples to the land since time immemorial, it also serves as a political reminder that refugees were once tied to a place of origin in similar yet distinct ways before they underwent the process of statelessness.

who have had to leave their homes, usually without passports and visas, and who therefore live outside the provisions of the nation-state."[2] While refugees lack citizenship but deserve the right of migration, Indigenous peoples have had settler citizenship imposed upon them even though they have always owned the right to their autochthonous status. And while both are essentially displaced natives, that is, displaced communities once connected to and having inhabited the territories they call home, the resettlement of one necessitates further displacement of the other. However, in comparing these two figures, what is revealed besides these fundamental differences is that their presence and "survivance," to borrow from Gerald Vizenor (Anishnaabe),[3] threatens the moral, political, and juridical authority of the settler nation-state. On the one hand, the figure of the refugee has proven to be a limit concept that renders the sovereign rule of the nation-state legible through a logic of exception, as pointed out by critical refugee studies scholars via Giorgio Agamben and Hannah Arendt.[4] Yet in a similar vein, the figure of Indigeneity throws the sovereign claims of the settler state into crisis, as the Introduction to this volume explains. Thus, theorizing Indigenous and refugee relation demonstrates how much settler nation-states need Indigenous peoples and refugees in order to wield sovereign control and hegemonic power over a range of subjects within and without their borders.

Even though the Indigenous and refugee person share many common experiences, how the category of the refugee has come to be defined helps explain why coterminous experiences of forced migration have remained undertheorized phenomena. As pointed out in critical refugee studies literature, protecting the refugee has relied upon circumscribing the category of the refugee, but often on the basis of race, gender, class, sexuality, and geopolitics.[5] For instance, Peter Nyers has argued that differentiating an economic migrant from the "bona fide" refugee rests upon liberal Western individual and patriarchal values, as the official UN definition privileges individual expressions of refugee resistance in the public realm (male refugees) that risk state persecution over those of refugee resistance in the private realm (female refugees).[6] Such a definition also clearly excludes internal or intrastate conflicts that have produced vast populations of internally displaced people – such as the Indigenous peoples in Canada, the US, Australia, New Zealand, and South Africa, or even the native inhabitants of the Indian subcontinent leading up to and after Partition.[7] Moreover, in the neoliberal era, lest scholars and policy makers run the risk of deterring Western states from maintaining their humanitarian obligations to help relieve the global refugee crisis by resettling more asylum seekers, critical analyses that argue for restricting instead of expanding the definition of the refugee from its UN definition paradoxically end up extending the global refugee crisis. As Laura Madokoro's and Alia Somani's historical analyses of early twentieth-century Chinese and Punjabi asylum seekers demonstrate in this collection, the juridical definition of the refugee has been anything but stable or universally applied. We suspect that part of the reason why the Indigenous and refugee relation remains so undertheorized is because categorizing the refugee has rested upon excluding a whole range of internal and cross-border displacements and migrations that native peoples from around the world have experienced because of the interconnected spread of imperial wars and empires, post-colonial state formations, and global capitalism. Thus, such a restrictive categorization has created more conceptual divisions between these communities, which obscures the experiences of displacement and dispossession that they may share.

Furthermore, "Indigenous" and "refugee" are not always mutually exclusive; in some instances, those referred to as "refugees" are at the same time undergoing their own process of forced de-indigenization. Although no clear definition of de-indigenization exists in current scholarly literature, we contend that it refers to processes and programs geared towards irrevocably separating Indigenous peoples from their languages, cultures, familial relationships, ways of knowing, and lands. It is also, of course, for many Indigenous communities and nations, centrally invested in rupturing the relationship between human and non-human beings. It is, indeed, the central goal of colonization. Therefore, when people are de-indigenized as a result of the enduring legacies of different yet coterminous colonial projects, forced from their homelands because of global destabilization caused by European and American colonization, inasmuch as they exist in distinct contexts, they have much in common, namely marginalization, impoverishment, and experiences of/with racism. When the complexities of Indigeneity and refugeeness are transported to settler colonies, where the distinction between Indigenous/non-Indigenous and colonized/colonizer is palpable and where colonization continues unabated, refugees are caught by an Indigenous/settler binary.

For Indigenous peoples colonized by the French, British, and then by Canada, the constant waves of settlement – irrespective of whether it is born through will or force – often feels like a continuation of centuries-deep colonial genocide intent on dispossessing Indigenous peoples and eradicating Indigenous lives.[8] Under assimilatory legislation commissioned as part of a wider genocidal project, the Canadian nation-state targeted Indigenous peoples for eradication. One of its most potent strategies for Indigenous erasure was the weaponization of Canadian citizenship, eventually coming to force Indigenous peoples into Canadian citizenship, as we discuss below. The question of Canadian citizenship, then, is somewhat of an "elephant in the room" in this discussion, whereby Canadian citizenship has been a mark of colonization for Indigenous peoples, while for refugees the possibility of eventual Canadian citizenship appears to promise safety and security.

In light of this and the cleavages produced by such seemingly oppositional positionalities, we, as authors who hail from otipemisiwak/ Métis and Sino-Vietnamese refugee backgrounds, will theorize a possible avenue to relationship building between Indigenous peoples and refugees. We contend that such relationship building is vital. It is vital not only in terms of learning to live alongside one another, but also in enabling us to develop an ethics of care and accountability to and for one another. It also removes the centre of focus from the deeply problematic nation-state and Canadian citizenship. We juxtapose our own families' migration narratives and the practice of what we refer to as "genealogical disclosure," and argue that this method can function as an accountability and relation-building tool.

Already a common praxis among Indigenous, feminist, and racialized scholars, genealogical disclosure – narrating who we are and where we come from at a deep level (meaning more than simply stating our positionality but offering *context* for it) – functions as a strategy of decolonial and anti-racist resistance for the authors to ethically situate their knowledge production and political commitments as scholars, teachers, and community allies. Genealogical disclosure, in short, is telling our stories in a manner that tells one another not just who we are but *how* we come to be who we are as people. This sits in stark contrast to storytelling for the purposes of institutions, or the "functional life writing" that Ebony Coletu writes about.[9] Genealogical disclosure involves sharing who we are and where we come from. Indeed, as the goal behind this storytelling practice is to situate Indigenous communities in relation with refugee communities, the empathy and understanding to be gained here also differ from the often traumatic and exploitative conditions of the refugee claimant who is forced to give an account of him-/herself that Donald Goellnicht cautions against in his chapter on cross-racial refugee narratives: when there is an oppressive power differential, the empathy exchanged can become an affect of consumption rather than care and compassion. Alternatively, we claim that the practice of genealogical disclosure, grounded in Indigenous kinship principles, performs an ethical and pedagogical role as it lays bare the

Indigenous and refugee person's rooted histories, responsibilities to each other, to their communities, and to the land and its sentient and non-sentient inhabitants.

To further elucidate the concept and practice of genealogical disclosure, we begin by telling our family migration stories. Taking the form of autobiographical vignettes placed in conversation with each other, our practice of genealogical disclosure echoes the autoethnographic and personal methodology practised by diaspora studies scholars such as Rey Chow and Christina Sharpe – but with a difference. For us, genealogical disclosure is a critical life narrative approach that engages with Indigenous kinship principles to enable and conceptualize relation building between Indigenous and refugee peoples.[10] Whereas autoethnography remains focused on the self, on narrating the self, genealogical disclosure bridges a person's past, present, and future in relation to the *people* that birth us, bind us, and care for us. It asks not just "who are you?" but "who do you come *from*?" and "who are you accountable to?"

The question typically asked of visibly racialized minorities – "Where are you from?" – resonates differently for Indigenous and refugee peoples. In an Indigenous context, such a question is intimately tied to Indigenous laws, grounding oneself in kinship relations and in place, and evokes both a concern and desire to ascertain a stranger's potential kinship connections to the land and home community. On the other hand, in a white and multi-racialized settler context, the question invokes/presumes a stranger's otherness on the basis of racial and colonial difference. As an otipemisiwak/Métis woman who is often read as singularly white, and as a visibly racialized Asian heterosexual cis-woman, we have woven together the following migration narratives in order to reflect on, re-envision, and recuperate this genealogical question as a relational practice that lays bare our political commitments to each other as friends, allies, and community members, thus modelling a critical practice that may inspire much-needed conversations on conceptualizing and building Indigenous and refugee relationalities.

Intersecting Disclosures: Indigenous Laws and Genealogical Disclosure

For otipemisiwak/Métis, this English-language concept of "genealogical disclosure" can best be understood through Indigenous laws specific to otipemisiwak/Métis. otipemisiwak/Métis are guided in life by what Métis scholars Brenda Macdougall and Anna Flaminio identify as nehiyaw (Cree) and Métis laws wahkohtowin and kiyokewin – kinship and visiting. Along with the action of storytelling, acimostakewin, wahkohtowin and kiyokewin strengthen the bonds that unite people, and bind Cree and otipemisiwak/Métis together across space and time. Flaminio writes that these laws involve "visiting and caring for our relations and our reciprocal obligations to treat each relative in a unique and respectful way."[11] Macdougall elaborates on wakhotowin as follows:

> As much as it is a worldview based on familial – especially an interfamilial – connectedness, wahkootowin also conveys an idea about the virtues that an individual should personify as a family member. The values critical to family relationships – such as reciprocity, mutual support, decency, and order – in turn influenced the behaviours, actions, and decision-making processes that shaped all a community's economic and political interactions ... Just as wahkootowin mediated interactions between people, it also extended to the natural and spiritual worlds, regulating relationships between humans and non-humans, the living and the dead, and humans and the natural environment.[12]

What this demonstrates is that otipemisiwak/Métis have codes of conduct that provide the foundation for building relationships across human and non-human, living and non-living. These, Flaminio asserts, are core Cree, otipemisiwak/Métis laws.

Undoubtedly, these foundational laws were extended to other humans, to non-Indigenous humans, and these lessons can thus today provide a pathway to relationship building with human beings who may be indigenous to *other* places and who find themselves recast upon their arrival to "Canada" as refugees. When Métis enact these protocols in relationship building outside of our immediate families and community relations, and even beyond interactions with other Indigenous peoples, it has the potential to build transformative relations with more recent arrivants to these lands now commonly referred to as Canada. If these laws provide the foundation for our relations and obligations to and for each other, then, potentially, they can enable us to build relations among, in the case of the authors working together in this piece, otipemisiwak/Métis and Sino-Vietnamese people. In order for this to work, then, we must answer the very placing/displacing question: "Where are you from?"

Jennifer

tansi! Jennifer nitishinakaso – I am of the otipemisiwak/Métis of Amiskwaciy-waskahikan (Beaver Hills House/Edmonton), Wabamun, Manitou Sakahigan (Lac Ste. Anne), and Mistahi Sakahigan (St. Albert). Those are the lands of the nehiyawak, Saulteaux, Nakoda, Métis, and the lands of notawiy (my father), nokum (my grandmother), and the homes of ni-chapanak (my great-grandparents), nitaniskotapanak (my great-great-grandparents and ancestors), and all of our relations before and after us. Although I have visited many times over the past decade, unlike most of this part of my Dad's family, I was not born in those lands, and have never lived there. Instead, I was born in a small town on the Pacific coast, and was raised in Haudenosaunee, Mississauga, and Neutral traditional territory on the south shores of Onitariio (the beautiful lake). I currently live in the treaty lands of the Mississauga Nation and teach Indigenous Studies-focused courses in the Department of Sociology at the University of Toronto Mississauga. For most of the time spent writing this piece, I lived in the homeland of the Omàmiwininiwak, the downriver people, the Algonquin Anishinaabeg, in the City of Ottawa, where I was the coordinator of the Indigenous Studies program in the School of Indigenous and Canadian Studies.

While I am otipemisiwak/Métis, I am also a third-generation immigrant by way of my paternal grandfather's Volgadeutsche family, ethnic Germans from the Volga River in the Samara district of Russia, who themselves moved into the Russian steppes on the invitation of Catherine the Great as part of the nation-building project of Russia. In essence, Russia sought to "people" its southern territorial claims. My grandfather was born shortly after his parents' arrival in Alberta, coming from Russia by way of Texas, Kansas, and Manitoba, and in the years that followed my great-grandparents' family back home in Russia would themselves become displaced ethnic minorities, as they were deported to Kazahkstan by Stalinist militia. In spite of initial attempts by Stalin to subject them to "Russification" (indoctrination into Russian language and culture), they were deemed no longer Russian; after hundreds of years away and some intermarriage, they were no longer considered "pure German" and were thus unwelcome in Germany. In addition to this, I am also a second-generation immigrant by way of my maternal grandfather, born into Victorian-era England, who arrived in Estevan, Saskatchewan, in the early 1900s, and who, like my Volgadeutsche family, did so on the promise of "free" land and a safer and more secure life. Through my maternal grandmother I also have ties to Great Britain, to the early Pennsylvania Dutch settlers who were bound to relationship and responsibility with Haudenosaunee through the Kaswentha (or Two Row wampum), and, because of my mother's adoption into an English Mennonite family, ties to ancestors I simply do not know much about.

Because my mother was adopted, the majority of stories I heard about my family, and the narratives I was given growing up, were tied to my paternal relations. As such, I have spent the past decade strengthening my relations on the prairies and gaining a greater understanding of what it means to say that I am of the otipemisiwak. I am not otipemisiwak or Métis because I am "mixed" – I am no more "mixed" than those whose heritages are Irish-Scottish, Sami-Russian, Igbo-Yoruba, or Ashante, Puerto Rican, and Jewish. To say that I am otipemisiwak or Métis because I am "mixed" means that I ground my sense of self in racialized and racializing binaries of Indianness and whiteness, categories that, as a human being committed to decolonization, anti-racism, and anti-neocolonialism, I soundly reject. I am otipemisiwak because I come from otipemisiwak and I share in the continuance of otipemisiwak family ties, memories, languages, and worldviews. It is from within this cultural context and learning from other otipemisiwak community members and scholars that principles of what wahkohtowin, kiyokewin, and acimostakewin came into my life.

Malissa

Whenever I begin a public talk on Indigenous and Asian relations, I often perform a version of the following land and community acknowledgment:

> Before I begin, I'd like to acknowledge my status as an uninvited guest on the territories of the Huron-Wendat, Mississauga, and Haudenosaunee peoples. These are the lands on which I currently live and work, though I've also started teaching on Anishnaabe and Algonquin territory as well. I also want to mention that the knowledge that informs my work has been shaped by my experiences as a second-generation settler descendant of Sino-Vietnamese refugees who have resettled on the territories of the Cree, Blackfoot, Métis, Nakado, and Tongva peoples.

What follows this preface is a territorial acknowledgment of the land upon which the public meeting or conference is taking place. The practice of territorial acknowledgment has become a scholarly and activist custom in recent years to acknowledge the Indigenous territory (or, if any, treaty) upon which public engagements in the academy are taking place, a trend that is being practised in activist spaces such as political rallies or even public readings and author interviews organized by local bookstores with a social justice mandate. This is typically a gesture of respect, and sometimes it carries a pedagogical function, as some of us sitting in such an audience may not know whose lands we are currently occupying. But recently, Indigenous academics like the Métis blogger and author Chelsea Vowel argue that, while performing these acknowledgments may powerfully disrupt and unsettle how settlers have come to relate to the land as being emptied of Indigenous presence or priority, once these acknowledgments become common practice in formal institutional spaces, they also run the risk of becoming tokenistic gestures that have little commitment to producing any real change.[13]

So, this is how I have come to perform this practice: I approach it as a practice of genealogical disclosure rather than a display of territorial knowledge that deserves an empty activist pat on the back. Anticipating but not waiting until someone questions my genealogical origins, I voluntarily disclose where I have been living and working and learning as an uninvited guest and I carefully detail where my diasporic community comes from. I reveal that my Canadian relatives migrated to this country as Sino-Vietnamese refugees under the auspices of the Canadian Private Sponsorship Program after the end of the Vietnam War, when they were pressured by post-war economic, political, and inter-ethnic instabilities to relocate on account of being economically privileged, ethnically Chinese, colonial intermediaries. I also list the communities that my family and I have been living among ever since they left Vietnam and Hong Kong as refugees of the Vietnam War. I do this to lay claim to the duties and responsibilities that I believe immigrants and refugees like my family and me have to these communities, just in case any members from these Indigenous communities may be listening in the audience and would like to ask me how I have been working to honour these relations, because otherwise who is this territorial acknowledgment really for? Coupled with a reflective territorial acknowledgment, this practice of genealogical disclosure is for me a gesture of respect and gratitude, but in laying claim to being an uninvited guest, it is also acknowledging a power differential. None of these communities invited my family and me to live in these places. As stateless refugees after prospering as colonial intermediaries in Vietnam, we have since been allocated our Canadian and American citizenship rights from settler-state powers that control and dominate the sovereignty and land rights of this list of communities and nations. Thus, I perform this disclosure to publicly announce the community displacements and debts that my family and I have incurred by simply living and working on these territories. Understandably, this practice is only a first step towards building Indigenous and refugee relations, a process that would require a lifelong commitment on our part to initiate more conversations and understanding between our communities if it is to accomplish any meaningful change. But in drawing out our connected yet distinct experiences of displacement and dispossession, this practice has the potential to inspire much-needed intergenerational solidarities among our communities.

The Intersecting Logics of Genealogical Interrogations

Jennifer

While "genealogical disclosure" has deep roots in Indigenous knowledge systems and laws, there remains a question as to whether it is constrained in some contexts, for some people. For instance, while some members of my Métis and Cree family may be racialized, I am perceived and thus treated as a white woman, except on just a handful of occasions. While I have been read as Indigenous a few times in my life and have experienced anti-Indigenous racism in those select instances, I overwhelmingly move through the world with the unearned advantages that perceptions of my whiteness accord me. In my daily life I do not endure the heavy weight of being subject to gazes that racialize me as a Native person, with intentions to relegate me to an inferior position, to dominate me, minimize me, and delegitimize my existence. That I am not racialized in this way does not mean that I am not Indigenous or that I am not impacted by racialization in certain ways. That I was born into economic poverty but have moved, however, through the world and into the professoriate and thus a different social class from the one I was raised in and that many Indigenous peoples continue to be oppressed by is in some part due to the whiteness that I carry. That I am perceived as non-threatening because of the structural power of whiteness certainly means that I face less exclusion on the basis of my appearance within academia and the wider world. In both places – academia and the wider world – I *offer* the answer to "Where are you from?" willingly; it never carries with it the weighty implications that I do not belong *here* – and that I am not a "true" Canadian who does not really belong.

Malissa

When I think back to all those times I've been asked, "Where are you from?" I can recall now with some amusement the unsatisfactory answers I have given, though not necessarily in the following order:

- I was born in Red Deer, Alberta, but I grew up in Edmonton.
- I've lived in Canada my whole life.
- My family came from Vietnam, but we're not Vietnamese.
- I'm Sino-Vietnamese.

Sometimes when I'm feeling lazy and lousy, I offer the following answers to my nosy inquisitors instead: "My ancestors are from China," or "I'm second-generation Chinese Canadian." But when I give these answers, answers so seemingly simple that they betray the complexity of what it has meant for people to come from China over the past two hundred years, I still find myself compelled to give more answers, even when more questions are not asked.

Then I remember those moments when I'm not even asked this vexing question, moments that bring up feelings of shame and indignation from being categorized correctly or incorrectly. Most women of Asian ancestry know what I'm talking about: those embarrassing moments of being accosted by men in public with an abrasive *ni hao?!* or *ahn nyeong hah seh yo!!!* These are the more aggressive moments when you'd prefer to be asked the vexing question instead. But my worst "I know where you are really from" moment happened to me on my way to the University of Alberta as an undergraduate student. I was on my way to class. I was sitting alone on the LRT when a man sat down across from me. We quickly exchanged polite smiles, but I could feel his intrusive stare, so I looked up and smiled politely again.

"What you got there in your thermos?" he asked.

"Excuse me?" I replied.

"Your thermos? What are you drinking out of it?"

"Oh, just coffee."

"Coffee? Why are you drinking coffee?"

Confused, I continued to stare at him, but I stopped smiling politely.

"You should be drinking tea, you know. It's a shame, you people losing your culture like that."

Repeated experiences with this genealogical interrogation have taught me that people were always less interested in learning about my cultural origins than they were in being able to identify my racial origins, a curiosity mostly driven by racial, sexual, and colonial logics.

Community/State Apprehensions and the Potentialities of Kinship and Friendship Making

When Indigenous and refugee peoples are asked to divulge their genealogical origins, the form of disclosure may range from the more compulsory to voluntary conditions. Whereas refugees are required to narrate their life stories as part of their legal application for political asylum, Indigenous peoples, when confronted with this outside of relationship-building contexts, may be called upon to meet institutionalized state demands in order to gain status recognition. While "genealogical disclosure" in English attends to these oppressive and institutional conditions, we are also reconceiving the individualistic framework behind the concept not solely to focus on the individual but to also recontextualize the individual and the way that both Indigenous and refugee peoples may situate themselves in relation to one another. As an Indigenous kinship-making approach, disclosing one's migration narrative has become for us a decisive and conscious effort to engage in the transparent situation of the Indigenous and refugee person in the world and the extension or direction of this place outward – to those not in the immediate familial or community network of the person.

Overwhelmingly, refugee programming by the Canadian government hinges on the notion of "resettlement," something that very clearly evokes the language of settlement that has been the hallmark of the colonization of Indigenous peoples. What we therefore propose is a commitment to relationship building that looks beyond the confines of the settler-preoccupied colonial state. We seek a way to refocus refugee attention towards the relationship with the original caretakers of the land and to recalibrate Indigenous approaches to community building towards refugees who now make up an increasing number of new arrivants to Canada. The literal and figurative face of Canada is changing, and if we do not foster pathways for connecting as Indigenous peoples and as refugees, we will both continue to be displaced within the nation that tries to place us. The crucial thing about genealogical disclosure – about being transparent about who we are and where we come from – is the hope that it will produce precisely the opposite result when it is discussed between Indigenous peoples and refugees from when it is invoked by white Canadians, whose primary motivation is to use it to displace and dislocate refugeed or racialized people from their version/vision of Canada/Canadianness. Rather, when enacted between Indigenous peoples and refugees, it promises to produce a more honest and transparent relationship that forges new pathways for feeling "at home" with one another.

It is precisely this ongoing commitment to honesty and mutual recognition (rather than state-based recognition) that will allow Indigenous peoples and refugees to come to care for one another and to develop reciprocal responsibilities to one another. While it can be argued that Indigenous peoples have no need or obligation to develop these relationships, as original caretakers, our commitment to our laws and to protecting our non-human relations requires us to find ways to engage. In fact, there is already evidence of this ongoing relationship building. In Winnipeg, Manitoba, tensions have increased between the Indigenous and refugee communities. For Indigenous peoples in Winnipeg's inner city, frustration flared up when a housing facility that used to be home for a number of local Indigenous families was reallocated to the Immigrant and Refugee Community Organization of Manitoba (IRCOM). IRCOM received roughly 14 million dollars for renovations to the facility and moved into it in September 2016. The following year, "a group of Indigenous children pepper-sprayed a group of young refugees" outside the building.[14]

In the wake of this incident, IRCOM began working with Jenna "Liiciious" Wirch, a local Anishinaabekwe who identifies as an advocate and community helper from the North End of Winnipeg. Wirch took on the role (one of many she holds) of community development worker tasked with helping to build relations between communities. In 2017, with financial support from the University of Manitoba, IRCOM participated in a two-day conference on "Building Bridges" between Indigenous peoples and refugees in Winnipeg. The conference brought people together in the Circle of Life Thunderbird House, a community gathering space operating under a council of Elders in the city. As a part of the conference programming, members of the Indigenous community and newcomers to Winnipeg were brought together in a circle to share and learn from one another.[15] The conference built on a history of relationship-building work already being undertaken in other areas of the city. For instance, in 2016, five Indigenous women and five so-called "newcomer women" were brought together for a ten-week "circle of reconciliation" wherein they learned about one another, worked to "break down the misconception, educate one another and make things better."[16] The Social Planning Council of Winnipeg's initiative brought Indigenous women together with newcomer women in vital conversation; as one participant, Rayne Graff, an Indigenous woman from Long Plain First Nation, noted, "I find in talking with people, they need to learn our history, so that they can understand why things are the way they are for us."[17] Particularly in Winnipeg, where poverty is acute and Indigenous and immigrant and refugee people face overlapping issues with respect to income security, housing, and health care access, the work of genealogical disclosure – as we see it already in action here – enables us to tell each other our stories, to break down stereotypes, to de-stigmatize one another, and to plan and develop pathways to support one another in our common and divergent struggles.

Malissa

Jennifer and I have known each other since we both started the PhD program at McMaster University in 2008, but we did not become close friends until we went on a road trip with our mentors Alice Te Punga Somerville and Nadine Attewell to the 2012 Native American Indigenous Studies Association (NAISA) conference on the territories of the Mohegan Sun tribe and other Native New England Peoples. Most road-trip experiences can either make or break lifelong friendships and alliances. It is obvious what our first NAISA road trip did for us intellectually and personally. This collaborative project is the culmination of all our conversations over the years about our research and our family migration narratives. Before we bonded on that trip, I did not even know that Jennifer was Métis. As I grew up in the inner-city districts of Edmonton's Chinatown and Boyle Street area, my encounters with Indigenous communities were only with the visibly racialized urban and impoverished Indigenous communities of these neighbourhoods; I did not realize that Jennifer's relations hailed from this region and the surrounding territories. When Jennifer first disclosed her family's migration narrative to me, I initially found it difficult to reconcile with my experiences with white supremacy and urban inner-city Indigenous communities. At the time, I remembered thinking quietly to myself that Jennifer did not "look" Indigenous, so how could she claim this racialized experience? But reading and listening to how she positions her white passing privilege in relation to her Métisness over the years, and rectifying my lack of knowledge on Indigenous critical issues since that time, has helped me better understand that Indigeneity is not only a racialized positionality; it is also a decolonial act of autochthonous resurgence complicated by over four hundred years of colonial contact and violence but made possible by the commitment of community members like that of my dear friend and colleague to maintain and renew relations with one's home community and all the beings that occupy that territory. In short, I have come to learn that being Indigenous takes work. Like most positionalities, one is not born Indigenous, not at least in the bio-physical sense.[18] One must also work at becoming and being Indigenous, a positionality that comes with a host of spiritual, ecological, and political obligations.

It is evident that relationship building between Indigenous and refugee peoples is more urgent than ever. The parallel yet distinct experiences of dispossession, forced migration, and the intergenerational traumas of war, residential school abuse, and the foster care system suggest such an obvious potential for inter-community solidarity and empathy. Yet discussions of Indigenous and refugee relationalities have remained curiously absent in Indigenous and critical refugee studies until quite recently.[19] For example, Yến Lê Espiritu has transitioned from theorizing the Vietnam War as a dyadic war between the United

States and Vietnam to a "*transpacific* war that inflicted collateral damage on the Vietnamese *and* also on indigenous and (formerly) colonized subjects in the circuits of US Empire."[20] This approach emerged out of her reflections on her own refugee flight route "from Vietnam to the Philippines to Guam and then to California, moving from one US military base to another," a transpacific route that revealed the reach and destruction of the US military empire in the Asia-Pacific region.[21] By critically juxtaposing the histories and experiences of refugee flight and Indigenous displacement and dispossession across the Asia-Pacific, Espiritu makes visible the interconnected structures and genealogies that refugee and Indigenous peoples have experienced, transcolonial intimacies that the categorical analysis of the Indigenous and refugee relation alone cannot reveal.[22]

In this chapter, Jennifer and I offer up the concept of genealogical disclosure as a similar strategy to decolonize Indigenous and refugee relations. It is a practice of both vulnerability and accountability, a detailing of our families' migration narratives to reveal to whom we are related, whom we live among. Where we come from tells a genealogy that requires a narrative format, a disclosure of the personal, a reveal of the relations we have or do not have to the places and communities we have come to settle among in order to build sustaining ways of life. Such storytelling practices contextualize us and demonstrate both the limits and the motivations behind our knowledge making and pedagogy, whether in the academy or in our communities. For refugees and descendants of refugees living with the intergenerational legacies of war and displacement, genealogical disclosure may be difficult if not near impossible for refugee families and communities that adamantly refuse to talk about the past, but that does not mean that the door to genealogical disclosure will remain closed indefinitely.

As a second-generation descendant of Sino-Vietnamese refugees, I did not learn about my family's migration narrative entirely from my elders. This narrative was provided to me in bits and pieces over the years, often in reluctant and curt answers to my repeated questionings. I also had to piece this narrative together through historical research and many informal conversations with other Vietnamese and Sino-Vietnamese refugees and their descendants. Thus, we thoroughly understand that the practice of genealogical disclosure is not for everyone, particularly for refugees and descendants still struggling with the effects of war, trauma, and displacement, those who remained stateless for many years and have been forced repeatedly to disclose their migration narrative to various state officials in their multiple applications for asylum. But as many critical refugee scholars have rightly pointed out, refugees are not abject, passive, voiceless, traumatized victims of war and circumstance.[23] Refugees are human beings who create literary and cultural production;[24] refugees are more than capable of demonstrating and organizing politically to better their living conditions in the camps or in their new places of settlement.[25] Consequently, we believe that refugees would be open to the practice of genealogical disclosure with Indigenous communities as a solidarity-building endeavour. To presume that refugees cannot embark on a process of self-decolonization in a settler colonial context is to assume that refugees would lack empathy and understanding for the experiences of Indigenous communities who have undergone parallel yet distinct processes of forced migration, military violence, and dispossession. And we believe that the mutual and voluntary practice of genealogical disclosure between and among Indigenous and refugee communities provides a first step towards achieving self-decolonization and relationship building between these communities.

Reading Displacement Together: Resituating Race, Empire, and Global Capitalism at the Meeting Point of Indigenous and Refugee Studies

In "Decolonizing Antiracism," Bonita Lawrence and Enakshi Dua appear to expect that anti-slavery activists like Frederick Douglass would acknowledge Indigenous peoples in their calls to freedom.[26] This presumed (rather too much, we think) that people who had been enslaved and who had long been denied access to education, and the ability to read and write, could *know* the extent of Indigenous peoples' marginalization or the complex histories of treaty relationships, when many well-schooled people *in the present*, with information widely available, do not know it. Key to the relationship building at the core of genealogical disclosure, if it is to work, is empathy and a reasonable dose of humility. These, too, find themselves embedded within the values, as previously outlined, that Macdougall identifies. This is reflected in Wirch's approach to relationship building between the Indigenous community of Winnipeg and the refugee community.[27] While Indigenous peoples hold a degree of resentment towards refugees because, as Wirch notes, people perceive refugee resettlement as "further colonization" wherein Indigenous peoples "are being displaced from our lands, from our food, from our waters. And it's wrong," she also notes that, ultimately, "we've all been colonized by the British."[28]

It is in this humble acknowledgment that the foundation is laid; beyond fear and anxiety wrought from centuries of oppression, *both* parties must come to see that there is far more that we share with each other – the legacies of imperialism – than what keeps us apart. Global imperialism and colonization have dispossessed Indigenous peoples of/from their homeland all over the world, and many of the arrivants to what is commonly called Canada have themselves been displaced over centuries in parallel and interconnected systems of displacement. People around the world have seen their families and communities forever torn asunder by European nation formation, by empire building, for centuries. Most acutely the rapacious greed of England, France, Spain, Germany, and the Netherlands precipitated a global destabilization and reorganization of people that would, throughout the 1800s and 1900s, drive the displacement of incalculable numbers of people, a process that persists to this day. The dawning of the Industrial Revolution, and with it accelerated modes of travel, enabled both the mass transportation *and* exportation of people seeking refuge from conflict, violence, poverty, and climatic changes wrought by what the late Powhatan-Renapé and Lenape scholar Jack Forbes referred to as "wétiko psychosis."[29]

The wétiko/windigo/wendigo/wendiigo/witiko is a central being in Métis, Cree, Anishinaabe, and other Indigenous people's cultures. As Anishinaabe writer Basil H. Johnston recounts, "weendigo" is

> [a] giant cannibal (or cannibals). These manitous came into being in winter and stalked villagers and beset wanderers. Ever hungry, they craved human flesh, which is the only substance that could sustain them. The irony is that having eaten human flesh, the Weendigoes grew in size, so their hunger and craving remained in proportion to their size; thus they were eternally starving.[30]

For Forbes, this cannibalistic figure exists on a much grander scale. He argues that all violence that human beings exact on one another and on our non-human relations, the environment we live in, is an extension of a wétiko disease, "the disease of aggression against other living things and, more precisely, the disease of the consuming of other creatures' lives and possessions."[31] Forbes frames wétiko disease as a consumptive psychological illness; those who are consumed by the disease in turn consume everything around them. Through this lens, then, "Anglo-American imperialism is a form of cannibalism designed to 'eat' Indians and also to consume Native people's land and resources."[32] When Europeans arrived on the shores of places such as Mi'kma'ki,[33] they were already infected, and this sickness was set in motion – or at minimum stoked – by global processes of imperialism. As such, the widespread global destabilization caused by wétiko psychosis has not been confined to Indigenous peoples here. It has uprooted Indigenous peoples from around the world and, often unwittingly, put them on the move. It displaces Indigenous peoples *and* people who become refugees.

Settler colonialism *is* therefore a consumptive sickness, and those who, from this perspective, fall victim to it are themselves, as well, infected. In the context of Canada as a settler colonial space, this process has bared its teeth in the attending commitment to race, racialization, and racism that has undergirded and enabled much of imperialism's work and has sought to keep those designated as "non-white," to borrow from Renisa Mawani, "in-between and out of place."[34] Canada has perpetuated and extended false notions of racial difference to commit genocide against Indigenous peoples while simultaneously manufacturing its national identity through an ethos of whiteness. This has been extended through Canada's enactment of highly restrictive immigration policies and practices that aimed to "Keep Canada White," an issue that Edward Woo Jin Lee takes on more extensively in this volume.[35] As numerous scholars note,[36] Canadian immigration policy grew from a foundation that distinguished "between *preferred* and *non-preferred* races from 1876 until the 1960s."[37] The process of creating a "white nation" was dependent upon two seemingly disparate yet interconnected movements – containing undesirable "internal" populations (such as Indigenous peoples and African people who were previously enslaved) and keeping undesirable "external" populations at bay. Thus, "the racialization/colonization of Aboriginal peoples and racialized land policies [that] enabled the appropriation of the Canadian 'nation's' territory" and "racialized immigration policies helped to establish and reproduce the 'nation's' population as white."[38]

With respect to Indigenous peoples, Canada enacted highly repressive legislation in the form of the 1876 Indian Act, intent on internally managing, civilizing, and assimilating Indigenous peoples. To state it plainly, enfranchisement provisions within the Indian Act translated to *forcing* Status Indians *into* Canadian citizenship. Indigenous peoples eligible for recognition by Canada as "Status Indians" under the Indian Act were compulsorily enfranchised for a number of reasons: for "serving in the Canadian armed forces, gaining a university education, for leaving reserves for long periods – for instance, for employment – and, for Aboriginal women, if they married non-Indian men or if their Indian husbands died or abandoned them."[39] Enfranchisement meant that Canada erased Indianness and thus "cancelled" present and future claims to the land by the land's original human inhabitants. Worse yet, enfranchisement separated families from one another; it defined what and who an Indian was and what and who an Indian was not; who could live on reserves and who could not. Enfranchisement went so far as to determine who could be buried next to whom.[40]

It was not until the post-Second World War period, in 1951, that the Indian Act received a major overhaul. The most obviously oppressive aspects of the Indian Act, such as the enfranchisement provisions concerning education that removed status from any Indian who attended a university, were repealed in light of the development of a global notion of human rights – a framework that would not look kindly upon Canada's use of things such as the pass system to manage and restrict the mobility of Indigenous peoples.[41] As a result of this genocidal project, Indigenous peoples are the only people in what is currently referred to by some as "Canada" to have been forcibly "made" Canadian.

Indigenous peoples are the only peoples who have been forced to become Canadian through state-engineered processes of civilization and assimilation, and yet this project was undertaken with a steadfast commitment to preserving and protecting Canada's whiteness. The historical dimensions of refugee relations within Canada reflect Canada's desire to manage its national commitment to whiteness. Canada steadfastly refused entry to refugees in the wake of the First World War. At the League of Nations, Canada initially refused to accept refugees unless they were able to do so on a temporary basis with a right of return, meaning that Canada could return refugees to their countries of origin once it deemed it suitable, necessary, or desirable to do so. And so, as peoples' relationships to their pockets of the earth have been severed through imperialist nation-building, people have been forced to flee. We find ourselves in a situation where, for their very survival, displaced people are made complicit in a system that demands Indigenous subjugation. They are displaced to a nation that has sought to make itself in the image of whiteness.

In spite of this, however, we contend that no one who arrives in the lands commonly called "Canada" today should be absolved of a responsibility to Indigenous peoples. The choice remains whether one remains complicit and allows their unknowingness to bolster complicity in settler colonialism, or seeks to move beyond complicity to respect, responsibility, and reciprocity. Rather than allow wétiko psychosis to continue to infect ourselves and future generations, we must work to form new relations, healing relationships, that see ourselves as connected rather than as apart. Genealogical disclosure is therefore our effort to elucidate a pathway to develop an ethic and practice of care *and* responsibility to and for one another, one that at its foundation must be honest about whose land we live on and who remain marked for death so that the rest of "us" may live.

Conclusion

We must recentre our activism around *how* we are; insofar as we focus on how people come to be where they are, we must place great emphasis on *how* people transform and allow themselves *to be transformed*. What does it meant to be a settler "today"? It essentially entails a continual violation of Indigenous peoples for the purposes of propping up an all-encompassing consumer society. How, then, can we learn from our complex pasts, the stories that we carry within each of us? What makes one a settler may not even be the behaviour of their ancestors, many of whom were "everyday people" unwittingly drawn into oppressive systems few understood. However, settlerhood is how you behave in the moment, in the present. That is, it involves asking yourself, "Once I have an understanding and a sense of obligation to anti-colonialism, anti-neocolonialism, and anti-racism, what am I going to do with it?" What does one do with the knowledge once gained? We will learn more effectively if we emphasize relations, especially if people are open and honest about who they are and how they have come to be on these lands. Doing so creates space to work through overlapping and intersecting traumas together, and to help heal and support one another. If we focus on what we hold in common with one another and look beyond the trauma wrought by the distinctions in our experiences under colonization, we may see that we share a common core – anchored in a deep commitment to kinship and the maintenance of our respective cultural lifeways.

What is at stake in acknowledging this? Even if we are to say in the next instant, "I am a settler," we would most certainly *not* evaporate and/or be pulled by fishhooks back to our "original lands." If we acknowledge that "I am afraid more people will come to my homeland and erase and displace me," we will neither halt the process nor further it. However, we will open the door for honest exchange. And yet we resist confronting these things for fear that, by admitting the complexities of our existences here, we sacrifice our ability to call it home. Worse yet, we may see ourselves as complicit in multiple forms of violence of which we once thought we were only the victims and survivors. If we do not speak as who we are, where we come from, and what we fear, we risk compromising our ability to build alliances and solidarities with one another, which are principally about *relationships* and about our survival with one another. To find ways to build relationships with one another and foment a sense of responsibility in the manner in which Indigenous peoples frame it, to one another and to the natural world around us, has never been more pressing, as with each passing day we become more aware of the threat that climate change poses to *all* of our survival.

NOTES

1 Drawing on the term "arrivant" from the Caribbean poet Kamau Brathwaite, Jodi Byrd (Chickasaw) has proposed the concept of "arrivant colonialism" to distinguish the genealogy of forced labour migration of African slaves and Asian coolies to the Americas from that of more voluntary settlers from Europe. See Byrd, *The Transit of Empire*.
2 Coleman et al., "Introduction," xiv.
3 In his seminal text, *Manifest Manners: Narratives on Postindian Survivance*, Gerald Vizenor theorizes the highly influential Indigenous Studies concept of "survivance," that is, Native survival and resistance, to counteract the damaging effects of literary, historical, and cultural representations of Native Americans as a dying and tragic race in the Western canon. As he puts it, "Survivance is an active sense of presence, the continuance of native stories, not a mere reaction, or a survivable name. Native survivance stories are renunciations of dominance, tragedy, and victimry" (vii).
4 See Nyers, *Rethinking Refugees*, 41; Yến Lê Espiritu, *Body Counts*, 22–3; Evyn Lê Espiritu, "Vexed Solidarities," 13.
5 Indeed, similar to the parallel and interconnected ways in which settler colonial societies, governed by a structure of what Iyko Day calls alien capitalism that exploits the land and racialized labour and denies entry and enfranchisement to Asian migrants, settler states like Canada adamantly refused to recognize displaced peoples from Asia and the South Pacific as refugees under the 1951 UN definition because they did not wish to be legally obligated to offer sanctuary to racially undesirable refugees; see Day, *Alien Capital*; Madokoro, *Elusive Refuge*, 25. As Madokoro further points out, the countries that participated in the drafting and revising of the 1951 UN definition of who constitutes a refugee "did so to protect their vested interests as countries who had received refugees or who might be called upon to receive refugees in the future," thus contributing to a humanitarian climate that was actually "conservative, cautious, and inclined to limitations and restrictions rather than expansive thinking about how to define and assist refugees" (*Elusive Refuge*, 30–1). For the original signatories of the 1951 UN Convention, applying the status of refugee to racialized, displaced persons outside of Europe was simply out of the question (ibid., 32; Price, *Orienting Canada*, 312).
6 Nyers, *Rethinking Refugees*, 47–50.

7 Ibid., 57; Madokoro, *Elusive Refuge*, 23; Chimni, "The Birth of a 'Discipline,'" 16.
8 In Canada, the term "Indigenous" is often used as blanket terminology – not unlike the term "refugee" – and thus it is important to acknowledge that the term Indigenous is a terminological placeholder for hundreds of distinct Indigenous nations whose stories of creation and histories of existence tie them, inseparably, to the land they live on. Also referred to as First Nations, Métis, and Inuit, or as "Aboriginal people" in accordance with the Canadian Constitution's s. 35 "Aboriginal rights" section, Indigenous peoples entangled with settler colonialism have a long history of displacement and dispossession precipitated by Canada's nation-building project.
9 Coletu, "Biographic Mediation," 384–5.
10 Our method of genealogical disclosure intersects with and departs from other autoethnographic and personal methodology approaches by blurring the boundaries of the self/other, native informant/ethnic community, academic/life-writing genre. We are less concerned with providing any essential truths or fully representing the views and concerns of our respective communities than we are with demonstrating how our connections to the communities that claim us may produce potential points of relationship building and solidarity by the mere juxtaposition of our family migration narratives. If the goal of diasporic autoethnographers, according to Azade Seyhan, was to chronicle the histories of the displaced lest their stories become lost and forgotten, our goal is to place our migration narratives side by side to elicit more awareness and discussion of the points of connection between and about these communities. See Seyhan, *Writing Outside the Nation*, 12.
11 Flaminio, *"Gladue" through "Wahkotowin"*, 114.
12 Macdougall, *One of the Family*, 8.
13 Vowel, "Beyond Territorial Acknowledgements."
14 Gilbert, "Amid Tensions."
15 Grabish, "Building Bridges."
16 Vitt, "'Us versus Them.'"
17 Ibid.
18 As taught to Jennifer during her pregnancy in 2016 by Métis elders and knowledge keepers Linda Boudreau, Annette Maurice, and Melanie Omeniho, one is very much born Métis, Cree, Mohawk, and Saulteaux in the non-physical sense of having lived in the spirit world with one's ancestors before arriving in the human world. Therefore, while one is not born "Indigenous," one is very much born Métis.
19 Y. Espiritu, *Body Counts*; Y. Espiritu, "Critical Refugee Studies and Native Pacific Studies"; E. Espiritu, "Vexed Solidarities."
20 Y. Espiritu, "Critical Refugee Studies," 483, emphasis in original.

21 Ibid.
22 Further, the methodology that she uses to uncover these seemingly unconnected experiences of imperial displacement (that is, US colonialism in the Philippines, US militarism in Guam, settler colonialism in California, and the Vietnam War) is structured around the concept of critical juxtaposing: "the deliberate bringing together of seemingly different historical events in an effort to reveal what would otherwise remain invisible" (Y. Espiritu, *Body Counts*, 47).
23 Nyers, Rethinking Refugees, 4; Y. Espiritu, *Body Counts*, 26; Soguk, *States and Strangers*, 8; Malkki, "Speechless Emissaries," 388–9.
24 Nguyen, "Refugee Gratitude"; Um, *From the Land of Shadows*.
25 Tang, *Unsettled*.
26 Lawrence and Dua, "Decolonizing Anti-Racism," 130.
27 Gilbert, "Amid Tensions."
28 Ibid.
29 Forbes, *Columbus and Other Cannibals*.
30 Johnston, *The Manitous*, 237.
31 Forbes, *Columbus and Other Cannibals*, 25.
32 Ibid.; Adese, "'You Just Censored Two Native Artists,'" 36.
33 Mi'kma'ki is the Mi'kmaq term for the traditional homeland of the Mi'kmaq.
34 Mawani, "In Between and Out of Place."
35 Hawkins, *Critical Years in Immigration*; Bannerji, "Geography Lessons"; Thobani, "Closing Ranks."
36 Bolaria and Li, *Racial Oppression in Canada*; Hawkins, *Critical Years in Immigration*; Stasiulis and Jhappan, "The Fractious Politics of a Settler Society"; Thobani, "Closing Ranks.".
37 Thobani, "Closing Ranks," 16.
38 Ibid., 16.
39 Crey, "Enfranchisement."
40 In light of enfranchisement provisions in the Indian Act, it is not surprising that Indigenous Studies has not historically spent much time focused on the status of refugees or the field of Refugee Studies. For First Nations people recognized as Indians under Canada's 1876 Indian Act legislation, attendance at university led to automatic enfranchisement. It is no surprise, then, as Indigenous peoples gradually made their way into universities, that academic writing was principally concerned with confronting positions that propagated the idea that we are innately inferior to those who came to the continent from Europe and who made aggressive claim to our lands and lives. Indigenous peoples working in the academy and writing within Indigenous Studies have perhaps been slower to theorize relationships with so-called "non-white" immigrants and refugee peoples,

who are sometimes subject to similar forces of violence, because of the need to remain committed to "survival scholarship," meaning the work needed to undo centuries of anti-Indigenous racism and erasure. At the same time, Indigenous Studies has centred on bringing Indigenous experiences and ways of living, being, and seeing the world to wider audiences.

41 Carter, "Controlling Indian Movement," 8–9; Barron, "The Indian Pass System in the Canadian West, 1882–1935"; Daschuk, *Clearing the Plains*.

REFERENCES

Adese, Jennifer. "'You Just Censored Two Native Artists': Art as Antidote, Resisting the Vancouver Olympics." *Public* 27, no. 53 (2016): 35–48.

Bannerji, Himani. "Geography Lessons: On Being an Insider/Outsider." In *Dangerous Territories: Struggles for Difference and Equality in Education*. Edited by Leslie G. Roman and Linda Eyre, 23–42. New York: Routledge, 1997.

Barron, F. Laurie. "The Indian Pass System in the Canadian West, 1882–1935." *Prairie Forum* 3, no. 1 (1988): 25–42.

Bolaria, B. Singh, and Peter S. Li. *Racial Oppression in Canada*. Aurora: Garamond Press, 1985.

Byrd, Jodi. *The Transit of Empire: Indigenous Critiques of Colonialism*. Minneapolis: University of Minnesota Press, 2011.

Carter, Sarah. "Controlling Indian Movement: The Pass System." *NeWest Review* 5 (1985): 8–9.

Chimni, B.S. "The Birth of a 'Discipline': From Refugee to Forced Migration Studies." *Journal of Refugee Studies* 22, no. 1 (2009): 11–29. https://doi.org/10.1093/jrs/fen051.

Coleman, Daniel, Erin Goheen Glanville, Wafaa Hasan, and Agnes Kramer-Hamstra. "Introduction." In *Countering Displacements: The Creativity and Resilience of Indigenous and Refugee-ed Peoples*. Edited by Daniel Coleman, Erin Goheen Glanville, Wafaa Hasan, and Agnes Kramer-Hamstra, ix–xlvii. Edmonton: University of Alberta Press, 2012.

Coletu, Ebony. "Biographic Mediation." *A/b: Auto/Biography Studies* 32 (2017): 384–5. https://doi.org/10.1080/08989575.2017.1289018.

Crey, Karmen. "Enfranchisement." https://indigenousfoundations.arts.ubc.ca/enfranchisement/.

Daschuk, James. *Clearing the Plains: Disease, Politics of Starvation, and the Loss of Aboriginal Life*. Regina: University of Regina, 2013.

Day, Iyko. *Alien Capital: Asian Racialization and the Logic of Settler Colonial Capitalism*. Durham, NC: Duke University Press, 2016.

Espiritu, Evyn Lê. "Vexed Solidarities: Vietnamese Israelis and the Question of Palestine." *Lit: Literature Interpretation Theory* 29, no. 1 (2018): 8–28.

Espiritu, Yến Lê. *Body Counts: The Vietnam War and Militarized Refugees*. Berkeley: University of California Press, 2014.

– "Critical Refugee Studies and Native Pacific Studies: A Transpacific Critique." *American Quarterly* 69, no. 3 (2017): 483–90. https://muse.jhu.edu/article/670049.

Flaminio, Anna. *"Gladue" through "Wahkotowin": Social History through Cree Kinship Lens in Corrections and Parole*. Saskatoon: University of Saskatchewan, 2013.

Forbes, Jack D. *Columbus and Other Cannibals: The Wétiko Disease of Exploitation, Imperialism, and Terrorism*. New York: Seven Stories Press, 2008.

Gilbert, Rose. "Amid Tensions, Refugees and Indigenous Canadians Seek Common Ground." *News Deeply*, 1 June 2018. https://www.newsdeeply.com/refugees/articles/2018/06/01/refugees-and-indigenous-canadians-seek-common-ground-amid-tensions.

Grabish, Austin. "Building Bridges: Winnipeg Newcomer, Indigenous Communities Come Together at Conference." *CBC News*, 13 May 2017. https://www.cbc.ca/news/canada/manitoba/indigenous-newcomers-come-together-winnipeg-1.3827740.

Hawkins, Freda. *Critical Years in Immigration: Canada and Australia Compared*. Montreal and Kingston: McGill-Queen's University Press, 1989.

Johnston, Basil H. *The Manitous: The Spiritual World of the Ojibway*. St. Paul: Minnesota Historical Society Press, 2001.

Lawrence, Bonita, and Enakshi Dua. "Decolonizing Anti-Racism." *Social Justice* 32, no. 4 (2005): 120–43.

Macdougall, Brenda. *One of the Family: Metis Culture in Nineteenth-Century Northwestern Saskatchewan*. Vancouver: UBC Press, 2010.

Madokoro, Laura. *Elusive Refuge*. Cambridge, MA: Harvard University Press, 2016.

Malkki, Liisa H. "Speechless Emissaries: Refugees, Humanitarianism, and Dehistoricization." *Cultural Anthropology* 11, no. 3 (1996): 377–404. https://www.jstor.org/stable/656300.

Mawani, Renisa. "In Between and Out of Place: Racial Hybridity, Liquor, and the Law in Late 19th and Early 20th Century British Columbia." *Canadian Journal of Law and Society* 15, no. 2 (2000): 9–38.

Nguyen, Vinh. "Refugee Gratitude: Narrating Success and Intersubjectivity in Kim Thúy's Ru." *Canadian Literature/Littérature Canadienne: A Quarterly of Criticism and Review* 219 (2013): 17–36.

Nyers, Peter. *Rethinking Refugees: Beyond States of Emergency*. New York: Routledge, 2006.

Price, John. *Orienting Canada: Race, Empire, and the Transpacific*. Vancouver: University of British Columbia Press, 2011.

Schlund-Vials, Cathy J. *War, Genocide, and Justice: Cambodian American Memory Work*. Minneapolis: University of Minnesota Press, 2012.

Seyhan, Azade. *Writing Outside the Nation*. Princeton: Princeton University Press, 2001.

Soguk, Nevzat. *States and Strangers: Refugees and Displacements of Statecraft*. Minneapolis: University of Minnesota Press, 1999.

Stasiulis, Daiva, and Radha Jhappan. "The Fractious Politics of a Settler Society: Canada." *Unsettling Settler Societies: Articulations of Gender, Race, Ethnicity and Class*, edited by Daiva Stasiulis and Nira Yuval-Davis, 95–131. London: SAGE Publications, 1995.

Tang, Eric. *Unsettled: Cambodian Refugees in the New York City Hyperghetto*. Philadelphia: Temple University Press, 2015.

Thobani, Sunera. "Closing Ranks: Racism and Sexism in Canada's Immigration Policy." *Race & Class* 42, no. 1 (2000): 35–55.

Um, Khatharya. *From the Land of Shadows: War, Revolution, and the Making of Cambodian Diaspora*. New York: New York University Press, 2015.

Vitt, Kaitlin. "'Us versus Them': Programs Mend Strained Relations between Indigenous, Newcomer Communities." *CBC News*, 12 November 2016. https://www.cbc.ca/news/canada/manitoba/indigenous-newcomer-relations-winnipeg-1.3845287.

Vizenor, Gerald. *Manifest Manners: Narratives on Postindian Survivance*. Lincoln: University of Nebraska Press, 1999.

Vowel, Chelsea. "Beyond Territorial Acknowledgments." *âpihtawikosisân* (blog), 23 September 2016. http://apihtawikosisan.com/2016/09/beyond-territorial-acknowledgments/.

6 Queer and Trans Migrants, Colonial Logics, and the Politics of Refusal

EDWARD OU JIN LEE

I was interested in the larger picture, in the discursive, material and moral territory that was simultaneously historical and contemporary ... and the ways in which *Kahnawakero:non*, the "people of Kahnawake," had *refused* the authority of the state at almost every turn. The ways in which their formation of the initial membership code ... was refused; the ways in which their interactions with border guards at the international boundary line were predicated upon a refusal; how refusal worked in everyday encounters to enunciate repeatedly to ourselves and to outsiders that "this is who we are, this who you are, these are my rights."

– Audra Simpson, "On Ethnographic Refusal"

[T]he path to the wild beyond is paved with refusal. In *The Undercommons* if we begin anywhere, we begin with the right to refuse what has been refused to you. Citing Gayatri Spivak, [Fred] Moten and [Stefano] Harney call this refusal the "first right" and it is a game-changing kind of refusal in that it signals that refusal of the choices as offered.

– Jack Halberstam, "The Wild Beyond"

Introduction

Through my research on and activism with (and as a part of) Queer, Trans,[1] Black, Indigenous, and other People of Colour (QTBIPOC) communities, I have been witness to innumerable acts of refusal. These acts of refusal were at times vocal and public assertions of space making and place taking, such as through QTIBPOC arts festivals or street demonstrations. In other moments, refusal manifested in more subtle ways of responding to state and institutional authorities in order to cross borders, access social services, and evade institutional violence.

According to Audra Simpson,[2] ethnographic refusal operates both as a critique of colonial modes of knowledge production and as a political strategy for Indigenous people to refuse to be "known" in a static and ritualistic manner by the white settler colonial state. These refusals are not only a response against something but are also a shift towards somewhere. The practice of refusal is generative both politically and theoretically, fostering the creation of new socialities as well as highlighting the "limits and possibilities, especially but not only of the state and other institutions."[3] Refusal also serves as an analytical strategy for intentionally withholding knowledge, thus rejecting a research process that reproduces the "possessor" versus "possession" dynamic and disrupting colonial epistemologies by shifting emphasis from the colonized and the enslaved and towards decoding the logics of white settler colonialism.[4]

My scholar-activism over the past decade has compelled me to deeply reflect upon how queer and trans migrants with precarious status, in particular, enact daily refusals to state practices of control, surveillance, detention, and deportation. Precarious status consists of temporary migrant categories (visitor, temporary worker, international student, refugee claimant, sponsored family member, undocumented, etc.) that include "authorized and unauthorized forms of non-citizenship that are institutionally produced and share a precarity rooted in the conditionality of presence and access."[5] An analytical focus on precarious status highlights the ways in which migrant categories are not "natural,"[6] but are produced by key actors within colonial nation-state formations.[7]

This is especially the case for the term "refugee," classifying individuals who flee violence and persecution as distinct from the (often labelled economic) "migrant," who supposedly migrates for other reasons. This classification produces a "refugee/migrant" binary,[8] which obscures the complex historical, geopolitical, and economic conditions that result in people, particularly from the global South, migrating to Canada, and does not neatly coincide with state-produced categories of the "student," "temporary worker," "refugee," etc. This binary also erases one of the few ways to access the inland refugee claim process – crossing the border with a temporary resident visa (TRV) as a student, worker, visitor, etc.[9]

Over the past decade, as many queer and trans migrants with precarious status continue to struggle for their survival and be detained, deported, and become undocumented, Canada has positioned itself as a global leader in lesbian, gay, bisexual, trans, queer, and intersex (LGBTQI) rights generally and a "safe haven" for LGBTQI refugees specifically.[10] The daily struggles of so many queer and trans migrants are subsumed by a prevailing narrative that frames Canada as a site of LGBTQI freedom in comparison to homophobic/transphobic and backward "Other" cultures, mostly situated within the global South.[11] Queer and trans migrants with precarious status, and in particular those seeking to gain refugee status, are often compelled to perform a script in which "the viewer or reader witnesses the migrant other's desire to be given the 'gift' of Canadian citizenship ... reborn into the liberatory democratic nation-state where they will be a model citizen, thus reinscribing a colonial, homonormative nationalist script."[12]

This script and the hyper-focus on how Canada is a "safe haven" for LGBTQI refugees obscure the ways in which queer and trans people from the global South are regularly blocked from obtaining a TRV to get to Canada.[13] Indeed, the Canadian immigration/colonization regime seems only interested in queer and trans migrants the moment they enter the refugee process.[14] In 2014, a *Toronto Star* article revealed that "gay rights advocates" from Uganda were refused visitor visas to enter Canada to participate in WorldPride (the international LGBTQ human rights and cultural festival) because of lack of travel history and insufficient funds.[15] State agents denied the advocates entry because of their sexual and gender identity and the likelihood that they would file in-land refugee claims. Indeed, the TRV eligibility requirements have been "used as a racialized, gendered, and sexualized tool to exclude queer and trans people from the Global South, in ways that prioritize economic concerns over humanitarian ones."[16]

And yet, many queer and trans migrants have traversed and rejected the migrant categories imposed upon them by the white settler colonial Canadian state. These acts of refusal by queer and trans migrants with precarious status align with the practice of refusal as a strategy within and against empire and coloniality as articulated by scholars who engage with Black, Indigenous, and diasporic critiques.[17] On a global scale, coloniality maps out a complex matrix of power, which decodes modernist notions of progress, civilization, market democracy, and development as inextricable from colonial logics of imposed settlement, genocide, resource extraction, labour exploitation, and racist classification.[18] Modernity's prevailing form of global governance – the nation-state – was established by Western powers and built on African slavery, Indigenous genocide in the Americas, and Asian indentured labour.[19] Practices of refusal push back against this colonial social order and gesture to decolonial ways of being and knowing.

In this chapter, I explore the relevance of the politics of refusal for queer and trans migrants with precarious status who refuse to be "known" by the Canadian "immigration/colonization regime."[20] Here, I refer to the "immigration/colonization regime" to denote the complex set of historical and ongoing relations that organize laws governing nationality in concert with immigration policy and the Indian Act. Notably, between 1917 and 1936, Canada had established the Department of Immigration and Colonization.[21] Although policies regarding immigration and Indigenous affairs are now understood to be separate, this chapter considers how settlement and colonization continue to be indivisible.

Moreover, the conditions that pushed queer and trans people living in the global South to become migrants with precarious status in Canada are intimately shaped by a global coloniality that intersects with, but is not reducible to, settler colonialism. Recent scholarship explores how sexuality and gender intersect with race, class, ability, and religion to produce colonial violence on a transnational scale, with particular impacts on queer and trans people in the global South and queer and trans people of colour who live in Western nation-states.[22] These processes of colonization and racialization are simultaneously gendered, classed, able-ized, and sexualized, resulting in an uneven and hierarchical distribution of life chances and exposure to death.

In the spirit of refusal politics, this chapter engages in "a deliberate shift in the unit of analysis, away from people and toward the relationships between people and institutions of power."[23] I contend that the Canadian immigration/colonization regime socially organizes the everyday lives of queer and trans migrants with precarious status from the global South.[24] As a ruling regime, the immigration/colonization regime coordinates and organizes people and activities at political, administrative, and institutional levels.[25] This racialized and gendered regime regulates and controls queer and trans migrant life through its political apparatus (politicians, legislative framework, etc.), administrative systems (such as the Canadian Border Services Agency or CBSA), and institutional bodies (police, hospitals, immigration, prisons, etc.).

Although this chapter draws from my previous research, and in particular my doctoral study, I also extend and align my analysis and politics within what Sirma Bilge describes as coalition building "between critical knowledge projects – making Native studies converse with queer and trans studies [and] with the intersectional project called queer/trans of colour critique, [to] shed light on how settler colonialism, sexual normativities, capitalism, patriarchy and nationalism reciprocate to structure society."[26] This chapter thus aims to contribute to a queer/trans of colour critique by challenging prevailing "refugee" knowledge projects. These projects naturalize the separation of refugees, migrants, and Indigenous peoples, and presume that migrants are cis and hetero while queer and trans people are (white) citizens and that queer and trans "refugees" are in need of pity from benevolent and generous white settler colonial nation-states.

In order to do so, I extend my previous research, which aimed to map out the ways in which queer and trans migrant life was socially organized. Through a critical methodological approach, I combine textual analysis of a public state speech with analysis from participant interviews with queer and trans migrants from across the global South (including Central and North Africa, Southeast and Western Asia, Central America, Mexico, and the Caribbean). I ground my methodology in reflexive research not only to situate myself as a researcher but also to expose my entry into the social processes and practice that constitute knowledge production.[27] As such, I also draw from my own experiences as a scholar-activist who is part of QTBIPOC communities and has previously supported queer and trans migrants.

In this chapter, I textually analyse the Speech from the Throne presented in 2013 by then Governor General David Johnston and, in particular, Johnston's use of the term "Canadians First." This ideological account of Canada reinforces ongoing white settler colonial logics that erase what Lisa Lowe[28] calls global histories of social violence. These violent histories, I suggest, also undergird Canadian nation-building. The use of "Canadians First" serves to both evoke and erase cisnormative[29] and heteronormative[30] social processes that were integral to histories of colonial violence and indeed the continuation of Canadian nation-building today, histories that have now been largely forgotten. These erasures intimately shape what and how we know what we know about the Canadian immigration/colonization regime and how it organizes the everyday lives of queer and trans migrants with precarious status.

Moreover, I explore how white settler colonial logics are central to the production of Canadian colonial citizenship and migrant precarity. I trace the historical continuities of the nineteenth- and twentieth-century Canada First movement[31] into the 2013 Speech from the Throne that valorizes white Canadian heterosexual and monogamous marriage between a cis man and a cis woman as the central pillar of white, settler colonial nation-building. I detail how the task of ensuring the safety of the Canadian family is achieved through the surveillance of those who transgress sexual and gender norms, such as sex workers, as well as through the punishment and removal of racialized and criminalized bodies of migrants who are simultaneously de-sexualized and de-gendered.

I also examine the production of migrant illegality by the Canadian immigration/colonization regime through the everyday experiences of queer and trans migrants. As migrants with precarious status from the global South are ideologically coded as frauds, criminals, and national security risks, there are particular consequences for queer and trans migrants. The colonial production of migrant illegality also reveals particular consequences for queer and trans migrants who are detained and/or become undocumented. At the same time, queer and trans migrants also refuse to be "known" by the immigration/colonization regime as "bogus" or "illegal." The refusal to be "ineligible" for refugee status, seen through border crossings and shifting migrant status, gestures to often untraceable decisions and actions taken by queer and trans migrants with precarious status to engage in the politics of refusal and to push back against a colonial regime organized to ensure their removal. Finally, I explore how the politics of refusal may gesture towards decolonial solidarities between queer and trans migrants from the global South and Indigenous people.

"Canadians First" T-Discourse: White Citizens, Heterocisnormative Families, and Racialized Others

In October 2013, Governor General David Johnston presented his Speech from the Throne, titled "Seizing Canada's Moment: Prosperity and Opportunity in an Uncertain World."[32] The Speech is an example of the immigration/colonization regime that socially organizes the everyday lives of queer and trans migrants with precarious status. Exemplified in Johnston's Speech is a "Canadians First" t-discourse promoting an ideological account of the relationship between citizens, newcomers, Indigenous peoples, and migrants with precarious status.[33] At the centre of this discourse is the protection of the white cis and hetero family: "families raise our children and build our communities. As our families succeed, Canada succeeds."[34] The central purpose of domestic and foreign policy is to protect citizens and, especially, to strengthen the heterocisnormative[35] nuclear family at the centre of the Canadian nation-building project.[36]

This family is defined against "New Canadians" and migrants, who must "work hard to learn our languages, our values, and our traditions, and in turn, are welcomed as equal members of the Canadian family."[37] The Canadian character is labelled "compassionate," "honourable," "loyal," "courageous," "confident," and "good," versus uncivilized "regimes that threaten their neighbours, slaughter their citizens, and imperil freedom." The comparison between the civilized Canadian family and potentially barbaric "New Canadians," who are immigrants and refugees, reinvigorates what Sedef Arat-Koç describes as the "clash of civilizations,"[38] highlighting an external threat that the nation must guard against. New Canadians must leave the "barbarism" of their former languages, values, and traditions, in order to be accepted into the "Canadian family."

At the same time, the Canada First t-discourse structures the immigration/colonization regime and is also premised on settler colonial processes that "Canadianize" (assimilate) European settlers into white society and justify the elimination of the "Indian," or Indigenous peoples, and the exclusion and/or containment of Black and Asian people.[39] The "white life for two" discourse regulated a white heterocisnormative middle-class domesticity through the promotion of sexual, moral, and racial purity *and* criminalization of non-normative sexualities and genders.[40] This criminalization was part of the colonial management of sexual relations that sought to destroy Indigenous ways of life, including the spiritual and central place of LGBTQ Indigenous and Two-Spirit peoples.[41] With the "disappearance" of Indigenous peoples, the assimilated Canadian family were described as inheritors of Canada from its "founders" and as the pioneers of a liberal democratic nation, rather than the architects of a settler colonial "white man's country"[42] predicated upon conquest, genocide, slavery, and indentured labour.

Moreover, the Canadian immigration/colonization regime used a wide array of immigration control mechanisms, such as disenfranchisement, the passport system, deportation, and border security, all designed to shift the line between the legal and illegal status of "undesirable" populations. This production of migrant illegality was fundamentally shaped by heterocisnormative processes that "contribute to drawing the line between legal and illegal immigration, along with associated modes of differential incorporation and citizenship, in ways that continually re-construct heterosexualized, gendered, racialized, cultural and imperial hierarchies."[43]

Indeed, a series of immigration controls was produced to maintain the racial, moral, and sexual purity of Canada's white settler society.[44] For example, the Immigration Act of 1906 also featured exclusion categories, notably Section 29, which excluded prostitutes and those "convicted of a crime involving moral turpitude."[45] The criminalization of sexual and gender transgressions became another colonial tool to contain and control racialized migrants, in particular those from China and British India, as "the intensifying prosecution of sodomy, public indecency and vagrancy[46] in the early twentieth century gave way to a great legal coherence of social figures that required governance."[47]

Production of the Immigration/Colonization Regime and Racialized Migrant Precarity

Of particular note, the more recent focus on "Canadians First" reinvigorates the fear of migrants, precarious or otherwise, "stealing" jobs from "hard-working" citizens. Ideologically produced as commodified objects, migrants with precarious status exist solely for the economic benefit of prosperous Canadian families. This t-discourse obscures the reality that Canadian "prosperity" can only be maintained by filling labour shortages. Canadians need these labour shortages to be filled as much as or more than any person may want to migrate to Canada with precarious status. It also erases the reciprocal character of precarious status, which involves both migrants and citizens.

The "Canadians First" t-discourse overlaps with the Immigration and Refugee Protection Act (IRPA) to further the colonial production of migrant precarity and illegality. In this case, the ideological account of the white colonial citizen is affirmed by the heterocisnormative family, which requires protection from migrants who are identified by the immigration/colonization regime as frauds, criminals, and security risks. In the section of the Speech titled "Promoting Canadian Values," the ideological code of Canadian "prosperity" is deployed in relation to "genuine" refugees versus "fraudulent asylum claimants." This section associates prosperity with freedom, in contrast to the assertion that the state had "inherited a broken immigration system and has worked hard to fix it ... our government has ... increased protection for genuine refugees; reduced the number of fraudulent asylum claimants and deported more than 100,000 illegal immigrants."[48] According to the Speech, Canadian prosperity is achieved by the increased surveillance of migrants to determine if they are "genuine" or "bogus," resulting in the deportation of "illegal immigrants."

The production of migrant illegality also reinforces an ideologically based linkage between migrants' precarious status and national security. Both the immigration and refugee objectives in the IRPA contain passages which prioritize the health, safety, and security of Canadians/colonial citizens.[49] Protecting the health and security of Canadians is reinforced through promoting "international justice and security by denying access to Canadian territory to persons, including refugee claimants, who are security risks or serious criminals."[50] This textual framing of migrants with precarious status as security risks justifies their detention and deportation, a framing that becomes more pronounced for those who file inland refugee claims. Published on the Citizenship and Immigration Canada (CIC) website,[51] this text describes detention and removal as key tools within the refugee system.[52]

The protection of the mythical white heterocisnormative family is also accomplished through the punishment of criminals and the maintenance of anti-sex-work laws.[53] Notably, cis women citizens who are prostitutes are not only framed as victims yet criminals but also construed as threats to community safety; in other words, the safety of the respectable Canadian family. Migrants who are framed as prostitutes or criminals pose an even greater threat to families, whose communities and institutions must be protected from abuse and infiltration. Only the "genuine" migrant is worthy of protection, while a "criminal" migrant is a threat warranting deportation. The Canadian family is thus produced in relation to the "bogus" migrant as security risk. The "bogus" migrant becomes a racialized and genderless threat to the security of the white and properly assimilated heterocisnormative family.

The production of the "genuine" migrant can be traced back to the passing of the 1976 Immigration Act and, within it, the "refugee" category. The inclusion of the refugee category within the Act was promoted by government actors as emblematic of Canada's humanitarian character, even as national security and economic concerns were consistently prioritized over refugee obligations.[54] The search for the "genuine" refugee raised the spectre of the "bogus refugee," discussed by Johanna Reynolds and Jennifer Hyndman earlier in this volume, and "system abusers," and reinvigorated neoliberal fears of frauds and criminals.[55] By the 1990s, Canada-US border agreements optimized the flow of goods, services, and "low-risk" travellers and increased enforcement measures to track "illegals," terrorists,[56] and criminals.[57] Canada transitioned from being explicitly articulated as a white settler colony to a liberal democratic nation-state,[58] as the term "colonization" was erased from Canadian immigration law. And yet, the colonial production of migrant illegality continued to be racialized, as migrants are targeted in the search for the "bogus" refugee, "terrorist," or "illegal immigrant." This ideological social order renders migrants with precarious status as lacking family, history, and geography, and thereby unworthy of full personhood. Within this colonial order, queer and trans migrants become part of a de-gendered and de-sexualized mass of racialized bodies unworthy of acceptance into the Canadian settler colonial family.

Settler Colonial Heterocisnormative Technologies of Immigration Control

Just as the colonial production of migrant precarity reproduced the labelling of migrants with precarious status as "bogus refugees," "terrorists," or "illegal immigrants," the 1990s also saw the emergence of refugee claims based on sexual orientation and, subsequently, gender identity and expression.[59] Since the 1990s, community activists, including LGBTQ migrants with precarious status, and scholars have advocated improvements to the refugee determination system, resulting in the recent implementation of guidelines based on Sexual Orientation and Gender Identity and Expression (SOGIE) by the Immigration and Refugee Board (IRB).[60] These guidelines require refugee decision makers to take into account SOGIE when analysing a claim, for example by not using stereotypes about LGBTQ people. Certainly, there are LGBTQ people from the global South who have been able to access the Canadian refugee claim process and succeed in gaining refugee status (and eventually citizenship).

However, Canadian media representations of the "LGBTQ refugee"[61] have reproduced the dominant narrative that frames queer and trans migrations as simply motivated by the desire to escape repression and seek freedom and liberation.[62] This script affirms the division between the "genuine" and the "bogus" LGBTQI refugee, valorizing some queer and trans migrants while rejecting others.[63] Indeed, with the exception of those who file refugee claims at the Canada-US border, the entry into Canada of migrants with precarious status from the global South is organized by Temporary Resident Visa (TRV) regulations.[64] The TRV imposes a racialized, gendered, and heterocisnormative system that obstructs people from the global South, including LGBTQI people, from being able to access the refugee claim process. These visa application forms also reproduce the gender binary, making it systematically more difficult for trans and gender non-conforming migrants to apply for a visa. These contemporary ways in which heterocisnormativity is embedded into technologies of immigration control are rooted within the historical colonial production of migrant illegality.

The Production of Migrant Illegality and the Everyday Realities of Queer and Trans Migrants

The settler colonial production of migrant illegality continues to organize the everyday lives of queer and trans migrants. In this section, I draw from interviews I conducted with queer and trans migrants with precarious status.[65] Mobilizing the analytic and politics of refusal, instead of focusing on individual narratives, I draw attention to the interactions between each person and the Canadian immigration/colonization regime. In particular, I examine the ways in which various text-based processes via politicians and laws/policies (i.e., the Immigration and

Refugee Protection Act) shaped their interactions with immigration authorities (border agents, etc.).

Gabi, Shayma, Ariel, Antonio, and Sage migrated to Canada from Mexico as well as North and Central Africa. Each of these people navigated various forms of precarious status upon arrival, including shifting from student or refugee claimant to undocumented status or from visitor to refugee claimant, etc. I situate their experiences within the production of migrant illegality. A CIC website video titled *Immigrating to Canada* states:

> some estimate ... around 80,000 to 120,000 illegal immigrants [are] currently in Canada. They may have come as tourists or clandestinely and then never [leave] ... to ensure that our immigration system is fair to those who have immigrated to Canada the legal way or may want to in the future, the Government of Canada will take every step to send illegal migrants back to their country of origin once they have exhausted their legal appeals.

This excerpt textually frames the figure of the "illegal" migrant as a subject position. People not only engage in illegal activity but also are "illegal." The "illegal immigrant" is closely linked to the circulation of the terms "genuine" and "bogus" migrant. Migrants deemed "bogus" are implicitly construed as "fraudulent" and a "security risk," a point that Reynolds and Hyndman also emphasize through their discourse analysis of policy documents and media reports.

Gabi migrated to Canada just a few months prior to the visa imposition on Mexican visitors. This visa imposition was applied in response to Mexicans who sought refugee status upon arrival. Although Gabi received a positive refugee decision, had she attempted to migrate to Canada after the visa imposition, she most likely would not have been able to obtain the visa. The ideological code of "genuine" was used as a device to differentiate between the "genuine" Mexican visitor and the "bogus" refugee. These ideological codes highlight the complex linkage between public discourse and government policy. Gabi described her arrival in Canada, at the airport, as the worst moment of her immigration process. In an interview, she recalls:

> these officers, they really discriminate me because I apply for refugee claim, but as well, I heard some comments about, like, all the people were coming and so people being arrested ... the agents, they ask me ... what's the reason of your visit to Canada and I say "oh, I need refugee" and then they say, they made a comment ... it was really kind of disgusting, they

said like "(some)one else," oh "bullshit" ... I wait in this attending room ... I spent around 12 hours waiting. They took my fingerprints.

Upon her return to the airport a few days later to process her claim, Gabi spoke with three immigration agents, as the first two agents pressured her to drop her refugee claim. The second officer went as far as to state, as Gabi described, "I'm gay, I have gay friends in Mexico, and they live very well, why don't you go back?" Gabi replied, "Well, I don't know who your friends are, I have friends in Mexico as well and let me tell you that the realities are pretty difficult."

The textual production of the "bogus" Mexican refugee emboldened the immigration agents to behave in a racist manner. Powerful state actors, such as Immigration Minister Jason Kenney, labelled all refugee claimants from Mexico as "bogus," abusing not only the "generous" system but also the generosity of Canadian citizens. This blanket assertion by the minister of "bogus refugees" from Mexico obscured the Mexicans, including those who were LGBTQ, who did receive positive refugee decisions. Also rendered invisible were complex forms of state and political violence faced by queer and trans people in Mexico, which were highlighted by the murders of refugees, in particular trans women, who had been refused entry and deported.[66] The reductive figure of the "bogus" Mexican refugee also obscures the complexity of diverse forms of migration, including the fact that thousands of Mexican migrants actually entered Canada as temporary workers,[67] some of whom eventually filed refugee claims. This points to the links between different types of precarious status and the ways in which migrants often shift between them. The queer and trans migrants from the global South who participated in my earlier study, as well as many that I have supported and/or known, shifted from various types of precarious status, fighting to find a way to become permanent residents. Although many eventually applied for refugee status, others chose not to, even if they could have, because they found another pathway from precarious status to permanent residency.

Prior to their arrival to Canada, Shayma and Ariel lived undocumented in the US for an extended period of time. With the support of a community organization, Ariel reached the Canada-US border and immediately filed a refugee claim with Canadian border officers. A few years later, their application was rejected, and they eventually became undocumented after their subsequent legal recourses proved unsuccessful. As a child, Shayma migrated to the US with her family, but everyone lost their status after the international student status of one of her parents expired. Shayma eventually received approval for a Canadian study permit and crossed the Canada-US border. However, she lost her status in Canada when her own study permit expired.

After their refugee claim was denied, Ariel was eventually given a removal order. Shayma's study permit expired, so she was able to remain undetected by the CBSA. Although she was not given a removal order, had the CBSA discovered her undocumented status, she could have been arrested, detained, and deported. For both Ariel and Shayma, becoming undocumented resulted in severe consequences, and they shared similar feelings of isolation, sadness, despair, depression, and anxiety. As Shayma explained,

> I'm like illegal this whole time and I'm working under the table and it's really bad ... I told myself that I would never make the mistake my parents made ... I'd never be that dumb, and look at me, I'm doing the exact same thing now and I can't believe I wasted this chance ... Canada was like, my big second chance and it's just, I just completely wasted it and now I'm the same thing and it's always gonna be like this.

Ariel similarly stated,

> You feel like you are invisible. You don't feel like you are a human. You feel like a monster or something ... zero. You feel like you are zero, like you don't belong, like, to a society. You don't belong to anywhere, so this is weird feelings and everything is not right, it's not fair.

Antonio's testimony about his experiences with being detained and deported resonates with Ariel's and Shayma's reflections. In this testimony, which was included in an article published in a journal titled *Building a Solidarity City,* Antonio described his first night at the detention centre:

> I was deeply moved as I walked through, meeting the eyes of the detained migrants who were filled with hopelessness and despair. These are people who, like me, had left their country to find a better life. And there we were, together, breathing sadness, solitude and despair into our lungs ... I didn't sleep that first night, submerged as I was in an ocean of sadness and frustration ... The next day ... looking at the building across the street, I could see children playing in a small yard surrounded by barbed wire and security walls, guarded by security officers. At that moment, I could no longer hold back my tears, imagining these children in the same conditions as me ... I was overwhelmed with an indescribable sorrow. All of a

sudden, I felt a hand touch my shoulder. Turning, I saw that it was a man from my dormitory. He was from Indonesia. He said that it was the price that we, the undocumented, had to pay.[68]

These everyday experiences reveal the ways in which the "Canadians First" t-discourse propels the immigration/colonization regime and imposes material practices of surveillance, detention, deportation, and loss of status on queer and trans migrants with precarious status. It is this same regime that continues to racially profile and over-incarcerate Black and Indigenous people. The safety and prosperity of the white heterocisnormative Canadian family depends on the expulsion of the "bogus" refugee and "illegal" migrant, who are de-sexualized, rendered genderless, and deprived of personhood. The only exceptions are the very few "genuine" LGBTQI refugees who are deemed worthy of Canada's protection. The regime publicly highlights the sexuality and gender of LGBTQI refugees so as to laud Canada as a benevolent nation – as, that is, a state of humanitarian exceptionalism, which claims to accept gender and sexual diversity, all the while maintaining a heterocisnormative national family.

The Politics of Refusal as a Response to the Immigration/Colonization Regime

Although queer and trans migrant lives are profoundly shaped by the immigration/colonization regime, they are not defined by it. Over and over again, the participants in my study refused the regime's attempts to stop them from entering Canada as well as to push them out. Indeed, Sage, Shayma, and Antonio actively refused the choices that the regime offered. Sage describes how they procured a fake passport to be able to get to the US:

> An individual sold me his passport because he had travelled to the US and he had a multiple entry visa ... I remember that he forced me to pay 500 dollars (US) ... I tried multiple times to take the plane ... they would trap me. I was almost taken to jail, but fortunately, there were people who helped me to find a [specific African country] passport, through government connections.[69]

Though repeatedly turned away at the airport, Sage was finally successful on the fourth attempt. Upon arrival in the US, Sage took a bus to the Canadian border and filed a refugee claim. Sage was allowed entry into Canada as a refugee claimant owing to family provisions (having a sister in Canada) under the auspices of the Canada-US Safe Third Country Agreement.

Because they lived in the US as undocumented persons, Shayma and her family worried about her entry into Canada as an international student. Shayma described her experience at the border:

> there's not a single stamp in it, like there's nothing in this passport, it hasn't been used at all ... so I guess she's a little suspicious and she's like, "where's your documentation from the US? Like you don't have anything, I see a French passport, but there's nothing" ... I just told her, "oh I thought all I needed was my passport, and this letter of approval, I didn't even realize I needed other things" and she literally said, I'll never forget this, she says "well, for all I know you're illegal" ... I feigned shock. I was like "oh well, I can assure that that's certainly not the case, I'm so sorry that I didn't bring these things, I mean I'll definitely have them mailed to me asap" and she was like, "yeah well you better because you can't be traveling back and forth across the border like this, without documentation" ... there was a moment where she kind of takes a moment to pause and think and then I see her sort of shrug and she prints the visa (laughs).[70]

It wasn't just the documents (study permit, passport) that validated Shayma's legal status. It was also the specific manner in which she engaged in dialogue with the border officer. Shayma played up her naïveté in order to convince the officer of her legal status, actively shaping how the officer was evaluating her documents. After becoming undocumented in Canada, Shayma eventually regained her student status and gained permanent residency. This experience reveals the pliability of precarious status and how "being illegal" is not necessarily a permanent condition.

Although Antonio's testimony was published after he was deported, this testimony also noted his public campaign to stay in Canada, which drew on the support of community and migrant justice groups. As someone who supported Antonio and participated in this campaign, I recall the state of crisis that we endured, especially Antonio, throughout the process. Those involved in the campaign ensured that Antonio had decision-making power over the direction of his campaign and thus control over his life, at a time when the state was violently limiting his life chances. Over time, I witnessed Antonio go from being in constant hiding to making daily decisions to survive, resist, and refuse the regime's authority over his life. As queer and trans migrants took leadership positions within the campaign, it became a crucial vehicle for organizing multiple interlinked queer, trans, and migrant communities in Montreal.

Antonio's, Gabi's, Shayma's, and Sage's everyday encounters with the immigration/colonization regime reveal how they refused the choices offered to them and refused to be known as "bogus" and "illegal." Their refusal to be "ineligible" at the airport or at the border reveals the powerful ways in which queer and trans migrants with precarious status engage in the politics of refusal. As a central feature of the immigration/colonization regime, the border is a key site of forgotten histories of social violence, naturalizing the Canadian nation-state and erasing Indigenous mapping of land on Turtle Island.[71] The colonial border remains a site of surveillance of racialized bodies, as the threat of Indigenous sovereignty folds "into the seemingly newer threat to settler sovereignty and security – the illegal alien, the always possible terrorist – rendering perhaps all bodies with color as border transgressors with the presumed intent to harm."[72] Although measures to restrict migration across borders are increasing, most notably through biometrics,[73] Shayma's, Ariel's, and Sage's migrations across borders contravened the colonial regime's desire to block "bogus" and "illegal" migrants from entry.

These acts of refusal were performed pre- and post-arrival and served as more than a survival strategy. They also signified a refusal of the immigration/colonization regime's textual framing of migrants with precarious status as undeserving of legal personhood. These refusals do not simply "constitute a revamping of resistance to accommodate critique," according to Carole McGranahan. Just as importantly, for McGranahan, "refusal as revenge, then, rejects external state and institutional structures."[74] These everyday refusals serve as a direct and collective response against colonial regimes organized to exclude and exploit migrants with precarious status, including those who are queer and trans.

Conclusion

The "Canadians First" t-discourse illuminates a historical continuity through its reproduction of white settler colonial logics, notably the tension between the desire for racial purity within a white (dominant) settler society and the need for a racialized and exploitable labour force. By foregrounding histories of colonial violence, often overlooked by official metanarratives, the mythology of innocent settlement is disrupted and immigration and colonization are reconstituted as intertwined. These histories also interrogate the contemporary valorization of the mythical white heterocisnormative nuclear Canadian family as "natural." Although the principle of white supremacy has been replaced by multiculturalism, the "Canadians First" t-discourse continues to reinforce racialized, gendered, and heterocisnormative hierarchies.

More recently, Adam Gaudry and Darryl Leroux have documented some newly formed québécois "Métis" groups who declare themselves to be "Québec's First Peoples," "representing the only truly authentic Indigenous people in Quebec."[75] The use of "First" thus remains a politically charged and potent tool to justify ongoing colonial practices of erasure, dispossession, and elimination. Certainly, there continues to be debate about whether or not Indigenous ways of conceptualizing nationhood inherently reproduce nationalism, the colonial state, and its borders.[76] Within this context, the use of the term "First Nations" becomes a tool to resist the ongoing white settler colonial project, rather than the sole way to conceptualize Indigenous sovereignty. "First" can thus be mobilized to erase Indigenous peoples or to resist ongoing colonial practices.

Over and over again, queer and trans migrants with precarious status from my study refused the authority of the immigration/colonization regime and its practices of exclusion, surveillance, and deportation. Instead, they found ways to get visas, cross borders, remain in Canada, and build informal support networks. These acts of refusal are related not only to white settler colonial logics but also to their own intergenerational histories of colonialism. All of the participants in my study referred to their parents and/or grandparents, most of whom lived in Asia or Africa during a time of anti-colonial struggle that forced British and French colonial rulers to withdraw, but that left in their wake nation-states formed to serve the political interests of the former colonizers.

Tracing the ways in which heterocisnormative processes inform coloniality on a global scale helps to situate the historical, social, economic, and political conditions of queer and trans migrations. This type of macro-analysis attends to the matrix of power that shapes post/neocolonial nation-states in the global South that drive out queer and trans people as well as the white settler nation-state that queer and trans migrants enter into upon arrival to Canada. An analytical focus at the scale of empire makes legible what Jodi Byrd describes as the "cacophonies of colonialism"[77] – interlacing colonial and imperial logics across geographies. Its analytical strength is also its major challenge. How can we engage with an analytical framework that attends to multiple colonial logics without erasing local, regional, and national specificities?

At the same time, queer and trans migrations are intrinsically shaped by the immigration/colonization regime. If the immigration regime is constitutive of the continued colonization of Turtle Island, how are queer and trans migrations either complicit in or actively contributing to the ongoing processes and practices of dispossession and elimination of Indigenous peoples? Highlighting some LGBTQI refugees as "good migrants" who are ideal candidates and deserving of Canadian citizenship and extolling the virtues of the refugee system as generous to LGBTQI refugees serves to obscure how the same white settler state contributes to underfund First Nations or fails to take accountability for missing and murdered Indigenous women. These strategies that reinforce the generosity of the citizen and, by extension, the state (or vice versa) also continue to erase the historical legacies of colonial violence that particularly impact Black, Indigenous, and other People of Color (BIPOC).

As implicated within the immigration/colonization regime, queer and trans migrants from the global South who enter Canada with precarious status must navigate this terrain (that was not of their making), often while fighting for their survival and existence. This is especially the case for Black queer and trans migrants from the global South. Anti-Black logics also informed the ways in which the participants in my study navigated their migration process and their everyday life. Central to coloniality is how modernity has defined the "civilized" human subject as white people/whiteness in relation to the non-human Black people/blackness.[78] Anti-black logics classify people on a hierarchical scale of humanness, since, as Rinaldo Walcott suggests, "the Black body is not the most abject body in a competition of abjection and oppression, but the Black body is a template of how the abjection by which the Human was produced."[79]

Indeed, multiple colonial logics overlap and operate simultaneously with the same or similar circulation of discourses, practices, and ideologies. Here, we can see the conjunctions between these logics. Linking these logics provides space to put "into conversation seemingly unrelated or dispersed phenomena ... in ways that shift radically our understanding of what is constitutive of the complex architecture of power, supremacy, and oppression."[80] However, an analysis on the scale of global colonialities risks flattening socio-historical and political differences particular to specific geographies. Thus, it is important to pay attention to the material realities of QTBIPOC and in particular those with precarious status, within specific geographic and political contexts. This is especially relevant in order to build knowledge about the ways in which queer and trans migrants engage in the politics of refusal.

Can making visible how queer and trans migrants with precarious status engage in everyday acts of refusal in response to colonial regimes gesture towards the building of decolonial politics? As Paola Bacchetta suggests, a queer decolonial politics deploys "strategies and tactics for resisting not just one or another relation of power at a time, but rather the ensemble of co-constitutive relations of power in question, inseparably ... it is to draw near to opening a space, and holding space, for the creative construction for other ways of life."[81] The intentional creation of a queer and trans decolonial politics can also reimagine vibrant and sustainable futures. In some ways, migrant justice campaigns by and for queer and trans migrants, such as individual anti-deportation campaigns and the recent campaign in Quebec called "Justice for Trans Migrants," evoke these political possibilities.

However, to what degree might campaigns build solidarities between migrants and Indigenous peoples? Recent anti-deportation campaigns have included the explicit participation of Indigenous peoples. Recently, Black Lives Matter Toronto activists travelled to the Standing Rock Indian Reservation to protest in solidarity with Indigenous tribes who protested the Dakota Access Pipeline (DAPL). A decolonial queer and trans politics thus cannot be limited to a nation-state's recognition and protection of sexual and gender identities.

Another strategy for a queer and trans decolonial politics may be entering into the heart of empire in order to reframe sites of exploitation as sites of possible coalitions and solidarities. The sites that bring migrants and Indigenous peoples together today (worksites, prisons, urban centres) may serve as the starting point for nurturing a decolonial politics. It is in the very sites through which the immigration/colonization regime aims to consolidate its power that queer and trans migrants from the global South and other BIPOC people may come together to foster a collective politics of refusal. Indeed, my research and activism suggest that these solidarities are already occurring, even if mostly unacknowledged. In some unexpected spaces and places, queer and trans migrants with precarious status bring forward their own critical analysis and strategies that "hint at political potentials, gesture to alternative narratives and enable an openness to multiple futures."[82]

NOTES

1 My use of the terms "queer" and "trans" recognizes their multiple usages as identity categories, theorizing (examining heteronormativity and cisnormativity) and espousing an anti-normative politics. I engage with these terms on multiple registers (i.e., identity, theory, politics). See

Lee, "Resituating 'Sexual and Gender Diversity' Within the Frame of Anti-racism and Anti-colonialism."
2 Simpson, *Mohawk Interruptus*.
3 McGranahan, "Theorizing Refusal," 319.
4 Tuck and Yang, "Unbecoming Claims."
5 Goldring and Landolt, eds., *Producing and Negotiating Non-Citizenship*, 3.
6 Ibid.
7 Fortier, "No One Is Illegal," 274; Lee, "The Social Organisation of Queer."
8 Macklin, "Disappearing Refugee."
9 Lee, "Responses to Structural Violence."
10 Lee, "Tracing the Coloniality of Queer and Trans Migrations."
11 Gosine, "Fobs, Banana Boy and the Gay Pretenders," 223; Driver, *Queer Youth Cultures*; Lee and Brotman, "Identity, Refugeeness, Belonging"; Murray, *Real Queer?*.
12 Murray, "Real Queer," 465.
13 Lee, "Tracing the Coloniality of Queer and Trans Migrations."
14 Lee, *The Social Organisation of Queer*; Lee, "Responses to Structural Violence."
15 Keung, "Ugandan Gay Activists Denied Visas to World Pride Conference."
16 Lee, "Responses to Structural Violence," 83.
17 Halberstam, "The Wild Beyond," 2; Harney and Moten, "The Undercommons," 1; McGranahan, "Theorizing Refusal"; Simpson, *Mohawk Interruptus*; Simpson, "On Ethnographic Refusal."
18 Quijano, "Coloniality of Power and Eurocentrism in Latin America"; Mignolo, *Local Histories/Global Designs*; Wynter, "Unsettling the Coloniality of Being/Power/Truth/Freedom."
19 Lowe, *The Intimacies of Four Continents*; Mignolo, *Local Histories/Global Designs*; Wynter, "Unsettling the Coloniality of Being/Power/Truth/Freedom."
20 Lee, "Tracing the Coloniality of Queer and Trans Migrations," 61.
21 Library and Archives Canada, *The Canadian State*.
22 Bakshi, Jivraj, and Posocco, *Decolonizing Sexualities*; Dutta and Roy, "Decolonizing Transgender in India"; Ekine and Abbas, *Queer African Reader*.
23 Tuck and Yang, "Unbecoming Claims," 851.
24 Lee, *The Social Organisation of Queer*.
25 Ng, "Exploring the Globalized Regime of Ruling from the Standpoint of Immigrant Workers."
26 Bilge, "Theoretical Coalitions and Multi-Issue Activism," 113.
27 Smith, *The Conceptual Practices of Power*; Smith, *Institutional Ethnography*.
28 Lowe, "The Intimacies of Four Continents."
29 Cisnormativity unpacks the ways in which social institutions and practices reproduce the gender binary as a societal norm, along with the erasure of

trans people. See Serano, *Whipping Girl*; Bauer et al., "'I Don't Think This Is Theoretical; This Is Our Lives.'"
30 "Heteronormativity" means the dominant norms, institutions, and practices that reproduce heterosexuality and monogamous marriage between a cis man and cis woman as natural and necessary. See Cohen, "Punks, Bulldaggers and Welfare Queens."
31 Mackey, *The House of Difference*.
32 Johnston, "Seizing Canada's Moment." This Speech was presented during the seventh year of Prime Minister Stephen Harper's nine years of minority and majority rule. Initially presented in Parliament, it was subsequently made publicly accessible through a Canadian government website and various mainstream media outlets.
33 An extension of Foucault's concept of discourse, "t-discourses" consider how texts mediate "practices and courses of actions ordered by them, and how they coordinate the activities of one with those of another or others" (D. Smith, *Writing the Social*, 158, citing Foucault, *The Archaeology of Knowledge*).
34 Johnston, "Seizing Canada's Moment," 13.
35 When heteronormative and cisnormative processes are interconnected.
36 To view scholarship that examines the role of the nuclear family within nation-building projects, please see Carty, "The Discourse of Empire and the Social Construction of Gender"; Carter, "The Importance of Being Monogamous"; Dua, "Beyond Diversity."
37 Johnston, "Seizing Canada's Moment," 19.
38 Arat-Koç, "The Disciplinary Boundaries of Canadian Identity after September 11," 34.
39 Devereux, *Growing a Race*; Thobani, *Exalted Subjects*; Valverde, *The Age of Light, Soap, and Water*.
40 Carter, "The Importance of Being Monogamous."
41 Prior to colonization, LGBTQ and Two-Spirit people occupied valued social positions within "the shared culture of a Native nation, which through kinship, economics, social life, or religion linked all Native people in relationship" (Morgensen, *Spaces between Us*, 135). See Cruz, "Medicine Bundle of Contradictions"; Metallic, "Finding Two-Spirit Identity"; and Meyer-Cook, "Two-Spirit People." The criminalization of non-normative sexualities and genders of Indigenous peoples was part of the gendered and sexualized violence enacted through laws and policies such as the Indian Act and the residential school system. See Anderson, *A Recognition of Being*, for more about how residential schools reshaped sexuality and gender; Metallic, "Finding Two-Spirit Identity"; Meyer-Cook and Labelle, "Namaji"; Meyer-Cook, "Two-Spirit People"; A. Smith, *Conquest*).

42 Dua, "Exclusion through Inclusion"; Price, *Orienting Canada*; Protocol Relating to the Status of Refugees, General Assembly.
43 Luibhéid, "Sexuality, Migration, and the Shifting Line between Legal and Illegal Status," 309. The state's response was informed by an earlier era, when white citizens sought to restrict Asian and Black migration. South Asian migrants came from land colonized by the British, and Black people were forcibly removed from their lands by the transatlantic slave trade that operated in concert with African colonization (Dua, "Exclusion through Inclusion"; Mackey, *The House of Difference*; Monture-Agnes, *Thunder in My Soul*).
44 Having first migrated to BC and California in the mid-nineteenth century to mine the gold fields, Chinese migrant men were then hired to build the railroads to reduce labour costs (Ngai, *Impossible Subjects*). During this time, the cross-gender practices of European settlers affirmed a type of white settler masculinity that coincided with "anti-immigrant politics, specifically the racializing, feminizing discourses that targeted Chinese residents for exclusion from the nation" (Sears, "All That Glitters," 384.)
45 Library and Archives Canada (LAC), Statutes of Canada. An Act Respecting Immigration and Immigrants, 1906. "Moral turpitude" included transgressive gender expression and sexual immorality, including "sodomy" (Canaday, *The Straight State*; Shah, *Stranger Intimacy*).
46 Vagrancy laws identified vagrants as those prone to "immorality," such as prostitution, gambling, intoxication, sodomy, and cross-dressing (Shah, *Stranger Intimacy*, 64).
47 Ibid., 151. One group targeted by these laws were South Asian migrant men, who were disproportionately incarcerated and put on trial for the crime of sodomy (Ingram, "Returning to the Scene of the Crime"). The prosecution of "sodomy," public indecency, and vagrancy operated in concert with the deportation regime, serving to deport South Asian men to a colonized India, and "affirmed Canada's sovereign right to regulate the mobility of British subjects within its borders ... and the exclusive allegiance of the nation to white settlers" (Shah, *Stranger Intimacy*, 219).
48 Johnston, "Seizing Canada's Moment," 20.
49 Immigration and Refugee Protection Act (IRPA), 2014.
50 Ibid., 4.
51 Detention, Removals and the New Assisted Voluntary Returns Program (CIC – DRAVRP), Backgrounder.
52 As the auditor general of Canada states, "detaining and removing those who would enter Canada illegally or who pose a threat to Canadians, the Canada Border Services Agency (CBSA) contributes to the safety and security of Canadians. In its detention and removal of those who are inadmissible, it also plays a key role in maintaining the integrity of Canada's

immigration and refugee programs and ensuring fairness for those who come to this country lawfully" (ibid.).
53 Johnston, "Seizing Canada's Moment," 12.
54 Aiken, "Of Gods and Monsters." Prior to the 1976 Immigration Act, Canada facilitated the entry of hundreds of thousands of Europeans while also limiting the entry of refugees classified as "non-preferred races," such as Jewish people (Iacovetta, *Gatekeepers*). From 1976 to 1986, Canada resettled over 150,000 refugees, mostly from Asia, and received the Nansen medal from the United Nations High Commissioner for Refugees (UNHCR) (Aiken, "Of Gods and Monsters"). The uneven manner in which refugees were included or excluded in Canada "demonstrated the extent to which ideologically defined security considerations together with a preference for White Europeans and for linking labor market needs to all admissions, were the primary drivers of domestic refugee policies" (ibid., 14). Although the inland refugee claim process was created in the 1980s, those who accessed it were framed as "self-selected" and "contrary to the constituent features of a genuine refugee: someone forced to leave a country through no personal fault in order to avoid state-sanctioned persecution – not voluntary, no choice" (Pratt, *Securing Borders*, 92). Soon after its implementation, a series of measures was implemented (visitor/transit visas, increased detention, search/seizure, carrier sanctions, etc.) to block migrants from filing refugee claims (Aiken, "Of Gods and Monsters"; Pratt, *Securing Borders*).
55 Arat-Koç, "Neoliberalism."
56 With the passage of Bill C-86 in 1992, "terrorism" became a central category of inadmissibility to "ensure that Canada does not become a safe haven for retired or active terrorists" (Aiken, 2001, 19). The events of 9/11 launched the "War on Terror" (Razack et al., *States of Race*) and fuelled an explicit framing of refugees as terrorists, resulting in additional security measures. Two months after 9/11, Canada passed the Immigration and Refugee Protection Act (IPRA), which included provisions to give ministers more discretionary power and limit appeal and review procedures (Dauvergne, *Making People Illegal*).
57 Pratt, *Securing Borders*.
58 Thobani, *Exalted Subjects*.
59 La Violette, "The Immutable Refugees."
60 Lee et al. "Knowledge and Policy about LGBTQI Migrants."
61 Jenicek, Lee, and Wong, "Dangerous Shortcuts."
62 Cantu, *The Sexuality of Migration*, xxv.
63 Murray, *Real Queer*.
64 In 2014, the CIC website described the TRV as "an official document issued by a Canadian visa office that is placed in your passport to show that

you have met the requirements for admission to Canada as temporary resident (either as a visitor, a student, or a worker)" (CIC – AVV, para 7, 2014). The TRV requirement is imposed on 147 countries, the vast majority of which are in Africa, Asia, and Central/South America (CIC – CTVR, 2014). In contrast, as of June 2014 there were 59 countries identified as visa-exempt, at least 11 of which are British overseas territories, including the UK (and British citizens who live anywhere), along with specific regions with close ties to the UK (e.g., Hong Kong) (CIC – CTVR, 2014). Out of the 48 remaining countries, the vast majority are in Europe, along with a small number in Asia (Brunei, Japan, Singapore, South Korea, Taiwan, and those with Israeli passports), the US, Australia, and New Zealand.

65 Lee, "The Social Organisation of Queer."
66 Ibid.; Burke, *Double Punishment*.
67 Visa Requirement for Mexico (CIC – VRM). Backgrounder (2014)
68 Lee, "The Social Organisation of Queer"; the citation is from Sanchez, "Testimony of a Deportee," paragraph 5.
69 Lee, "The Social Organisation of Queer," 172.
70 Ibid., 173.
71 This includes the Jay Treaty of 1794, in which the Mohawk, Oneida, Onondaga, Cayuga, Seneca, and Tuscarora Nations had "the right to traverse the boundaries of the US-British divide freely and without levy" (Simpson, *Mohawk Interruptus*, 133). The treaty, however, implicitly suggests that Canada and the US have the power to control who can cross the border (ibid.).
72 Simpson, *Mohawk Interruptus*, 123.
73 Chan and Chunn, *Racialization, Crime and Criminal Justice in Canada*. Since the fingerprinting of refugee claimants began in 1992 (Arat-Koç, "Neoliberalism"), the use of biometrics has expanded to include biometrically enhanced passports, permanent resident cards, and international fingerprint databases. Indeed, border enforcement serves as a key mechanism to facilitate the entry of migrants while blocking anyone who may be deemed an external threat.
74 McGranahan, "Theorizing Refusal," 322.
75 Gaudry and Leroux, "White Settler Revisionism and Making Metis Everywhere," 132.
76 Fortier, "No One Is Illegal"; Lawrence and Dua, "Decolonizing Antiracism"; Sharma and Wright, "Decolonizing Resistance."
77 Byrd, *The Transit of Empire*, 14.
78 Mugabo, "On Rocks and Hard Places"; Sexton, "The Vel of Slavery"; Walcott, "The Problem of the Human."
79 Walcott, "The Problem of the Human," 100.
80 Bilge, "Theoretical Coalitions and Multi-Issue Activism," 113.

81 Bacchetta, "QTPOC Critiques of 'Post-Raciality,' Segregationality, Coloniality and Capitalism in France," 278.
82 Manalansan, "The 'Stuff' of Archives," 106.

REFERENCES

Aiken, S.J. "Of Gods and Monsters: National Security and Canadian Refugee Policy." *Revue québécoise de droit international* 14 (2001): 7–36. http://www.sqdi.org/fr/revue-collection-v14n2-1.html.

Anderson, Kim. *A Recognition of Being: Reconstructing Native Womanhood.* Toronto: Sumach Press, 2000.

Arat-Koç, Sedef. "The Disciplinary Boundaries of Canadian Identity after September 11: Civilizational Identity, Multiculturalism, and the Challenge of Anti-imperialist Feminism." *Social Justice* 32, no. 4 (2005): 32–49.

– "Neoliberalism, State Restructuring and Immigration: Changes in Canadian Policies in the 1990s." *Journal of Canadian Studies* 34, no. 2 (1999): 31–56.

Bacchetta, Paola. "QTPOC Critiques of 'Post-Raciality,' Segregationality, Coloniality and Capitalism in France." In *Decolonizing Sexualities: Transnational Perspectives, Critical Interventions*. Edited by Sandeep Bakshi, Suhraiya Jivraj, and Silvia Posocco, 264–81. Oxford: Counterpress, 2016.

Bakshi, Sandeep, Suhraiya Jivraj, and Silvia Posocco, eds. *Decolonizing Sexualities: Transnational Perspectives, Critical Interventions*. Oxford: Counterpress, 2016.

Bauer, Greta R., Rebecca Hammond, Robb Travers, Mathias Kaay, Karin M. Hohendel, and Michelle Boyce. "'I Don't Think This Is Theoretical; This Is Our Lives': How Erasure Impacts Health Care for Transgender People." *Journal of the Association of Nurses in AIDS Care* 20, no. 5 (2009): 348–61.

Bilge, Sirma. "Theoretical Coalitions and Multi-Issue Activism." In *Decolonizing Sexualities: Transnational Perspectives, Critical Interventions*, 108–22. Edited by Sandeep Bakshi, Suhraiya Jivraj and Silvia Posocco. Oxford: Counterpress, 2016.

Burke, Nora Butler. *Double Punishment: Immigration Penalty in the Daily Lives of Migrant Trans Women*. Montreal: Concordia University, 2016.

Byrd, Jodi. *The Transit of Empire: Indigenous Critiques of Colonialism*. Minneapolis: University of Minnesota Press, 2011.

Canaday, M. *The Straight State: Sexuality and Citizenship in Twentieth-Century America*. Princeton and Oxford: Princeton University Press, 2009.

Cantu, Lionel. *The Sexuality of Migration: Border Crossings and Mexican Immigrant Men*. New York: New York University Press, 2009.

Carter, Sarah. *The Importance of Being Monogamous: Marriage and Nation Building in Western Canada to 1915*. Edmonton: University of Alberta Press, 2008.

Carty, Lisa. "The Discourse of Empire and the Social Construction of Gender." In *Scratching the Surface: Canadian Anti-Racist Feminist Thought*. Edited by Enakshi Dua and Angela Robertson, 35–48. Toronto: Women's Press, 1999.

Chan, Wendy, and Dorothy Chunn. *Racialization, Crime and Criminal Justice in Canada*. Toronto: University of Toronto Press, 2014.

Cohen, Cathy. "Punks, Bulldaggers and Welfare Queens: The Radical Potential of Queer Politics?" *Feminist Theory* 4, no. 3 (1997): 359–64.

Cruz, L.E. "Medicine Bundle of Contradictions: Female-Man, Mi'kmaq/Acadian/Irish Diasporas, Invisible DisAbilities, Masculine-Feminist." In *Feminism FOR REAL: Deconstructing the Academic Industrial Complex of Feminism*. Edited by J. Yee. Ottawa: Canadian Centre for Policy Alternatives, 2010.

Dauvergne, C. *Making People Illegal: What Globalization Means for Migration and the Law*. Cambridge: Cambridge University Press, 2008.

Detention, Removals and the New Assisted Voluntary Returns Program (CIC – DRAVRP), Backgrounder. Department of Citizenship and Immigration Canada, 2014. http://www.cic.gc.ca/english/department/media/backgrounders/2010/2010-03-30c.asp. Accessed May 2015.

Devereux, Cecily. *Growing a Race: Nellie L. McClung and the Fiction of Eugenic Feminism*. Montreal and Kingston: McGill-Queen's University Press, 2006.

Driver, Susan. *Queer Youth Cultures*. Albany: SUNY Press, 2008.

Dua, Enakshi. "Beyond Diversity: Exploring the Ways in Which the Discourse of Race Has Shaped the Institution of the Nuclear Family." In *Scratching the Surface: Canadian Anti-Racist Feminist Thought*. Edited by Enakshi Dua and Angela Robertson, 237–59. Toronto: Women's Press, 1999.

– "Exclusion through Inclusion: Female Asian Migration in the Making of Canada as a White Settler Nation." *Gender, Place and Culture* 14, no. 4 (2007): 445–66. https://doi.org/10.1080/09663690701439751.

Dutta, Aniruddha, and Raina Roy. "Decolonizing Transgender in India: Some Reflections." *Transgender Studies Quarterly* 1, no. 3 (2014): 320–37.

Ekine, Sokari, and H. Abbas. *Queer African Reader*. Dakar: Pambazuka Press, 2013.

Fortier, Craig. "No One Is Illegal: Movements and Anti-Colonial Struggles from within the Nation-State." In *Producing and Negotiating Non-Citizenship: Precarious Legal Status in Canada*. Edited by Luin Goldring and Patricia Landolt, 274–90. Toronto: University of Toronto Press, 2013.

Foucault, Michel. *The Archaeology of Knowledge*. New York: Pantheon Books, 1972.

Gaudry, Adam, and Darryl Leroux. "White Settler Revisionism and Making Metis Everywhere: The Evocation of Metissage in Quebec and Nova Scotia." *Critical Ethnic Studies* 3, no. 1 (2017): 116–42.

Goldring, Luin, and Patricia Landolt, eds. *Producing and Negotiating Non-Citizenship: Precarious Legal Status in Canada*. Toronto: University of Toronto Press, 2013.

Gosine, Andil. "Fobs, Banana Boy and the Gay Pretenders." In *Queer Youth Cultures*. Edited by Susan Driver. Albany: SUNY Press, 2008.

Halberstam, Jack. "The Wild Beyond: With and for the Undercommons." In *The Undercommons: Fugitive Planning and Black Study*. Edited by Stefano Harney and Fred Moten, 2–14. Brooklyn: Autonomedia, 2013.

Harney, Stefano, and Fred Moten, eds. *The Undercommons: Fugitive Planning and Black Study*. Brooklyn: Autonomedia, 2013.

Iacovetta, F. *Gatekeepers: Reshaping Immigrant Lives in Cold War Canada*. Toronto: Between the Lines, 2006.

Immigrating to Canada (CIC – IC), Video Centre, 2014. http://www.cic.gc.ca/english/department/media/multimedia/video/immcan/immcan.asp.

Ingram, Gordon. "Returning to the Scene of the Crime: Uses of Trial Dossiers on Consensual Male Homosexuality for Urban Research, with Examples from Twentieth-Century British Columbia." *GLQ: A Journal of Lesbian and Gay Studies* 10, no. 1 (2003): 77–110. https://doi.org/10.1215/10642684-10-1-77.

Jenicek, Ainsley, Edward Lee, and Alan Wong. "Dangerous Shortcuts: Media Representations of Sexual Minority Refugees in the Post 9/11 Canadian Press." *Canadian Journal of Communications* 34, no. 4 (2009): 635–58.

Johnston, David. "Seizing Canada's Moment: Prosperity and Opportunity in an Uncertain World." Speech from the Throne: Full Speech. http://speech.gc.ca/eng/full-speech, 2013. Accessed May 2015.

Keung, Nicolas. "Ugandan Gay Activists Denied Visas to World Pride Conference." *thestar.com*, 2014. http://www.thestar.com/news/gta/2014/05/22/ugandan_gay_activists_denied_visas_to_world_pride_conference.html.

La Violette, Nicole. "The Immutable Refugees: Sexual Orientation in Canada (A.G.) v. Ward." *University of Toronto Faculty of Law Review* 55, no. 1 (1997): 1–41.

Lawrence, Bonita, and Enakshi Dua. "Decolonizing Antiracism." *Journal of Social Justice* 32, no. 4 (2005): 120–43.

Lee, Edward Ou Jin. "Resituating 'Sexual and Gender Diversity' within the Frame of Anti-Racism and Anti-Colonialism." In *Canada without Racism: Envisioning the End of Racism*. Edited by Liza Lorenzetti, David Este, and Christa Sato, 201–30. Winnipeg: Fernwood Publishing, 2018.

– "Responses to Structural Violence: The Everyday Ways in Which Queer and Trans Migrants with Precarious Status Respond to and Resist the Canadian Immigration Regime." *International Journal of Child, Youth and Family Studies* 10, no. 1 (2019): 70–94.

– "The Social Organisation of Queer/Trans Migrations: The Everyday Experiences of Queer and Trans Migrants with Precarious Status." PhD diss., McGill University Libraries, 2015.

- "Tracing the Coloniality of Queer and Trans Migrations: Resituating Heterocisnormative Violence in the Global South and Encounters with Migrant Visa Ineligibility to Canada." *Refuge: Canada's Journal on Refugees* 34, no. 1 (2018): 60–74.
Lee, Edward Ou Jin, and Shari Brotman. "Identity, Refugeeness, Belonging: Experiences of Sexual Minority Refugees in Canada." *Canadian Review of Sociology* 48, no. 3 (2011): 241–74.
Lee, Edward Ou Jin, O. Kamgain, T. Hafford-Letchfield, H. Gleeson, A. Pullen-Sansfaçon, and F. Luu. "Knowledge and Policy about LGBTQI Migrants: A Scoping Review of the Canadian and Global Context." *Journal of International Migration and Integration* (2020). https://doi.org/10.1007/s12134-020-00771-4.
Library and Archives Canada (LAC). *The Canadian State*. 2014. Retrieved from http://www.collectionscanada.gc.ca/canadian-state/023012-1616-e.html
- Statutes of Canada. An Act Respecting Immigration and Immigrants, 1906. Ottawa: SC 6 Edward VII, Chapter 19, 1906. http://www.pier21.ca/research/immigration-history/immigration-act-1906.
Lowe, Lisa. *The Intimacies of Four Continents*. Durham, NC: Duke University Press, 2015.
- "The Intimacies of Four Continents." In *Haunted by Empire: Geographies of Intimacy in North American History*. Edited by Laura Ann Stoler, 191–212. Durham, NC, and London: Duke University Press, 2006.
Luibhéid, Eithne. "Sexuality, Migration, and the Shifting Line between Legal and Illegal Status." *GLQ: A Journal of Lesbian and Gay Studies* 14, no. 2–3 (2008): 89–315.
Mackey, Eva. *The House of Difference: Cultural Politics and National Identity in Canada*. Toronto: University of Toronto Press, 2002.
Macklin, Audrey. "Disappearing Refugee: Reflections on the Canada-US Safe Third Country Agreement." *Columbia Human Rights Law Review* 36 (2005): 365–426.
Manalansan, Martin, IV. "The 'Stuff' of Archives: Mess, Migration and Queer Lives." *Radical History Review* 120 (2014): 94–107.
McGranahan, Carole. "Theorizing Refusal: An Introduction." *Cultural Anthropology* 31, no. 3 (2016): 319–25.
Metallic, G. "Finding Two-Spirit Identity: An Autoethnography." MSW, ISP. McGill University, 2013.
Meyer-Cook, F. "Two-Spirit People: Traditional Pluralism and Human Rights." In *Homosexualités: Variations linguistiques et culturelles*. Edited by S. Brotman and J.J. Levy, 245–80. Quebec City: Presses de l'Université du Québec, Coll. Santé et Société, 2008.

Meyer-Cook, F., and D. Labelle, D. "Namaji: Two-Spirit Organizing in Montreal, Canada." *Journal of Gay and Lesbian Social Services* 16, no. 1 (2004): 29-51. https://doi.org/10.1300/J041v16n01_02.

Mignolo, Walter D. *Local Histories/Global Designs: Coloniality, Subaltern Knowledges, and Border Thinking*. Princeton: Princeton University Press, 2012.

Monture-Agnes, P. *Thunder in My Soul: A Mohawk Woman Speaks*. Halifax: Fernwood Publishing, 1995

Morgensen, S.L. *Spaces between Us: Queer Settler Colonialism and Indigenous Decolonization*. Minneapolis: University of Minnesota Press, 2011.

Mugabo, Délice. "On Rocks and Hard Places: A Reflection on Antiblackness in Organizing against Islamophobia." *Critical Ethnic Studies* 2, no. 2 (2016): 159–83.

Murray, David A.B. *Real Queer?: Sexual Orientation and Gender Identity Refugees in the Canadian Refugee Apparatus*. London: Pickering and Chatto Publishers, 2015.

– "Real Queer: 'Authentic' LGBT Refugee Claimants and Homonationalism in the Canadian Refugee System." *Anthropologica* (2014): 21–32.

Ng, Roxana. "Exploring the Globalized Regime of Ruling from the Standpoint of Immigrant Workers." In *Sociology for Changing the World: Social Movements/Social Research*. Edited by Caelie Frampton, Gary Kinsman, A.K. Thompson, and Kate Tilleczek, 174–88. Halifax: Fernwood Publishing, 2006.

Ngai, M.M. *Impossible Subjects: Illegal Aliens and the Making of Modern America*. Princeton and Oxford: Princeton University Press, 2004.

Pratt, Anne. *Securing Borders: Detention and Deportation in Canada*. Vancouver: University of British Columbia Press, 2005.

Price, Jim. *Orienting Canada: Race, Empire and the Transpacific*. Vancouver: University of British Columbia Press, 2011.

Protocol Relating to the Status of Refugees, General Assembly. United Nations, 2198 (XXI) Sess. (1967).

Quijano, Anibal. "Coloniality of Power and Eurocentrism in Latin America." *International Sociology* 15, no. 2 (2000): 215–32.

Razack, S., S. Thobani, and M. Smith, eds. *States of Race: Critical Race Feminism for the 21st Century*. Toronto: Between the Lines, 2010.

Sanchez, M. "Testimony of a Deportee." In *Building a Solidarity City*, 2013. https://www.solidarityacrossborders.org/en/solidarity-city/solidarity-city-journal/testimony-of-a-deportee.

Sears, Claire. "All That Glitters: Trans-ing California's Gold Rush Migrations." *GLQ* 14, no. 2–3 (2008): 383– 402. https://doi.org/10.1215/10642684-2007-038.

Serano, Julia. *Whipping Girl: A Transsexual Woman on Sexism and the Scapegoating of Femininity*. Emeryville: Seal, 2007.

Sexton, Jared. "The Vel of Slavery: Tracking the Figure of the Unsovereign." *Critical Sociology* (2014): 1–15.
Shah, Nayan. *Stranger Intimacy: Contesting Race, Sexuality and the Law in the North American West*. Berkeley: University of California Press, 2011.
Sharma, Nandita, and Cynthia Wright. "Decolonizing Resistance: Challenging Colonial States." *Social Justice* 35, no. 3 (2009): 120–38.
Simpson, Audra. *Mohawk Interruptus: Political Life across the Borders of Settler States*. Durham, NC: Duke University Press, 2014.
– "On Ethnographic Refusal: Indigeneity, 'Voice' and Colonial Citizenship." *Junctures: The Journal for Thematic Dialogue* 9 (2007): 67–80.
Smith, A. *Conquest: Sexual Violence and American Indian Genocide*. Cambridge, MA: South End Press, 2005.
Smith, Dorothy. *The Conceptual Practices of Power: A Feminist Sociology of Knowledge*. Toronto: University of Toronto Press, 1990.
– *Institutional Ethnography: A Sociology for People*. Lanham, MD: AltaMira, 2005.
– *Writing the Social: Critique, Theory and Investigations*. Toronto: University of Toronto Press, 1999.
Thobani, Sunera. *Exalted Subjects: Studies in the Making of Race and Nation in Canada*. Toronto: University of Toronto Press, 2007.
Tuck, Eve, and K. Wayne Yang. "Unbecoming Claims: Pedagogies of Refusal in Qualitative Research." *Qualitative Inquiry* 20, no. 6 (2014): 811–18.
Valverde, Mariana. *The Age of Light, Soap, and Water: Moral Reform in English Canada, 1885–1925*. Toronto: University of Toronto Press, 2008.
Visa Requirement for Mexico (CIC – VRM). Backgrounder, 2014. http://www.cic.gc.ca/english/department/media/backgrounders/2009/2009-07-13.asp.
Walcott, Rinaldo. "The Problem of the Human: Black Ontologies and the Coloniality of Our Being." In *Postcoloniality – Decoloniality – Black Critique*. Edited by Sabine Broeck and Carsten Junker, 93–108. New York: Campus Verlag, 2013.
Wynter, Sylvia. "Unsettling the Coloniality of Being/Power/Truth/Freedom: Towards the Human, after Man, Its Overrepresentation – An Argument." *CR: The Centennial Review* 3, no. 3 (2003): 257–337.

7 Producing the Figure of the "Super-Refugee" through Discourses of Success, Exceptionalism, Ableism, and Inspiration

GADA MAHROUSE

In the wake of US President Donald Trump's anti-migrant campaign election platform and his subsequent 2017 executive order, which restricted entry of immigrants and refugees from Iraq, Iran, Libya, Somalia, Sudan, Syria, and Yemen,[1] it was publicized that Steve Jobs, the famous CEO and founder of Apple (one of the world's largest and richest multinational technology companies), was the son of a Syrian migrant.[2] The narrative about Jobs's origins was circulated by those who were opposed to Trump's exclusionary policies to contest the expressions of fear, panic, anxiety, and insecurity about the arrival of refugees.[3] By pointing to Jobs's tremendous success, those who circulated his origin story meant it as a reminder and illustration of the potential contributions that refugees and migrants can make. Organizations and individuals who advocate for refugees are also increasingly putting forward similar narratives. In fact, a Google search of the term "inspirational refugees" turns up tens of thousands of hits in which UNHCR refugees are hailed for being resilient, determined, and/or successful. A speaker series initiative in Canada called "REF Talks" is but one example. Its stated goal is to "connect the Canadian public with personal stories of refugees and celebrate their success, their contributions and accomplishments in their host country."[4]

This chapter questions the inadvertent effects of the inspirational refugee narrative. While recognizing the good intentions behind its circulation, I ask: what is activated through such discourses of inspiration and success? To answer this question, I develop an intersectional analytic framework that brings together key tenets from Critical Refugee Studies, Critical Race Studies, and Critical Disability Studies. Borrowing mainly from Critical Disability Scholars who have worked with the notion of the inspirational "supercrip" – a term used to describe how individuals with disabilities are required to display perseverance, bravery, or extraordinary feats to be positively acknowledged[5] – I demonstrate that a parallel figure is actively being constructed: *the super-refugee*.[6] Furthermore, positing this figuration as having both constitutive and generative effects,[7] I caution against its circulation. I argue that, although it is used by refugee supporters to contest xenophobic and racist thinking, it perpetuates discourses of individualism and responsibility that fold back into neoliberal, capitalist, and ableist understandings that can limit, rather than empower, refugees in the West. To be clear, my aim is not to make any claims on individual abilities or to diminish any accomplishments or success. Rather it is to consider how stories of refugee success are (co)produced, circulated, and received by host communities and what the insatiable appetite for these super-refugee stories reveals about liberal Western understandings, expectations, and responsibilities.

The chapter is divided into three parts. First, I develop an intersectional theoretical framework for thinking about refugees, race, and disability. Next, I focus on three widely circulated stories on inspirational super-refugees and look at some patterns that emerge within them. In the third part, I contemplate discourses of investment and indebtedness as corollaries of the inspirational super-refugee narrative to expose the neoliberal underpinnings that it reinforces, and the complicities and responsibilities that it obscures. I conclude by calling for more public acceptance for the unexceptional in the circulation of refugee narratives.

Refugees, Race, and Disability: An Intersectional Analytic

The theoretical underpinnings of this chapter are firmly situated within the principles of Critical Refugee Studies as described in the Introduction to this book. Namely, I begin from the premises that refugee reception is a highly racialized process, and with a critique of traditional international humanitarian regimes to elucidate how the state, citizens, and refugees are co-produced. This approach is informed by Peter Nyers's considerations on "how the category of the 'refugee' has been invented and naturalized as being a 'problem' for the international system of states."[8] The analysis that follows is mainly rooted in Yen Lê Espiritu's call for critical attention to "the trope of the 'good refugee' and the myth of 'the nation of refuge.'"[9] Importantly, Espiritu observes that such positive representations are often linked to economic utility.[10] Thematically, this chapter engages with some of the key concepts explored elsewhere in this book, including *exceptionality* and *exceptionalism*, both in terms of individuals and the nation-state (Nguyen and Phu; Madakoro), representations of *good* and *deserving* refugees (Reynolds and Hyndman), and refugee *narratives* vis-à-vis their ability to draw *empathy* (Goellnicht). Lastly, along with the other authors in this book who employ intersectional frameworks for their analyses, I aim to encourage more dialogue between distinct critical fields of inquiry and to highlight how they can inform each other.

As critical projects, the fields of Critical Disability Studies (CDS), Critical Refugee Studies (CRS), and Critical Race Theory (CRT) share the fundamental objectives of demonstrating how exclusion is normalized for some members of society and shifting the paradigmatic views that perpetuate these exclusions. For instance, CDS scholars have unsettled the dominant frame of disability as a medical problem faced by individual people and have instead argued for a focus on how the world treats disabled people.[11] In so doing, they have exposed the problematic ways in which disability is often seen as a flaw or tragic condition that must be overcome. CRS scholars have similarly challenged the tendency to locate responsibility (whether for success or failure) with refugees, rather than questioning the structural violence that led to their displacement.[12] CRT scholars have contributed in significant ways to both CDS and CRS by showing how nations police their borders through racialized and gendered discourses of refugees as threats or victims and how power relations produce pity-based responses that mask our complicity in furthering the vulnerability of people with disabilities.[13]

Despite their overlapping political goals of exposing systems of power, the disciplinary nature of academic thinking has largely restricted our ability to *cross-pollinate* these fields of knowledge, thereby significantly limiting our ability to see the connections between them. To illustrate the potential of going beyond single-issue and disciplinary approaches, I begin by highlighting the meaningful ways in which the intersections between race, disability, and refugees have been critically theorized in current studies and then proceed to call for further explorations.

Important to the development of an intersectional framework on disability, race, and refugees is Mimi Thi Nguyen's work, which shows that a vocabulary of illness is used to represent stateless peoples and refugee bodies as disabled or abnormal.[14] As Nguyen explains, because of their disenfranchisement, refugees are often discursively constructed as damaged subjects. Maria Pisani and Shaun Grech make a similar claim, showing that there are important parallels between "illegal" bodies and disabled bodies in the sense that both are seen as unproductive and as unwanted burdens.[15]

The parallels between disability and refugees are also explored in Nirmala Erevelles's sustained examination of disability and difference.

Erevelles points out that a salient resemblance exists between the "making" of dis/ability and the "making" of refugees.[16] The intersection of CDS and CRS and CRT, Erevelles argues, offers important insights on hierarchies of power. Indeed, in discussing exclusions of people with cognitive/severe disabilities, Erevelles found it necessary to forge a link between CRT and CDS to advance an argument that the "disciplinary practices produced within the material conditions of late capitalism enact in complex and contradictory ways the 'racialization of disability' and the 'dis-abilization of race.'"[17] Erevelles further points out that theorists in both areas have grappled "with the ideological terms and material conditions necessary to (re)negotiate their participation in civil society without reifying the hegemonic structures of white supremacy and ableism that persist."[18] The resemblances between disability and race are also taken up by Jasbir Puar, who makes connections between disability, debility, and capacity. Puar uses the notion of debility to go beyond the ability/disability binary in order to "addre[ss] injury and bodily exclusion that are endemic rather than epidemic or exceptional."[19]

Building on these significant intersectional approaches, my interest in bringing CDS, CRS, and CRT further into conversation is also modelled after scholarship that has effectively fused CDS with a number of fields, including transnational feminist theories,[20] critical race theories,[21] queer theories,[22] and combinations thereof.[23] Indeed, the coming together of CRS, CRT, and CDS could have an added advantage for exploring what Pisani and Grech describe as the ontological and practical invisibility of people with disabilities within studies of forced migration.[24] As they argue, disability and forced migration are rarely put together, whether in policy, research, or practice, and "the connections have only infrequently been made with the implication that those working in migration remain unaware of and uneducated in disability; and those working in disability, remain uninformed about and uneducated in migration."[25] Accordingly, the intersectional analytic I am proposing would allow us to see the remarkable similarities in the ways certain non-normative marginalized figures are represented. For instance, it is noteworthy that media representations of both refugees and people with disabilities tend to fall into good or bad archetypes.[26]

The Production of Super-Refugees

The potential for an intersectional framework for examining inspirational refugee narratives can best be illustrated through two stories, both involving refugees with disabilities. The first is that of a teenaged

Syrian refugee named Nujeen Mustafa who has cerebral palsy. After she was photographed smiling as she was being lifted in her wheelchair from a dinghy that had landed on the coast of Greece, Mustafa was propelled into the spotlight.[27] The public soon learned that she and her older sister fled Syria, travelled over sixteen months across the Mediterranean through Eastern Europe, and ended up in Germany.[28] As one reporter in the *Telegraph* newspaper put it, "the 3,500 mile journey from Aleppo to Cologne is a feat for any able bodied person but a miracle considering Nujeen did it in a rickety old wheelchair."[29]

Sympathetic and admiring responses to her story were immediate. Mustafa was featured on "Last Week Tonight with John Oliver," and she has been interviewed by many leading news media outlets.[30] In 2017 Mustafa published a co-authored memoir entitled *Nujeen: One Girl's Journey from War Torn Syria in a Wheelchair*.[31] In the media, Mustafa is consistently lauded for her "determination" and eternal "optimism."[32] For example, in response to a reporter's question about how she managed to stay upbeat in the face of so many setbacks, Mustafa replied, "I thought of everything as a big adventure."[33] Reports are also sprinkled with endearing facts about her, such as that she taught herself English by watching American soap operas.

In the Canadian context, Hani Al Moulia's story circulates in similar ways. He was first brought to Western media attention when Melissa Fleming, the head of communications and chief spokesperson for the United Nations High Commissioner for Refugees (UNHCR), mentioned him in a TEDGlobal talk she gave in 2015.[34] Admiring some photographs Al Moulia took while he was in a refugee camp in Lebanon, Fleming pointed out that his talent is particularly impressive because he has a visual impairment that renders him legally blind. Al Moulia and his family were eventually resettled to Regina, Saskatchewan in 2015.[35] Since then, like Mustafa, Al Moulia has been regularly featured in news media, usually described as "upbeat" and as someone who "never lost his enthusiasm for life and his drive to succeed."[36] In another striking similarity to Mustafa, we learn the endearing detail that he taught himself English reading Dan Brown novels and listening to American rap music.

Of course, Mustafa's and Al Moulia's respective experiences of fleeing Syria and resettling in Germany and Canada are much more complex and fraught with contradiction, ambivalence, and nuance than what I have sketched out here. In presenting their stories in these crude, broad strokes, my aim is to highlight how their experiences are flattened in the media and illustrate what reporters tend to emphasize – a point to which I will return. For now, by focusing on Mustafa and Al Moulia, my objective (albeit obvious and perhaps clumsy) is to show that, given their evident physical disabilities and because they are represented through their refusal to be limited by them, the term "supercrip" can easily be applied to them.[37] Indeed, as Sami Schalk's work helps to elucidate, they are constructed through the specific narrative structures of overcoming limitations and achieving unlikely success.[38]

Rather than being quick to celebrate them and circulate their success, however, CDS scholarship insists that we ought to question the implications of such inspirational narratives.[39] As Danielle Peers points out, these representations, which are framed by motivational rhetoric, "create unrealistically high expectations of what *all* disabled people should accomplish" and subsequently "serve to justify the vilification of particular disabled people who do not manage to overcome, often writing them off as stubborn or lazy and therefore deserving of the poverty or lack of care that they may experience."[40] We must therefore ask how such stories work to erase or invalidate the difficulties that they and others have faced.

Having shown the simultaneous and analogous production of supercrips who become super-refugees through Mustafa and Al Moulia, I want to bring in a third story. It is one that Canadian Prime Minister Justin Trudeau told in his address to the United Nations 2016 Leaders' Summit on Refugees about the Hadhads, a Syrian family who established a successful business in a small town in Nova Scotia. Trudeau explained that the Hadhad family had been in a refugee camp in Lebanon for three years before coming to Canada, and that they managed to open a small chocolate factory just eight months after their arrival. The epitome of their success was demonstrated, Trudeau emphasized, in the fact that they were now employing Canadians. In his speech, Trudeau urged that "we have to recall stories like this one when we're trying to think of solutions to help the 65 million displaced persons worldwide."[41] In Canada, the Hadhad story has been incredibly popular. Mostly, it is narrated as through an emphasis on how they went from being refugees to successful entrepreneurs in under a year.

In considering these three stories side by side, one notices similar patterns in their production. For instance, it is not incidental that the stories of the Hadhads, Mustafa, and Al Moulia were first constructed by prominent political leaders or media outlets. Mustafa was propelled into the limelight by a BBC journalist, Al Moulia's story gained prominence through Melissa Fleming of the UNHCR, and the Hadhads became known internationally when Trudeau invoked them in his speech.

Another point of commonality between them is how quickly the popularity of these stories intensified. As mentioned earlier, among other media outlets and platforms that she has been given, public interest in Mustafa has resulted in the publication of her memoir.[42] In Canada, Al Moulia has been appointed to the Prime Minister's Youth Council and has been a featured speaker at an event that brings together celebrated presenters to inspire youth. Since Fleming's speech, Al Moulia has also been the subject of several documentary films.[43] Similarly, the Hadhad chocolate company website indicates that Tareq Hadhad has done over one hundred interviews with different news teams and organizations, and there is a link on his site for those who want to book him as a speaker.[44] Moreover, Mustafa, Al Moulia, and Tareq Hadhad have all been featured on the TEDTalks platform – whose motto is "ideas worth spreading."

A question that therefore emerges is: why does the Western public have such a voracious appetite for these narratives? One answer to this question comes from critical humanitarian scholarship on affective regimes of communication.[45] Writing about the positive and hopeful portrayals in humanitarian campaigns and the ways in which suffering is communicated to Western societies, Lili Chouliaraki argues that media-savvy and sceptical publics increasingly take notice of how the message is communicated and not just the message itself.[46] This suggests that the simple humanitarian message that refugees need our support is no longer sufficient to engage the public. Instead, we expect to be won over by the way the message is told. Drawing from this, one can start to see why the stories of the Hadhads, Mustafa, and Al Moulia are so enjoyable and gratifying. Although we do learn about hardships they endured, their positivity and upbeat determination are emphasized, qualities that grab our attention and leave an impression. It is important, for instance, that Mustafa's and Al Moulia's disabilities were pre-existing and not caused by war. This means that we can hear their stories without being reminded of atrocities and terror. As Jennifer Terry's work reveals, these stories "sanitize" the realities of war.[47] Terry's work also leads us to question the rescue impulse associated with the idea that "we can enhance" these indivduals. For example, the public may assume that now that she is the West, Mustafa may be able to access a better wheelchair than the "rickety" one she left Syria in.

Put simply, super-refugee stories do not delve deeply into war and its aftermath, but are instead consistently presented as relatable, affirming tales of "never giving up." They are articulated in ways that resemble and reinforce what earlier studies on representations of refugees and immigrants have shown – a very particular narrative structure whereby they first shed light on the refugees' devastating plights (in these cases, a perilous journey across the Mediterranean or life in a refugee camp), followed by some aspect of the refugees' resilience and determination.[48] Writing about the proliferation of the "genre" of inspirational stories and their narrative structure, Puar notes their proselytizing tone and ethos on turning injury into transgression, triumph, and success.[49] These scripts are so formulaic that Karissa Singh, the founder of the UK social media campaign "Post Ref Racism," offers a type of recipe of the elements that make "catchy" stories about refugees that resonate with the British public and become "shareable": 1) "relate it to the local or the familiar," 2) "choose a talented subject," and 3) "make it a firsthand account."[50]

Critical scholars have advised that in "hearing" these stories, one must bear in mind the high material stakes of their being told in a particular way. For example, writing about her experience of being evaluated for classification as a Para-Olympian, CDS scholar Danielle Peers refers to the interrogational dynamics she undergoes as an enforced "confessional," and observes that she is expected to convey feelings and experiences in ways that match up with the format of those asking the questions.[51] Peers's work closely echoes studies on asylum claims processes. For example, focusing on migration officials in Sweden, Åsa Wettergren shows that feelings of sympathy or resentment play a vital role in the emotional evaluation used to determine the claims. As Wettergren explains: "It is likelier after all that an officer will accept and positively repair the gaps of a story if she or he finds the applicant sympathetic, and, vice-versa, that she or he will look for contradictions and incoherence if she or he feels resentment."[52] These disparate works and sites reveal that, for asylum seekers and people with disabilities, a comparable scripted process of narrating stories exists. More importantly, it is the listeners' emotional identification with the stories that has tremendous bearing on how the narrator is treated.

While such stories may not empower refugees, Vinh Nguyen's work has shown that they certainly "confirm liberal ideals of freedom, democracy, and equality" in ways that perpetuate national mythologies.[53] Trudeau's deployment of the Hadhad story is the clearest example of this. Undeniably, his speech given at the UN is one example of how the current Canadian government has effectively positioned itself as welcoming of refugees in contrast to the United States. In narrating the Hadhads' success as a typical rag-to-riches story, Trudeau buttresses the larger story of Canada as an extraordinarily humanitarian nation-state.⁵⁴ As Nguyen and Phu point out in the Introduction, it is not difficult to see how such stories benefit the state in ways that are consistent with how Canada has been previously recognized for its "exceptional history of welcoming refugees."⁵⁵

The national mythologies shaped through Al Moulia's story are also revealing. In fact, Al Moulia's appointment to Canada's Youth Council is somewhat ironic in light of Canadian immigration responses to other cases involving disability. As one report by a group called Global Disability Watch reveals,⁵⁶ Canada has a common practice of denying residency to persons with disabilities and members of their families. Describing the case of Nico Montoya, a child from Cost Rica with Down Syndrome whose family was denied permanent residency in Canada because of his disability, the report shows how disabled immigrants are assessed and often rejected according to an economic calculation of what they will cost Canadian taxpayers. Celebrating Al Moulia as a refugee with a disability therefore falsely implies that, when it comes to immigrants and refugees with disabilities, Canada is a "land of opportunity."

Additionally, a CDS framework alerts us to the need to be cautious of how these types of stories obscure very real differences in refugees' circumstances. As Schalk writes: "people represented in glorified supercrip narratives are not only those 'who enjoy extraordinary and compensating qualities,' but also those with extraordinary and compensating *'circumstances'* – such as having race, gender, or class privilege."⁵⁷ The Hadhads' success in terms of relative social positioning and circumstances is a good illustration of this point. It is important to note that the Hadhads, as one of the few refugee families in a very small town, received significantly greater community support than refugee families who have settled in large cities. In fact, several unusual circumstances – seldom mentioned in accounts of the Hadhads' story – undoubtedly facilitated their success. Namely, they were a middle-class business-owning family with skills, professional knowledge, and cultural capital. In addition, as one in-depth report indicates,⁵⁸ a community member in the town where they were resettled helped them to find the specialized equipment they needed, and local carpenters, plumbers, and electricians pitched in to help build them a small factory. Without diminishing the Hadhads' hard work and determination, we must recognize that it would not have been possible for most other Syrian refugees to achieve that type of success in such a limited time. In other words, their individual success story is told in a way that elides some of the significant material conditions, relative privileges, and unevenly distributed structural advantages that enabled their success.

Thus, like their supercrip counterparts, one can see that inspirational stories of super-refugees similarly entrench a notion of responsibility at the level of the individual and not on society. As Prem Kumar Rajaram's work on the incorporation of refugee voices in humanitarian campaigns reveals, stories like these do not necessarily empower refugees or challenge the power relations within international development/aid frameworks.[59] In fact, because "refugee voices" types of campaigns fail to contextualize the stories that are told, they tend to exaggerate, objectify, and essentialize.[60] Furthermore, although super-refugee stories may be considered authentic and reliable insofar as they are often narrated by the refugees themselves, it is more accurate to think of them as speech acts that fit into an established framework, one that is predetermined by the discourses of gratitude and indebtedness.

Puar's work shows us that these success narratives work squarely within the normative logics of neoliberalism. As Puar asks, "which debilitated bodies can be reinvigorated for neoliberalism, available and valuable enough for rehabilitation, and which cannot be?" The distinction, Puar points out, is that "the conditions that make disability endemic as opposed to exceptional are already ones of entrenched economic, racial, political, and social disenfranchisement."[61] This echoes the racialized "model minority" discourses that Espiritu discusses in her book on Vietnamese refugees in the US. As she explains, since the Second World War, social citizenship in the United States has been defined as "the civic duty of the individual to reduce his or her burden on society."[62] It is this idea of individualism and its two corollaries – investment and debt – that I will explore next.

Investment and Indebtedness

The analogous structure of inspirational supercrip and super-refugee narratives also compels us to ask how they advance and reinforce notions of individualism in ways that assign the obligations of rehabilitation, adaptation, and successful integration to refugees. One salient example of this individualizing imperative can be seen in the earlier mentioned video-recorded TEDGlobal talk by Melissa Fleming of the UNHCR.[63] Under the auspices of helping refugees "thrive and not just survive," Fleming encourages countries to accept refugees lest they risk "missing investment opportunities," and suggests that we ought to see refugee camps "as centers of excellence." Fleming's video, which has been viewed more than a million times, reveals that the most sympathetic framings of refugees have come to rely on neoliberal notions of the "worth" of refugees and posits their acceptance in terms of how we may profit from them.

A critique of this notion of worth has been powerfully articulated in an essay written by Dina Nayeri, an Iranian American novelist and short story writer whose family fled Iran.[64] Nayeri, who first settled in Europe and then in the US, has been dubbed the "ungrateful refugee." She makes a lucid point about how glorifying refugees who succeed in the West is an iteration of the racialized politics of gratitude:

> I've seen a troubling change in the way people make the case for refugees. Even those on the left talk about how immigrants make America great. They point to photographs of happy refugees turned good citizens, listing their contributions, as if that is the price of existing in the same country, on the same earth. Friends often use me as an example. They say in posts or conversations: "Look at Dina. She lived as a refugee and look how much stuff she's done." As if that's proof that letting in refugees has a good, healthy return on investment.

Nayeri's observation reveals that an upshot of the refugee success narrative is the discourse of debt and gratitude. The ubiquity of these discourses is also evident in a statement that Lina Arafeh, a Syrian refugee now settled in Canada, made in a radio interview:

> Every single day I send my kids to school saying you have to prove yourself, you cannot waste the time, you have to show them that you are doing well. You want to contribute something to Canada and the future so that they don't regret it.[65]

Arefeh's simple words reveal a sense of obligatory overachievement as a form of debt payment.

These discourses of investment and debt have been theorized by those who have interrogated the logic of gratitude as it applies to refugees. For instance, Mimi Thi Nguyen has put forth the idea of "the gift of freedom" to describe the perpetual sense of indebtedness which refugees are made to feel for having been given a new start.[66] Most importantly, Nguyen's work makes clear that this "gift" can easily be withdrawn. The compulsory disposition of gratitude also comes through in the writing of Carolina Moulin,[67] who argues that part of the implicit agreement of offering protection to refugees is gratitude and docility – i.e., they are expected to not make demands. In sum, we must consider the implications of characterizing refugees in terms such as "determination," "enthusiasm," and "drive." These characteristics and the inspirational super-refugee narratives in which they are embedded frame discussions of resettlement by emphasizing what we can gain from them, rather than our political and legal duty to protect.

Conclusion: Resisting the Neoliberal Impulse

This chapter began with the narrative about Steve Jobs's success. Recalling that it was circulated at a time when many were looking for ways to oppose Trump's anti-migrant and anti-refugee policies, I want to end by questioning the strategic political uses of stories of super-refugees. In light of the open hostility and racism about and towards refugees, to what extent might these narratives challenge prejudices? To answer this question, I turn to work by CDS scholar Jan Grue, who offers important insights into how we respond to such narratives by highlighting the inadvertent costs and consequences of their circulation. Writing about representations of inspirational people with disabilities, Grue questions whether it is "*a priori* a bad thing to depict people with impairment succeeding at a task or displaying physical capabilities ... [or] as potential role models, whether for people with similar impairments or for a general audience?"[68] While she concedes that the answer to these questions might very well be "no," she points out that the main concern with discourses of empowerment and inspiration is that they falsely tell "variants of the same simple story: disabled people are capable of anything."[69] This suggests that positive depictions of hyper-resilient, determined super-refugees should not simply be understood as a type of counter-discourse to the racialized hostility and fear. Moreover, while they may result in more tolerance towards refugees in the West, they do not meaningfully alter the dominant paradigm. Rather, as the feel-good accounts of Mustafa, Al Moulia, and the Hadhads show, these narratives indulge Western hosts' feelings that "we" rescued the "Other." More importantly, they present refugeeness as a condition that arouses emotion but not transformation.[70]

At the same time, a nuanced reading of these narratives reveals that their effects are complex in the sense that they are not always entirely oppressive and problematic for refugees themselves. Vinh Nguyen has pointed out that these stories may have therapeutic and even spiritual effects for some. Similarly, Schalk has noted that from the perspective of people with disabilities, "supercrip representations can be *both* empowering and disempowering."[71] While appreciating this, as I have argued throughout, CDS offers us some useful ways to contemplate these narratives. Indeed, super-refugee stories similarly raise questions about the pressure to overcompensate and excel, and reveal that a type of debt is often being performed through them. The pressure to succeed can also be experienced as an expectation associated with gratitude. Through inspirational stories of super-refugees, the public comes to believe that socio-historical circumstances can and should be overcome, and the demarcation between those considered deserving and undeserving is reinforced. As Didier Fassin warns, these distinctions push us to see the protection of refugees more as a favour than as an obligation.[72] Indeed, whether or not refugees are supported by Western governments should not depend on whether or not we are moved by their stories, or whether or not they can demonstrate being worthy investments who one day will adequately reimburse their host country.

As wars and imperialisms continue to produce more refugees, we must therefore be wary of representations forwarding the idea that, with some positivity and determination, refugees can and will overcome the circumstances they have been dealt. Rather than being seduced by the "thrive" narrative, in order to divest from neoliberal and individualizing impulses we must advance unconditional acceptance of those who are merely trying to survive. Indeed, the case for unexceptionality vis-à-vis refugees is gaining momentum. In an opinion piece published in the *Daily Telegraph*, youth commentator Seb Starcevic responds to the success stories that idealize refugees by asking "what about the other 99 per cent?" Starcevic writes, "I'd be interested in learning more about the unexceptional refugee. Average grades, average goals, average in every way."[73] Hearing more of these stories of the unexceptional refugees might illuminate the day-to-day challenges faced by most and help to identify ways they can be better supported. That is, rather than focusing on the extraordinary feats of "super-refugees," we might better understand the historical, global, political, and social forces that produce them.

NOTES

1 Colloquially referred to as the "Muslim ban," it temporarily halted entry by nationals of these seven Muslim-majority countries for 90 days, suspended refugee resettlement for 120 days, banned all Syrian refugees indefinitely, and attempted to restrict the United States' refugee quota by half. See Executive Order 13769 of 27 January 2017; Merica, "Trump Signs Executive Order to Keep Out 'Radical Islamic Terrorists.'"
2 This was first posted on Twitter by tech entrepreneur David Galbraith, who pointed out that Steve Jobs shared Syrian heritage with Aylan Kurdi,

the three-year-old whose dead body was photographed washed up on the Mediterranean shore. The tweet was shared more than eleven thousand times. See also Ahuja, "Banksy's Steve Jobs Mural Spotlights Refugee Crisis."

3 For more on this climate of fear and anxiety, see Bauman, *Strangers at Our Door*.
4 See https://www.unhcr.ca/news-stories/special-features/ref-talks-canada/.
5 Jaeger and Bowman, *Understanding Disability*; Chrisman, "A Reflection on Inspiration"; Schalk, "Reevaluating the Supercrip"; Clare, "Stolen Bodies, Reclaimed Bodies."
6 Although most words beginning with the "super-" prefix are written as one word, I use the hyphen to draw attention to the incongruity between the two words.
7 I use Castaneda's notion of figuration, which emphasizes the relation between the semiotic and the material practices. As Castaneda explains, "to use figuration as a descriptive tool is to unpack the domains of practice and significance that are built into each figure" (*Figurations*, 3).
8 Nyers, "Emergency or Emerging Identities?"
9 Espiritu, *Body Counts*, 2.
10 See also Roberts and Mahtani, "Neoliberalizing Race, Racing Neoliberalism," 250.
11 Clare, "Stolen Bodies, Reclaimed Bodies."
12 Espiritu, *Body Counts*, 2, emphasis in original.
13 Razack, "The Perils of Storytelling for Refugee Women," 167–8; Razack, *Looking White People in the Eye*. For more on this, see Goellnicht in this book.
14 For this argument, Nguyen draws from Hannah Arendt (*The Gift of Freedom*, 60).
15 Pisani and Grech, "Disability and Forced Migration," 426.
16 Erevelles, *Disability and Difference in Global Contexts*. She is referring to both psychological and physical disabilities.
17 Ibid., 150.
18 Ibid., 153.
19 Puar, *The Right to Maim*, xvii.
20 Erevelles and Nguyen, "Disability, Girlhood, and Vulnerability in Transnational Contexts."
21 Connor, "Not So Strange Bedfellows"; Annamma, Connor, and Ferri, "Dis/Ability Critical Race Studies (DisCrit)."
22 McRuer, *Crip Theory*.
23 Puar, *The Right to Maim*.
24 Pisani and Grech, "Disability and Forced Migration," 426.

25 Ibid., 422.
26 Hadley, "Cheats, Charity Cases and Inspirations." Media representations of refugees are explored further in Johanna Reynolds and Jennifer Hyndman's chapter. Importantly, these representations are gendered. Negative ones, usually of single men, summon up refugees as invaders, fraudulent opportunists, or threats to national security. In contrast, more sympathetic representations usually feature women and children refugees as helpless, vulnerable victims deserving of assistance or rescue. See Silveira, "The Representation of (Illegal) Migrants in the British News"; Berry, Garcia-Blanco, and Moore, "Press Coverage of the Refugee and Migrant Crisis in the EU"; Kaye, "Redefining the Refugee"; Szczepanik, "The 'Good' and 'Bad' Refugees?"; Parker, "'Unwanted Invaders.'"
27 Fergal Keane first interviewed Mustafa for BBC News in 2015 (Keane, "Migrant Crisis).
28 "Meet Nujeen Mustafa."
29 Smith, "From Syria to Cologne in a Wheelchair."
30 In Canada, she was the focus of a story in *Maclean's* magazine and she has been interviewed on the nationally broadcast CBC radio show "The Current."
31 The book was written with journalist Christine Lamb, who also co-authored *I Am Malala: The Girl Who Stood Up for Education and Was Shot by the Taliban*, the memoir of the Pakistani activist and Nobel Peace prize laureate Malala Yousafzai. In fact, Mustafa has been dubbed as the "new Malala."
32 Le Blond, "Fresh Hope in Germany for Syrian Girl Who Fled Home in a Wheelchair."
33 O'Connor, "Nujeen Mustafa."
34 Fleming, "Let's Help Refugees Thrive, Not Just Survive."
35 Canadian Journalists for Free Expression, "Finding Refuge."
36 Johne, "Legally Blind Photographer Hani Al Moulia Brings Refugee Crisis into Focus."
37 Chrisman, "A Reflection on Inspiration," 173.
38 Schalk, "Reevaluating the Supercrip," 76. Schalk also draws attention to the work of Amit Kana, who has explored the somewhat contradictory messages in supercrip narratives, noting that "it is used in reference to representations of disabled people who are presented as extraordinary for doing something ordinary as well as representations of disabled people who are presented as extraordinary for doing something exceptional or rare" (79).
39 Chrisman, "A Reflection on Inspiration."
40 Peers, "From Inhalation to Inspiration," 332, emphasis in original.
41 Liberal Party of Canada, "A Syrian Refugee Success Story."

42 Mustafa and Lamb, *Nujeen*.
43 Both Kevin Newman for CTV's *W5* and Zahra Mackaoui's "Through My Eyes: Hani's Journey" follow Al Moulia's journey from the camps in Lebanon to Canada.
44 "Peace by Chocolate."
45 Fassin, *Humanitarian Reason*; Wettergren, "Mobilization and the Moral Shock"; Ticktin, *Casualties of Care*.
46 Chouliaraki, *The Ironic Spectator*, 56.
47 Terry, *Attachments to War*.
48 Vinh Nguyen, "Refugee Gratitude"; Malkki, "Speechless Emissaries."
49 Puar, *The Right to Maim*, 7.
50 Singh, "The Refugee Stories Captivating the UK Twittersphere."
51 Peers "Interrogating Disability."
52 Wettergren, "Mobilization and the Moral Shock," 180.
53 Vinh Nguyen, "Refugee Gratitude," 17.
54 Ibid.
55 In 1986, the UNHCR awarded "the people of Canada" the Nansen Refugee Award "in recognition of their essential and constant contribution to the cause of refugees within their country and around the world." This marked the first and only occasion the award was presented to the citizens of a country (UNHCR, "Refugee Resettlement Facts [Fact Sheet]").
56 Spagnuolo and Nazami, "Canada's Dismal Treatment of Disabled Immigrants or 'How to Build a Disability-Free Country."
57 Schalk, "Reevaluating the Supercrip," 80, emphasis in original.
58 Kassam, "Isam and the Chocolate Factory." Tareq Hadhad is trained as a physician.
59 Rajaram, "Humanitarianism and Representations of the Refugee."
60 Ibid.
61 Puar, *The Right to Maim*, 13 and 16.
62 Espiritu, *Body Counts*, 94.
63 Fleming, "Let's Help Refugees Thrive, Not Just Survive."
64 "The Current," "Expecting Gratitude from Refugees Can Be Toxic, Says Author."
65 Ibid.
66 Mimi T. Nguyen, *The Gift of Freedom*.
67 Moulin, "Ungrateful Subjects?"
68 Grue, "The Problem with Inspiration Porn," 839–40, emphasis in original.
69 Ibid., 846.
70 Erevelles, *Disability and Difference in Global Contexts*, 128.
71 Nguyen, "Refugee Gratitude"; Schalk, "Reevaluating the Supercrip," 75.
72 Fassin, *Humanitarian Reason*.

73 Seb Starcevic, https://www.dailytelegraph.com.au/rendezview
/guess-what-mediocre-refugees-are-people-too/news-story/570c87c
1f6f4211eb7b7de0163a1bd3e.

REFERENCES

Ahuja, Masuma. "Banksy's Steve Jobs Mural Spotlights Refugee Crisis." *CNN*, 4 January 2016. http://www.cnn.com/style/article/banksy-steve-jobs-graffiti/index.html.
Annamma, Subini A., David Connor, and Beth Ferri. "Dis/Ability Critical Race Studies (DisCrit): Theorizing at the Intersections of Race and Dis/Ability." *Race Ethnicity and Education* 16, no. 1 (2013): 1–31.
Bauman, Zygmunt. *Strangers at Our Door*. Malden: Polity Press, 2016.
Berry, Mike, Inaki Garcia-Blanco, and Kerry Moore. "Press Coverage of the Refugee and Migrant Crisis in the EU: A Content Analysis of Five European Countries." UNHCR. December 2015. http://www.unhcr.org/56bb369c9.html.
Canadian Journalists for Free Expression. "Finding Refuge: The Story of Hany [sic] Al Moulia, Syrian Refugee." http://www.cjfe.org/almoulia. Accessed 24 September 2018.
Castaneda, Claudia. *Figurations: Child, Bodies, Worlds*. Durham, NC: Duke University Press, 2002.
Chouliaraki, Lilie. *The Ironic Spectator: Solidarity in the Age of Post-Humanitarianism*. Malden: Polity Press, 2013.
Chrisman, Wendy L. "A Reflection on Inspiration: A Recuperative Call for Emotion in Disability Studies." *Journal of Literary & Cultural Disability Studies* 5, no. 2 (2011): 163–84.
Citizenship and Immigration Canada. "Remembering the Journey to Canada of Vietnamese Refugees [Poster]." http://www.cic.gc.ca/english/pdf/pub/Vietnamese-Journey-Poster.pdf. Accessed 24 September 2018.
Clare, Eli. "Stolen Bodies, Reclaimed Bodies: Disability and Queerness." *Public Culture* 13, no. 3 (2001): 359–65.
Connor, David J. "Not So Strange Bedfellows: The Promise of Disability Studies and Critical Race Theory." In *Disability and the Politics of Education: An International Reader*. Edited by Susan L. Gabel and Scot Danforth, 451–76. New York: Peter Lang, 2008.
"The Current." "Expecting Gratitude from Refugees Can Be Toxic, Says Author." CBC Radio, 3 May 2017. http://www.cbc.ca/radio/thecurrent/the-current-for-may-3-2017-1.4095703/expecting-gratitude-from-refugees-can-be-toxic-says-author-1.4095737.
Erevelles, Nirmala. *Disability and Difference in Global Contexts: Enabling a Transformative Body Politic*. New York: Palgrave Macmillan, 2011.

Erevelles, Nirmala, and Xuan Thuy Nguyen. "Disability, Girlhood, and Vulnerability in Transnational Contexts." *Girlhood Studies* 9, no. 1 (2016): 3–20.

Espiritu, Yến Lê. *Body Counts: The Vietnam War and Militarized Refuge(es)*. Oakland: University of California Press, 2014.

Executive Order 13769 of 27 January 2017, "Protecting the Nation from Foreign Terrorist Entry into the United States." Code of Federal Regulations, Title 3 (2017) 82:20 Federal Register 8977. https://www.gpo.gov/fdsys/pkg/FR-2017-02-01/pdf/2017-02281.pdf.

Fassin, Didier. *Humanitarian Reason: A Moral History of the Present*. Translated by Rachel Gomme. Berkeley: University of California Press, 2011.

Fleming, Melissa. "Let's Help Refugees Thrive, Not Just Survive." *TEDGlobal*. October 2014. https://www.ted.com/talks/melissa_fleming_let_s_help_refugees_thrive_not_just_survive.

Grue, Jan. "The Problem with Inspiration Porn: A Tentative Definition and a Provisional Critique." *Disability and Society* 31, no. 6 (2016): 838–49.

Hadley, Bree. "Cheats, Charity Cases and Inspirations: Disrupting the Circulation of Disability-Based Memes Online." *Disability and Society* 31, no. 5 (2016): 676–92.

Jaeger, Paul T., and Cynthia Ann Bowman. *Understanding Disability: Inclusion, Access, Diversity, and Civil Rights*. Westport: Praeger, 2005.

Johne, Marjo. "Legally Blind Photographer Hani Al Moulia Brings Refugee Crisis into Focus." *Globe and Mail*, 13 October 2016. https://www.theglobeandmail.com/life/giving/legally-blind-photographer-hani-al-moulia-brings-refugee-crisis-into-focus/article32350212.

Kassam, Ashifa. "Isam and the Chocolate Factory: Syrian Refugees Relaunch Family Business in Canada." *Guardian*, 12 May 2017, World news. https://www.theguardian.com/world/2017/may/12/hadhad-family-peace-by-chocolates-syrian-refugees-canada.

Kaye, Ron. "Redefining the Refugee: The UK Media Portrayal of Asylum Seekers." In *The New Migration in Europe: Social Constructions and Social Realities*. Edited by Khalid Koser and Helma Lutz, 163–82. New York: St. Martin's Press, 1998.

Keane, Fergal. "Migrant Crisis: 'You Should Fight for What You Want in This World' BBC News." YouTube video. Posted by BBC News, 17 September 2015. https://www.youtube.com/watch?v=DwD3bosbDdQ.

Le Blond, Josie. "Fresh Hope in Germany for Syrian Girl Who Fled Home in a Wheelchair." UNHCR, 12 May 2017. http://www.unhcr.org/news/stories/2017/5/58dd189f4/fresh-hope-germany-syrian-girl-fled-home-wheelchair.html.

Liberal Party of Canada. "A Syrian Refugee Success Story: The Hadhad Family." Last modified 23 September 2016. https://www.liberal.ca/a-syrian-refugee-success-story-the-hadhad-family.

Malkki, Liisa H. "Speechless Emissaries: Refugees, Humanitarianism, and Dehistoricization." *Cultural Anthropology* 11, no. 3 (1996): 377–404.

McRuer, Robert. *Crip Theory: Cultural Signs of Queerness and Disability*. New York: New York University Press, 2006.

"Meet Nujeen Mustafa: The Girl Who Fled War-Torn Syria in a Wheelchair." YouTube video. Posted by "Vision.ae," 11 April 2017. https://www.youtube.com/watch?v=itlmubG4HbY.

Merica, Dan. "Trump Signs Executive Order to Keep Out 'Radical Islamic Terrorists.'" CNN, 30 January 2017. http://www.cnn.com/2017/01/27/politics/trump-plans-to-sign-executive-action-on-refugees-extreme-vetting.

Moulin, Carolina. "Ungrateful Subjects? Refugee Protests and the Logic of Gratitude." In *Citizenship, Migrant Activism and the Politics of Movement*. Edited by Peter Nyers and Kim Rygiel. New York: Routledge, 2012.

Mustafa, Nujeen, and Christina Lamb. *Nujeen: One Girl's Incredible Journey from War-Torn Syria in a Wheelchair*. New York: HarperCollins 2016.

Nguyen, Mimi T. *The Gift of Freedom: War, Debt, and Other Refugee Passages*. Durham, NC: Duke University Press, 2012.

Nguyen, Vinh. "Refugee Gratitude: Narrating Success and Intersubjectivity in Kim Thúy's *Ru*." *Canadian Literature* 219 (2013): 17–36.

Nyers, Peter. "Emergency or Emerging Identities? Refugees and Transformations in World Order." *Millennium Journal of International Studies* 28, no. 1 (1999): 1–26.

O'Connor, Joanne. "Nujeen Mustafa: 'Sometimes It's Good to Be Unaware. Maybe I Was Too Young to Realise the Danger.'" *Guardian*, 20 December 2015. https://www.theguardian.com/world/2015/dec/20/nujeen-mustafa-interview-syrian-refugee.

Parker, Samuel. "'Unwanted Invaders': The Representation of Refugees and Asylum Seekers in the UK and Australian Print Media." *eSharp 23: Myth and Nation* (2015).

"Peace by Chocolate: A Syrian Family Tradition." https://www.peacebychocolate.ca.

Peers, Danielle. "From Inhalation to Inspiration: A Genealogical Auto-ethnography of a Supercrip." In *Foucault and the Government of Disability*. Edited by Shelley Tremain, 331–49. Ann Arbor: University of Michigan Press, 2015.

— "Interrogating Disability: The (De)Composition of a Recovering Paralympian." *Qualitative Research in Sport, Exercise and Health* 4, no. 2 (2012): 175–88.

Pisani, Maria, and Shaun Grech. "Disability and Forced Migration: Critical Intersectionalities." *Disability and the Global South* 2, no. 1 (2015): 421–41.

Puar, Jasbir K. *The Right to Maim: Debility, Capacity, Disability*. Durham, NC: Duke University Press, 2017.

Rajaram, Prem Kumar. "Humanitarianism and Representations of the Refugee." *Journal of Refugee Studies* 15, no. 3 (2002): 247–64.

Ray, Carolyn. "Sweet Success: How the Hadhads Went from Refugees to Employers in 1 Year." *CBC News*, 7 January 2017. https://www.cbc.ca/news/canada/nova-scotia/peace-by-chocolate-hadhads-celebrate-year-one-in-antigonish-1.3925779.

Razack, Sherene. *Looking White People in the Eye*. Toronto: University of Toronto Press, 1999.

– "The Perils of Storytelling for Refugee Women." In *Development and Diaspora: Gender and the Refugee Experience*. Edited by Victoria Foote, Helene Moussa, Penny Van Esterik, and Wenona Giles, 164–74. Dundas, ON: Artemis Enterprises, 1996.

"REF Talks Canada." UNHCR Canada. Last modified 2018. https://www.unhcr.ca/news-stories/special-features/ref-talks-canada/

Roberts, David J., and Minelle Mahtani. "Neoliberalizing Race, Racing Neoliberalism: Placing 'Race' in Neoliberal Discourses." *Antipode* 42, no. 2 (2010): 248–57.

Schalk, Sami. "Reevaluating the Supercrip." *Journal of Literary and Cultural Disability Studies* 10, no. 1 (2016): 71–86.

Silveira, Carolina. "The Representation of (Illegal) Migrants in the British News." *Networking Knowledge: Journal of the MeCCSA Postgraduate Network* 9, no. 4 (2016). http://www.ojs.meccsa.org.uk/index.php/netknow/article/view/449.

Singh, Karissa. "The Refugee Stories Captivating the UK Twittersphere." Forced Migration Forum. 24 February 2017. https://forcedmigrationforum.com/2017/02/24/the-refugee-stories-captivating-the-uk-twittersphere.

Smith, Saphora. "From Syria to Cologne in a Wheelchair: Why 17-Year-Old Nujeen Is Malala's New Hero." *Telegraph*, 27 October 2016. http://www.telegraph.co.uk/women/life/from-syria-to-cologne-in-a-wheelchair-why-17-year-old-nujeen-is.

Spagnuolo, Natalie, and Hadayt Nazami. "Canada's Dismal Treatment of Disabled Immigrants or 'How to Build a Disability-Free Country." Global Disability Watch. 14 November 2016. http://globaldisability.org/2016/11/14/canadas-dismal-treatment-disabled-immigrants-build-disability-free-country.

Szczepanik, Marta. "The 'Good' and 'Bad' Refugees? Imagined Refugeehood(s) in the Media Coverage of the Migration Crisis." *Journal of Identity and Migration Studies* 10, no. 2 (2016): 23–33.

Terry, Jennifer. *Attachments to War: Biomedical Logics and Violence in Twenty-First-Century America*. Durham, NC: Duke University Press, 2017.

Ticktin, Miriam I. *Casualties of Care: Immigration and the Politics of Humanitarianism in France*. Berkeley: University of California Press, 2011.

Titchkosky, Tanya. "The Ends of the Body as Pedagogic Possibility." *Review of Education, Pedagogy, and Cultural Studies* 34, no. 3–4 (2012): 82–93.
UNHCR. "1986 The People of Canada." Last modified 2018. http://www.unhcr.org/subsites/nansen/4ad5dc559/1986-people-canada.html?query=1986%20nansen%20award.
– "Refugee Resettlement Facts [Fact sheet]." Last modified April 2017. http://www.unhcr.ca/wp-content/uploads/2017/04/Canadian-Resettlement-Fact-Sheet-ENG-April-2017.pdf.
Walker, Peter, and Adam Withnall. "Donald Trump's Muslim Ban: Steve Jobs Was Son of Syrian Migrant." *Independent*, 25 January 2017. https://www.independent.co.uk/news/world/americas/donald-trump-muslim-ban-steve-jobs-apple-son-of-syrian-migrant-refugee-mexico-border-wall-a7544636.html
We Day. "Empowering a Generation of Change-Makers." https://www.we.org/we-day/what-is-we-day.
Wettergren, Åsa. "Mobilization and the Moral Shock: Adbusters Media Foundation." In *Emotions and Social Movements*. Edited by Helena Flam and Debra King, 99–118. New York: Routledge, 2005.

8 Cross-Racial Refugee Fiction: Dionne Brand's *What We All Long For*

DONALD GOELLNICHT

Refugee Fiction

Narrative, or storytelling, is central to the process of claiming refugee status in any modern political system that abides by the UN's 1951 Convention Relating to the Status of Refugees; indeed, the asylum seeker often has nothing but their story on which to base their claim for asylum, since they usually flee their home country without documents or other forms of evidence to support their claims. The ability for refugees to narrate their stories in a hearing before a refugee board panel has been an integral part of the refugee determination process in Canada since 1985, but such storytelling has never been a simple process of narrating "the facts." Marita Eastmond insightfully explains the relationship between truth/facts, experience, and representation in the refugee's narration process, dividing it into parts: "*life as lived*, the flow of events that touch on a person's life; *life as experienced*, how the person perceives and ascribes meaning to what happens, drawing on previous experience and cultural repertoires; and *life as told*, how experience is framed and articulated in a particular context and to a particular audience."[1] She stresses that "What is remembered and told is also situational, shaped not least through the contingencies of the encounter between narrator and listener and the power relationship between them,"[2] so much so that it may be impossible to ever reconstruct "life as lived." As Carrie Dawson points out, the many impediments to a claimant narrating her story "include language barriers, the difficulties of testifying to trauma, cultural and gendered injunctions against speaking about the source of that trauma, the inquisitorial nature of hearings, and the prescriptive nature of the written submission upon which the hearing is based [in Canada]."[3] Such barriers not only impede the claimant who is expected to produce testimony; they also impede the listener's ability to "hear" and understand the claimant's story.[4]

The narrative that will be "acceptable" or convincing to a Refugee Board will be built on verifiable facts, credibility, and consistency, drawing on such narrative techniques as coherence and linear chronology, together with ideological stability, all of which are considered essential to "truth telling" in this type of bureaucratic performance. In reality, however, most refugees are the "survivors" of traumatic experiences in their home countries (what they are fleeing), in their temporary places of refuge (often an enclosed camp), and in their host countries (which often put them through new traumas such as detention and other forms of discrimination). There is a considerable body of theory demonstrating that traumatic memory is usually fragmented, messy, incoherent, repressed, elided, silenced, maybe even forgotten in aid of psychic survival. John Chr. Knudsen observes that for those suffering from trauma and depression, laconic speech and silence are common responses to the requirement to testify about flight,[5] while Rousseau, Crépeau, Foxen, and Houle point out that accounts of experience can be altered by trauma in ways that include distorted spatial and temporal perception, dissociation, memory blockage, and difficulty concentrating.[6] Y-Dang Troeung, following Aihwa Ong and others, has complicated the matter further by raising the important question of whether Western psychiatric approaches to the workings of trauma are adequate to comprehending – and assisting – Southeast Asians, whose understanding of trauma often operates within a Buddhist spiritual epistemology.[7]

In the face of broad evidence of the difficulties that refugees encounter in producing a narrative that will genuinely represent their experience and satisfy the demands of the host state, which is usually looking to find "holes" or discrepancies in the claimant's narrative, this chapter asks whether the creative writer might have a particular responsibility to convincingly represent refugee experience in a way that the refugee often cannot, for both political and psychological reasons, and in the process to make the listener to refugee narratives more understanding and empathetic. This chapter will focus on the possibilities and problems involved in cross-racial fictional narratives, those in which the race of the author does not match up with the race of the refugee characters being depicted. These issues will be taken up in relation to Dionne Brand's celebrated novel *What We All Long For*, which narrates a Vietnamese refugee family's story from a position outside the Vietnamese ethnic/national community. Finally, in considering these issues, the chapter will also consider the related question of whether the goal of understanding via fictional narrative which leads to empathy and compassion might itself be a misguided objective that places too much restriction on the artist/writer, assumes the right of the listener/audience/reader to intrude into the intimate memories of refugees, and diverts attention from the ethical responsibilities of nation-states. In turning to Brand's novel, the chapter examines an alternative genre to the discursive regimes of state policy that define and police refugees, to media representations of refugees, and to fictional or life-writing narratives produced by refugees themselves. Rather, the focus rests on the potentialities and possibilities of what might be called refugee-ally fiction or, to use Brand's term, "kinship" fiction.

Art provides an alternative way of exploring refugee narratives, one freed of the life-or-death burden often carried by actual refugee narratives delivered before a state tribunal and, accordingly, liberated to experiment with different ways of representing refugee subjectivity and experience. While the refugee narrative presented to a tribunal must be factual, linear, clear, and consistent, fictional representations often gain their power from a licence to imagine refugee subjectivity and especially the psychic states caused by refugee trauma. A significant aspect of this discursive strategy is the literary form employed, which is often fragmentary, incoherent, elliptical, and meditative, designed to create understanding of the refugee's mental state, even if that involves an understanding that the refugee's mental state cannot be grasped, known, or understood, or needs to be grasped and understood within a different cultural or religious epistemology. Its telling also grants the refugee subject an agency that transcends victimhood. An excellent illustration of this type of literary form, similar in some ways to Brand's *What We All Long For*, is Madeleine Thien's *Dogs at the Perimeter*, a novel about the horrors of the Khmer Rouge genocide in Cambodia and a refugee who survives such catastrophic trauma to live in Canada. Thien herself is not of Cambodian background or a refugee. Guy Beauregard points out that *Dogs at the Perimeter* was often poorly reviewed, "variously characterized ... as 'sometimes confusing reading' (Lalonde), 'difficult to follow' (Grubisic), 'convoluted' (Gordon), 'abrupt' and 'bewildering' (Foran), and 'disjointed, impressionistic, almost incoherent' (Marchand)."[8] Beauregard argues convincingly that "reading Thien's novel ... opens up space for us to rethink the critical language we need to read difficult histories across the North and the South, even as such a language remains persistently out of reach."[9]

Dionne Brand reviewed *Dogs at the Perimeter* and, not surprisingly, she praises rather than critiques the difficulty Thien's fictional form poses for the reader: "Thien's project is a bold and difficult one. It is the project of our age, one that resists narrative, one that overwhelms narrative;

one that is ultimately impossible to narrate fully, namely to traverse that place that human beings traverse at the soul's murkiest."[10] Brand's bold proclamation calls into question once more the very possibility of refugee claimants narrating their "whole truth" before a refugee board, not because they are intentionally lying but because their monumental trauma cannot be fully narrated. Yet Brand does not see this as a sign of defeat for the novelist; rather, the novelist must find new ways of telling these stories of unspeakable trauma. As she says, "what [Thien] also seems to tell us is that to describe human despair in despairing language or documentary language or journalistic language has already numbed us and so these details need another means of transport so that we may not look away. The genocide of the Khmer Rouge has become iconic, evacuated of the real, and Thien's narrative strives to shift our gaze back to the real."[11] The role of the fiction writer, rather than being diminished, is enhanced; a profound responsibility falls on her "to shift our gaze back to the real" by using narrative techniques that "transport" us to the truth rather than simply showing or telling us that truth. At the same time, though, Brand knows that such narrative transport cannot end in successful resolution, must inevitably come to an inconclusive close:

> We are left with the accumulation of stories of brokenness, of silences in the face of damage. "Every day we woke on a knife edge and ran along it," the narrator [of *Dogs at the Perimeter*] says. Not many of us in North America know this knife's edge, although some certainly have known and do. Many of us have not experienced the utter failure of a state, the arbitrary cruelties and the clinical bloodiness that follow. Oceans away, we inhabit a discourse of innocence even when we are deeply implicated.[12]

Brand here implicates the West, including Canada, in the Cambodian genocide and other such profound atrocities, resulting from Western colonial/imperial projects, that produce refugees in the first place. She thus discloses the ethical responsibility of Western states that would cast themselves simply as innocent humanitarian saviours of refugees. Authors, she suggests, have a gift to portray these "stories of brokenness, of silence," but also a responsibility to uncover those who are culpable in the name of justice: "Thien points us to the imagination as salve. Yet the imagination can also produce the catastrophic."[13]

What We All Long For

In an attempt to understand what fiction might contribute to the representation of refugee subjectivity, I turn now to a more sustained reading of *What We All Long For*, a novel that presents and argues for cross-racial kinship. Brand is a Black lesbian feminist, originally from the Caribbean, who has been established in Canada for many years, a celebrated author and activist who has won several awards for her poetry and fiction. I argue that this type of cross-racial narration, embodying what Brand calls the "kinship" created by literature, can offer a more resistant position from which to be critical of the Canadian state and its self-conception as an exceptional site of humanitarian refuge. *What We All Long For* charts the attempts of four young protagonists of colour, living in downtown Toronto, to forge a future-oriented, multicultural community that differs from – but is inevitably haunted by – their parents' transnational migrant – immigrant and refugee – pasts. Brand's multicultural imperative is evident in the four second-generation Canadian protagonists and the one Vietnamese narrator in the novel who share the narrative spotlight: Tuyen, a Vietnamese Canadian; Carla, a mixed-race, Italian-Jamaican Canadian; Jackie, a Black Canadian whose parents have migrated from Halifax to Toronto; Oku, a Black Caribbean Canadian of undisclosed national origin; and Quy, Tuyen's brother, who reminisces about his experiences as a refugee in Southeast Asia for most of the novel. Brand thus disperses the novel's centre of consciousness across a variety of registers of difference and across a number of borders, producing a narrative whose form establishes a collective identity. It is important to acknowledge, too, that her four Torontonian protagonists of colour represent half of the contemporary city, as roughly 50 per cent of Toronto's population is made up of "visible minorities." The novel constitutes a powerful example of a narrative that transports us to the real, with Brand focusing on the psychic dangers of both remembering and forgetting the past. She writes back to statist power by capturing in fiction the traumatic past that usually cannot be conveyed in conventional narratives.

Brand's creation of Vietnamese voices and characters from a position outside of the Vietnamese Canadian community may be viewed in at least two ways: as cultural appropriation or as a "transgressive text." Appropriation of voice emerged as a controversial issue in Canada in the late 1980s and 1990s, focused initially on the question of whether non-Indigenous writers should tell Indigenous stories (which often involve sacred cultural knowledge) or write in Indigenous voices, but then expanded to tackle the issue of white writers dealing with communities of colour more broadly.[14] This debate exploded again recently with the "appropriation prize" debacle in 2017.[15] Writing about American literature, Shelley Fisher Fishkin takes a very different approach to this issue. In her article "Desegregating American Literary Studies,"

Fishkin complains about "the essentialist paradigms that are the inheritance of a segregated curriculum" and posits the concept of "transgressive texts," in which the race of the author and of her/his protagonist(s) do not align, as texts that challenge such segregation.[16] Her argument is premised on the claim that "we are all hurt by an identity politics that assumes that only black writers may be relied upon to write truthfully about African Americans, or that only white writers may be depended upon to tell the truths about whites";[17] she further suggests that this logic can be extended to the writing of other racialized groups. In a similar vein, but shifting attention from creative writing to scholarly projects more broadly, Colleen Lye poses an important question: "In embracing pluralism and cosmopolitanism ... how can we guard against an ever-greater dependency on biological notions of identity to help us order our epistemological projects?"[18] Lye argues that Asian American scholars need to generate theories "of speaking not of identity but of form, of trying to investigate race and nation through the relationship between aesthetic and social modalities of form."[19] I consider Brand's novel to be engaging in such an investigation of race and the Canadian nation through its aesthetic form.

With its cross-racial voices, *What We All Long For* has been praised as Brand's most positively multicultural novel, in which she presents Toronto as a forward-looking place where young people from different racial, sexual, and class backgrounds can come together to forge a future. But such an exclusive view downplays or ignores the novel's careful attention to the parents' traumatic pasts, especially that of Tuyen's Vietnamese parents, as well as its privileging of the narrative of the lost refugee brother, Quy. Quy functions as the allegorical embodiment of the loss involved in diasporic scattering, literalizing the catastrophic trauma that haunts survivors.[20] Brand, like Agamben, to whom I will turn at the conclusion of this chapter, insists on the figure of the refugee who haunts the present, as the ground upon which to create her globalized urban space of *critical* multiculturalism.[21]

Part of Brand's establishing a generation of critical multicultural subjects in Toronto involves eschewing all ethnic classifications and identities in favour of an identity grounded, not in the old nation to which traditional diasporans look homeward nostalgically, nor in the contemporary Canadian nation-state. Rather, Brand's young protagonists' subjectivities are located in the postmodern city, with an emphasis on the present and the future; in form, as several critics have observed, hers is a novel of the critically multicultural, postmodern, global city. Her protagonists claim that they consciously break with their parents' backward-looking nostalgia that searches for an identity grounded in some pure ethnic consciousness carried with them from the past: "Most days they smoked outside school together, planning and dreaming their own dreams of what they would be if only they could get out of school and leave home. No more stories of what might have been, no more diatribes on what would happen back home, down east, down the islands, over the South China Sea, not another sentence that began in the past that had never been their past."[22]

But just as they do not cling to their parents' diasporic longing for homeland, neither do they naïvely buy into official multiculturalism's soapy message of Canada as a tolerant, colour-blind or post-racial society where difference is simply celebrated and where asylum seekers are welcomed from various parts of the world. They know that "they weren't the required race" – i.e., white – to succeed in Canada, and they refuse to "act the brown-noser, act the fool" (47) in order to be accepted or tolerated. They are aware of the limitations and discriminations they face, but they still operate with hope in the future, looking forward, racing across the city, rather than remaining static or looking backwards to the past. No matter what difficulties they face – and there are many – they maintain a faith in their abilities to forge a future based on cultural hybridity or syncretism, continuously built and rebuilt in the negotiations across forms of difference grounded in race, ethnicity, gender, sexuality, and class. *What We All Long For* operates, then, in opposition to the kind of official multicultural narrative that is employed by the state to fix racial and ethnic identities in the project of managing racialized and ethnicized communities. Drawing on the centrality of critique in interdisciplinary fields like "critical race studies," "critical ethnic studies," and "critical refugee studies," the term "critical multiculturalism" as applied to Brand's novel captures the importance of interrogating the underlying imperatives of official state multiculturalism to manage racialized minorities so as to maintain white privilege and supremacy, while also attending to forms of intersectional alliance and agency across difference that are created among racialized and other disadvantaged communities.

This sense of hope and futurity, as I noted earlier, is the aspect of Brand's novel that has caught the attention of critics so powerfully. Diana Brydon exemplifies this dominant approach:

> The shift in Dionne Brand's work from a diasporic mourning of loss in *A Map to the Door of No Return* to the more multiply constituted engagements of *What We All Long For* ... may be the most remarked upon change in direction in postcolonial Canadian thinking about the need to form new ways of connecting beyond the loyalties of the past and the potential of

Toronto as a global city. Brand's second generation Torontonians are closer to Hardt and Negri's multitude than to the immigrants, exiles or diasporas of an earlier generation; their communal links are more rhizomatic than genealogical; yet they are also fully rooted in their own time and place.[23]

Kit Dobson goes so far as to claim that Brand now views notions of belonging and of home as a nostalgic trap for feminists of colour.[24] Joanne Leow is one of the few critics who have tempered this celebratory view of the novel, pointing to the dark side of its globalizing vision that emerges in Quy's narrative, which she labels "a kind of pessimistic ballast to the novel."[25] I too will argue that Quy's presence in the novel disrupts the futurity that the younger generation embraces, reminding them – and us as readers – of the past losses that remain unreconciled and that continue to haunt the present and future.

While I can agree that there is a new-found optimism evident in this novel, I remain concerned about the binary opposition that is implicitly established when critics read the first-generation parents – immigrants, migrants, refugees, exiles – as deluded, as inevitably inferior, doomed to failure because they hold on melancholically to the past or repress it in order simply to survive. According to Dobson, the parents' generation is "split between feelings of limited belonging to the nation-state and intense nostalgia"[26] for the lost home, affects that undermine any sense of achievement and belonging in Canada. Their powerful melancholia, their intense loss, is not a choice they can make; it cannot be dismissed so easily.

Brand emphasizes the significance of traumatic pasts in the way that the different sets of parents are given unequal coverage in the text: perhaps surprisingly, it is not Carla's Black Jamaican father or Jackie's Black Haligonian parents or Oku's Black Caribbean (probably Trinidadian) parents who are the narrative focus, although Brand's brief evocations of them are brilliant, at times Morrisonian in their calling up of specific histories that inevitably accompany migrants to large global cities; rather, it is the difficult life of the Vietnamese refugee family that gets the most attention in Brand's portrayal of the older generation. Tuyen, her parents, Tuan and Cam, and her siblings are the central family, and her missing brother Quy, who was literally lost in the confusion of dispersal as the family escaped Vietnam by boat, emerges from the outset as an important character, one who poses a significant challenge to the optimism of his generation. He is the only first-person narrator in the novel; he is the first character to be identified by name; and his sections are the only ones that have a titular name: *Quy*. Indeed, as Brand explains, the name Quy means "precious" in Vietnamese (65).[27] His narrative is thus privileged, giving us through the first-person voice an *apparently* unmediated and accurate representation of Vietnameseness and refugeeness: a seemingly authentic, first-person refugee account. His narrative erupts periodically to disrupt the Toronto narrative – as the transnational Asian narrative moves to intersect with the Toronto one. Quy is the allegorical embodiment of the loss involved in diasporic scattering, yet that loss is temporarily regained when he finds his way to Toronto years later as a young man, only to be lost again as he is left dying at the end of the novel before he can be reunited with his grieving parents. Quy performs in an embodied way the kind of repetition compulsion symptomatic of catastrophic trauma. As Cathy Caruth observes, trauma cannot be comprehended at the moment of the traumatic event, nor can it be worked through later, so it continues to haunt the survivors long after the event, even, according to Marianne Hirsch and others, passing down to the next generation.[28]

At the same time as Brand suggests the authenticity of Quy's story, however, she also undermines any such sense of certainty we as readers may think we have achieved. She does this by turning Quy from an innocent child into a skilled con artist when, as a virtual orphan, he is "adopted" in the Malaysian refugee camp Pulau Bidong by a Buddhist monk who trains him in the strategies of how to survive by means of con games. Given Quy's expertise in conning his audience, his reliability as a narrator becomes dubious, which is why his sister, Tuyen, remains suspicious of his story – a move that invites readers to exercise similar caution, notwithstanding Quy's "authenticity" as a refugee. From the outset, Quy asserts that Pulau Bidong was "A place where identity was watery, up for grabs" (9). Much later, he tells us outright: "I'm not a person to be trusted. People always trust me, though" (218), and we are left to question whether the resurrected man who arrives in Toronto years later is the boy who was lost in the South China Sea. Arriving off the coast of BC, claiming refugee status, and being taken into detention, Quy proclaims: "There's something to anonymity, stereotype, being part of the hordes. It can be a camouflage. Did I tell the Amnesty people who I was? Who I'd been? No. What for? ... Yes, I'm innocent of all things. Yes, I'm guilty of all things" (286–7). In a bold move, Brand complicates and problematizes the relationship of the present to the past in narrating refugee experience: the refugee subject continues to haunt and shape the present, yet access to that past is never unmediated and wholly reliable. The refugee can use this unreliability to her/his advantage, to reclaim a form of agency, as Quy does, by being the trickster, by telling the parts of his story that will work to his advantage in different situations; but the refugee is also held hostage to her/his traumatic past that often cannot, in the end, be papered over.

For this very reason, Tuyen's parents, like Quy, have learned to keep their complicated family history separate from their official refugee story, as Brand so eloquently emphasizes:

> Only when they arrived in Toronto would they fully construct their departure as resistance to communism. That is the story the authorities needed in order to fill out the appropriate forms. They needed terror, and indeed Tuan and Cam had had that; they needed loss, and Tuan and Cam had had that too. And perhaps with this encouragement, this coaxing of their story into a coherent wholeness, they were at least officially comforted that the true horror was not losing their boy but the forces of communism, Vietnam itself, which they were battling. Whatever the official story, her mother's cache of photographs told another, a parallel story, a set of *possible stories*, an exquisite corpse. (225)

The exquisite corpse in the form of Quy is precisely what arrives in Toronto to haunt the family, to unsettle their official anti-communist narrative required by the Canadian state and to remind them of the "true horror" of losing their son. The exquisite corpse lying in the roadway near their Richmond Hill home – the house a symbol of their official story of refugee "success" – is the past they cannot face and yet cannot live without.

With these parallel stories, "a set of possible stories," Brand illustrates not that some refugee stories are lies, but rather that there are layers and layers of truths, some personal and intimate, others more acceptable – often for ideological reasons – to state institutions like refugee boards. She evidences the fact that for the refugee, past trauma is almost never "past"; it haunts the present, sometimes erupting violently into the "here" of everyday life in Canada, refusing to be contained in a neat, acceptable narrative of what happened "over there." Her novel is, then, not simply a counter-narrative to the official requirement for coherent, linear, factual narratives of refugee experience; it calls into question the very method of narrative required by refugee boards to determine legitimacy. Asylum seekers are compelled to choose between these various truths in order to navigate through a difficult system; the fiction writer, however, can reveal these different narrative frames as a way of helping readers to understand the impossible choices asylum seekers face as they attempt to deal with their own psychic and material wounds while producing a narrative that will meet the expectations of the laws of receiving states.

"Kinship" and Empathy

Despite the brilliant complications and complexities of her aesthetic form – or perhaps because she is fearful that revealing these complexities and complications will make some readers suspicious of refugee claims – Brand also insists on the empathy that a cross-racial narrative can generate. She emphasizes the Vietnamese narrative in *What We All Long For* as a transgressive text, in which she as a Black writer has produced what may very well have been the first Vietnamese Canadian novel. She is proud of having written a novel that at least some Vietnamese Canadians identify with. In her convocation address at Wilfrid Laurier University, where she received an Honorary Doctorate of Letters degree in June 2012, Brand tells a story that exemplifies empathy as an effect of her novel:

> At a reading once in Calgary of my last novel, *What We All Long For*, a woman waited in the book line and when she approached me I noticed she was in tears. And the book was in part about a Vietnamese family who had arrived in Toronto after the Vietnam War, and who were wrecked and broken after losing their son in the crush and panic of that time. And the woman who approached me weeping asked me, when she got to me: "How did you know? How did you know?" I was taken aback but then understood what she was saying and rose to comfort her. She had been a refugee from Vietnam herself and found a similarity between herself and the characters in the book. Kinship, that is what literature means!

Here, Brand is not claiming that she has produced in her novel an authentic Vietnamese Canadian narrative or refugee narrative, whatever that might be (even though she did a great deal of research on the Vietnamese narrative). Rather, she claims that her text gets the Vietnamese story *right enough* that it has the affective power to resonate with Vietnamese refugees. It creates a sense of kinship across lines such as race, gender, sexuality, and class. I suggested earlier that Brand may be able to achieve this affective response of empathy because she is herself a Black lesbian feminist immigrant to Canada from the Caribbean, someone who knows the experience of outsider status, of state and personal discrimination, of abjection and the claiming of agency. Freed of any need to produce a narrative of refugee gratitude, she is able to be more critical of the Canadian nation and to dispel notions of Canadian exceptionalism in the treatment of refugees and other migrants. She is also free to explore many of the "possible stories" that refugees can tell, to exhume and examine the "exquisite corpse" of the refugee's past without the coroner's imperative to produce a set of facts that will stand up in court. In the process, she wants her novel to create understanding of the asylum seeker's extreme plight and thus to produce empathy and compassion in her readers. Empathy, however, is a contested concept in refugee studies.

Empathy is usually invoked as the necessary or desired affect for those in the host country to feel towards those seeking refuge; indeed, many scholars consider empathy to be essential to our understanding of refugee subjectivity. Bridget Hayden, for example, states: "The significant factor that distinguishes a refugee from other people who cross borders, people who are internally displaced, or indeed from those who have not moved at all but live in abysmal conditions, is the sense of responsibility and either pity or empathy we feel for them. 'Refugee,' like all other such categories, is a relational term."[29] Caroline Wake also considers empathy as significant in theatre that performs the "witnessing" of asylum seekers: "the figure of the performing witness refers to the observer who becomes so ethically and *empathetically* engaged in or by a performance that he or she is transformed from a passive watcher into an active witness."[30]

Some feminist and queer theorists, however, reject the importance of empathy and understanding across categories of difference on psychological and ideological grounds. Patti Lather, drawing on the work of Douglas Crimp, Elizabeth Ellsworth, and Doris Sommer, argues that the concept of empathy leading to understanding constitutes a liberal move that is "premised on structures that all people share" and that "reduces otherness to sameness within a personalized culture."[31] Such a move towards empathy, she claims, collapses genuine, messy difference between observer and observed, reader and text, rejects "counter-practices of queering, disidentifying, denaturalizing and defamiliarizing," and thus enacts the very kind of imperial violence, the voyeuristic right to know the Other, that it claims to oppose.[32]

Discussing the role of empathy specifically in the context of actual women refugee claimants in Canada, Sherene Razack writes:

> given the fact that most judges come from dominant groups, they are unlikely to be able to empathize with marginalized groups. In any event, in the area of discrimination ... [Toni] Massaro points out that empathy is not the ultimate goal. It is not enough to try to find ways to communicate to the judge that discrimination is hurtful. It is equally necessary to convince him or her that an action is morally wrong and requires legal sanction.[33]

Razack also stresses that empathy replicates colonial/imperial power relations between North and South, the West and "the Orient," observing that "Tolerance, understanding and compassion are not situations that easily lead to respect ... [T]hese words conceal relations of power and a position of superiority – who is tolerating whom, who enjoys the power and position to be compassionate?"; they also "support the dichotomy of civilized, ordered North/uncivilized, chaotic South" so that "the Immigration Board members [can] see themselves in their 'appropriate' roles as saviours."[34]

Razack bases her critique of empathy on an approach to refugee claims that is grounded in the moral responsibility of Western countries like Canada to accept their complicity or agency in causing or exacerbating the conflicts that produce refugee crises in the first place. In other words, she argues for an approach that focuses on large structural issues rather than small interpersonal ones. Razack's dismissal of empathy, understanding, and compassion is also predicated on the assumption that the observer, audience member, judge, or refugee board member is white, straight, and patriarchal. This raises for me two questions: Can art that tackles refugee issues effectively focus on large structural injustices or is the strength of art to represent the interpersonal, to operate in an affective register? Second, what happens to the dynamics of power between narrator and listener when the writer creating the story of Others is not white, straight, patriarchal but instead occupies some form of minoritized subjectivity, as Brand does?[35] Razack herself offers something of an indirect answer to this second question in a later article titled "Stealing the Pain of Others: Reflections on Canadian Humanitarian Responses." Here, Razack, building on the work of Saidiya Hartman, Susan Sontag, Sara Ahmed, and others, continues to critique empathy as an affect of consumption, one that allows the Western audience/reader to maintain a sense of superiority, of humanity, by feeding off of or "stealing" the pain of Others – African American slaves, victims of the Rwandan genocide, etc. – who are viewed as inhuman. She distinguishes, however, between white Western artists/narrators and famous slave narrative author Harriet Jacobs/Linda Brent: "Jacobs is a survivor witness while the others are observers once removed. And we, in turn, as consumers of their narratives, are once more distanced."[36] Brand, I would argue, is herself something of a "survivor witness" who uses empathy to convey the experiences of Others, but who also makes us aware of the gaps that we cannot cross in coming to an "understanding" of Others' stories.

I would not want to claim that understanding, empathy, and compassion, which, as Brand emphasizes with her concept of "kinship," can be particular strengths of literary and artistic creation, should replace responsibility to refugees based on state moral and legal obligation. Yet, I do not consider these two approaches to be mutually exclusive. Affects, operating at the interpersonal level, can be strong motivators to moral and political action, as many feminist and queer theorists have long argued. But perhaps more importantly, Brand offers us at the close of *What We All Long For* an example of what can happen when cross-racial understanding and empathy fail. It is no accident that Quy is savagely beaten and left "half-dead by the road" (317) by Jamal, Carla's brother, who is Black, and Bashir, "the son of an ex-Somali" (315). That these two young men, who are themselves oppressed by racist state institutions, see Quy only as "an Asian guy" who possesses a "Beamer X5" that they want to steal, speaks to the failure of cross-racial understanding and compassion that could lead to meaningful alliances – and perhaps also to the ways in which the white state manages not just to keep racialized communities divided but also to have them violently victimize each other.

What Brand achieves through her narrative of Vietnamese refugees is similar to what Nam Le does in his short-story collection, *The Boat*, where he explores what I have called elsewhere "refugee cosmopolitanism" through writing stories about non-Asian subjects that reflect back on that refugee condition.[37] Like Le, Brand takes the position that our political response to refugees should be empathy rather than a demand for certain knowledge or authenticity. In "Beyond Human Rights," building on Hannah Arendt's theorization of the refugee, Agamben states:

> If we want to be equal to the absolutely new tasks ahead, we will have to abandon decidedly, without reserve, the fundamental conceptions through which we have so far represented the subjects of the political (Man, the Citizen and its rights, but also the sovereign people, the worker, and so forth) and build our political philosophy anew starting from the one and only figure of the refugee.[38]

As the limit-case of humanity, stripped of human rights which are guaranteed to citizens by belonging to a nation-state, the refugee, Agamben's figure of bare or sacred life, becomes the test of our abilities to extend human compassion and to accept the human rights of those who no longer belong to a nation-state, those who are outcast and suspended in statelessness. Brand takes up these concerns, inviting her readers to respond ethically to the refugee's extreme but decidedly human condition, to behave as a cosmopolitan humanitarian engaged with abjected cosmopolitan subjects rather than as a suspicious national subject obsessed with security.[39]

It is no accident, then, that Brand maintains the important figure of the refugee as the ground upon which to create her globalized urban space of critical multiculturalism. To the extent that the Vietnamese refugee is the most visible figure of the refugee in the late twentieth century (as the Syrian refugee has become at the start of the twenty-first century), *What We All Long For* acts as a text that argues for cross-cultural syncretism, opens up possibilities for acceptance without certain knowledge, and tells stories that connect us. It prepares the reader, the judge, the refugee board member to listen for the gaps, erasures, repressions, forgettings in testimonial narratives with understanding, if not certainty, and without retributive judgment, thus contributing to a more humane form of hearing. Further, creative fictional representations offer a different way of telling refugee narratives, not bound by state and ideological demands or the weight of private trauma. Cross-racial narratives, written by an author from outside the refugee community, shift our understanding of "refugee narrative" away from an essentialist or biologically determined understanding of the term, by which only refugees can tell their stories. Refugee narratives of this kind free the refugee from always having to provide "testimony," from always having to tell her story to others, to relive trauma, as a condition of existence. Rather, others (creative writers) have to learn (to research, imagine, feel) the refugees' stories and to represent these stories to a national community of readers. In this way, producing "refugee narrative" becomes a profound ethical responsibility.

NOTES

1 Eastmond, "Stories as Lived Experience." Eastmond adds a fourth category: "*life as text*, the researcher's interpretation and representation of the story," which would have to take into account the role of scholars.
2 Ibid., 248–9.
3 Dawson, "The Refugee's Body of Knowledge," 56–7. This chapter is in part an attempt to explore the bold claims that Dawson makes, in this article, for art being an avenue to "a refugee determination process that is both expeditious and humane" (68).
4 There is a large body of research on the difficulties of understanding and assessing refugee narratives within the context of asylum-seeking processes; see, for example, Kirmayer, "Failures of Imagination"; Shuman and Bohmer, "Representing Trauma"; Herlihy and Turner, "The Psychology of Seeking Protection."

Cross-Racial Refugee Fiction   209

5 Knudsen, "When Trust Is on Trial," 13.
6 Rousseau et al., "The Complexity of Determining Refugeehood," 43.
7 Troeung, "Witnessing Cambodia's Disappeared." See also Ong, *Buddha Is Hiding*.
8 Beauregard, "Interwoven Temporalities."
9 Ibid., 169–70.
10 Brand, "Running on the Knife's Edge."
11 Ibid.
12 Ibid.
13 Ibid.
14 For a sustained treatment of this topic, see Ziff and Rao, eds., *Borrowed Power*, especially Part 2 with essays by Lenore Keeshig-Tobias, Rosemary J. Coombe, M. Nourbese Philip, Kwame Dawes, and Joane Cardinal-Shubert.
15 On the "appropriation prize," which morphed into a false debate about "free speech," see Edwards, "What Can We Learn from Canada's 'Appropriation Prize' Literary Fiasco?"
16 Fishkin, "Desegregating American Literary Studies," 128.
17 Ibid., 128.
18 Lye, "In Dialogue with Asian American Studies," 4.
19 Ibid., 6–7.
20 See Chu, "The Repetition Compulsion Revisited."
21 Brand produces a form of writing, an aesthetics, that I would label "critical multiculturalism," or what Rinaldo Walcott calls "everyday multiculturalism." Walcott "invoke[s] Himani Bannerji's term 'popular multiculturalism' or everyday multiculturalism, which are inextricably different from official multiculturalism" in that "Everyday or popular multiculturalism requires us to think about the lives people make across differences and, importantly, connections that produce new modes of relationality and being"; he identifies this modality as central to *What We All Long For* (Walcott, "Against Institution," 19–20).
22 Brand, *What We All Long For*, 47; all future references are to this edition, and page numbers are given in the text in parentheses.
23 Brydon, "Canadian Writers Negotiating Home within Global Imaginaries," 12. See also Dobson, who writes: "Dionne Brand's 2005 novel *What We All Long For* represents a generational shift in the politics of being in Canadian space. In it, young, poor, and racialized characters navigate their lives and loves within the urban space of the Greater Toronto Area ... The daily reality of being non-white within Canada gives them strong anti-national political consciousnesses ... [This] younger generation ... feels little belonging to either the Canadian nation or to their ancestral homes; for them, finding community is a specifically urban project, and they seek to fracture notions of belonging through a focus on the component parts

of that very word: being and longing ... The protagonists of the novel, recognizing the city's incomplete nature, see it as a battleground, as a space for political action and for the creation of a viable sense of self – a space for building culture from below" ("'Struggle Work,'" 88–9).

24 Dobson, *Transnational Canadas*, 185.
25 Leow, "Beyond the Multiculture," 196.
26 Dobson, *Transnational Canadas*, 188.
27 "Quý" means "precious" and is used for Vietnamese names, while "quỷ" means "demon, devil, ghost," a meaning that also resonates for Brand's narrative.
28 See Caruth, *Unclaimed Experience*, and Hirsch, *Family Frames*. In her more recent work *Literature in the Ashes of History*, Caruth shifts focus somewhat in her theory of trauma, with a new emphasis on "Freud's enigmatic move in the theory of trauma from the drive for death to the drive for life, from the reformulating of life around the witness to death to the possibility of witnessing and making history in creative acts of life" (5), a move that resonates with Brand's interest in the younger generation's "creative acts of life."
29 Hayden, "What's in a Name?" 478.
30 Wake, "Through the (In)Visible Witness in *Through the Wire*," 188.
31 Lather, "Against Empathy, Voice and Authenticity," 19.
32 Ibid.
33 Razack, "The Perils of Storytelling for Refugee Women," 167–8.
34 Ibid., 171–2. Rousseau and Foxen come to similar conclusions in their study of affect within the Canadian refugee determination system: "From the IRB [Immigration and Refugee Board] member's side, concepts of empathy and compassion are used to confirm the benevolent image that they, as representatives of a humane system, want to project. Here the unilateral gift of refuge to a helpless victim who is seen as having nothing to offer, reinforces the myth that maintains the hegemony of the system" (Rousseau and Foxen, "Look Me in the Eye," 88).
35 See Troeung, for a discussion of Kim Echlin's cross-racial narrative in *The Disappeared* and, in particular, Echlin's views on storytelling and empathy; Troeung quotes Echlin as stating that "it is the power of imagination that lets us transcend our own personal experience, to have empathy with others and to really encounter the bigger world" ("Witnessing Cambodia's Disappeared," 152).
36 Razack, "Stealing the Pain of Others," 390.
37 Goellnicht, "'Ethnic Literature's Hot.'"
38 Agamben, "Beyond Human Rights," 159.
39 On "abject cosmopolitanism," see Nyers, "Abject Cosmopolitanism."

REFERENCES

Agamben, Giorgio. "Beyond Human Rights." In *Radical Thought in Italy: A Potential Politics*. Edited by Paolo Virno and Michael Hardt, 159–64. Minneapolis: University of Minnesota Press, 1996.

Beauregard, Guy. "Interwoven Temporalities: Reading Madeleine Thien's *Dogs at the Perimeter*." *Studies in Canadian Literature* 39, no. 2 (2014): 169–89.

Brand, Dionne. "Convocation Address." Wilfrid Laurier University, June 2012.

– "Running on the Knife's Edge." Review of *Dogs at the Perimeter*, by Madeleine Thien. *Literary Review of Canada*, December 2011, http://reviewcanada.ca/magazine/2011/12/running-on-the-knifes-edge.

– *What We All Long For*. Toronto: Vintage Canada, 2005.

Brydon, Diana. "Canadian Writers Negotiating Home within Global Imaginaries." Keynote address for "Moving Cultures, Shifting Identities" conference at Flinders University, Australia, 2007, 12.

Caruth, Cathy. *Literature in the Ashes of History*. Baltimore: Johns Hopkins University Press, 2013.

– *Unclaimed Experience: Trauma, Narrative, and History*. Baltimore: Johns Hopkins University Press, 1996.

Chu, James A. "The Repetition Compulsion Revisited: Reliving Dissociated Trauma." *Psychotherapy: Theory, Research, Practice, Training* 28, no. 2 (Summer 1991): 327–32.

Dawson, Carrie. "The Refugee's Body of Knowledge: Storytelling and Silence in the Work of Francisco-Fernando Granados." *Topia: Canadian Journal of Cultural Studies* 29 (2013): 55–72.

Dobson, Kit. "'Struggle Work': Global and Urban Citizenship in Dionne Brand's *What We All Long For*." *Studies in Canadian Literature* 31, no. 2 (2006): 88–104.

– *Transnational Canadas: Anglo-Canadian Literature and Globalization*. Waterloo: Wilfrid Laurier University Press, 2009.

Eastmond, Marita. "Stories as Lived Experience: Narratives in Forced Migration Research." *Journal of Refugee Studies* 20, no. 2 (2007): 248–64.

Edwards, Stassa. "What Can We Learn from Canada's 'Appropriation Prize' Literary Fiasco?" *Jezebel*, 16 May 2017. https://jezebel.com/what-can-we-learn-from-canadas-appropriation-prize-lite-1795175192.

Fishkin, Shelley Fisher. "Desegregating American Literary Studies." In *Aesthetics in a Multicultural Age*. Edited by Emory Elliott et al., 121–34. Oxford: Oxford University Press, 2002.

Goellnicht, Donald. "'Ethnic Literature's Hot': Asian American Literature, Refugee Cosmopolitanism, and Nam Le's *The Boat*." *Journal of Asian American Studies* 15, no. 2 (2012): 197–224.

Hayden, Bridget. "What's in a Name? The Nature of the Individual in Refugee Studies." *Journal of Refugee Studies* 19, no. 4 (2006): 471–87.

Herlihy, Jane, and Stuart W. Turner. "The Psychology of Seeking Protection." *International Journal of Refugee Law* 21, no. 2 (2009): 171–92.

Hirsch, Marianne. *Family Frames: Photography, Narrative, and Postmemory*. Cambridge, MA: Harvard University Press, 1997.

Kirmayer, Lawrence. "Failures of Imagination: The Refugee's Narrative in Psychiatry." *Anthropology and Medicine* 10, no. 2 (2003): 167–85.

Knudsen, John Chr. "When Trust Is on Trial: Negotiating Refugee Narratives." In *Mistrusting Refugees*. Edited by E. Valentine Daniel and John Chr. Knudsen, 13–35. Berkeley: University of California Press, 1995.

Lather, Patti. "Against Empathy, Voice and Authenticity." In *Voice in Qualitative Inquiry: Challenging Conventional, Interpretive, and Critical Conceptions in Qualitative Research*. Edited by Alesia Jackson and Lisa Mazzei, 17–26. New York: Routledge, 2008.

Leow, Joanne. "Beyond the Multiculture: Transnational Toronto in Dionne Brand's *What We All Long For*." *Studies in Canadian Literature* 37, no. 2 (2012): 192–212.

Lye, Colleen. "In Dialogue with Asian American Studies." *Representations* 99, no. 1 (2007): 1–12.

Nyers, Peter. "Abject Cosmopolitanism: The Politics of Protection in the Anti-Deportation Movement." *Third World Quarterly* 24, no. 6 (2003): 1069–93.

Ong, Aihwa. *Buddha Is Hiding: Refugees, Citizenship, the New America*. Berkeley: University of California Press, 2003.

Razack, Sherene. "The Perils of Storytelling for Refugee Women." In *Development and Diaspora: Gender and the Refugee Experience*. Edited by Victoria Foote, Helene Moussa, Penny Van Esterik, and Wenona Giles, 164–74. Dundas, ON: Artemis Enterprises, 1996.

– "Stealing the Pain of Others: Reflections on Canadian Humanitarian Responses." *Review of Education, Pedagogy, and Cultural Studies* 29, no. 4 (2007): 375–94.

Rousseau, Cecile, Francois Crépeau, Patricia Foxen, and France Houle. "The Complexity of Determining Refugeehood: A Multidisciplinary Analysis of the Decision-Making Process of the Canadian Immigration and Refugee Board." *Journal of Refugee Studies* 15, no. 1 (2002): 43–70.

Rousseau, Cecile, and Patricia Foxen. "Look Me in the Eye: Empathy and the Transmission of Trauma in the Refugee Determination Process." *Transcultural Psychiatry* 47, no. 1 (2010): 70–92.

Shuman, Amy, and Carol Bohmer. "Representing Trauma: Political Asylum Narrative." *Journal of American Folklore* 117, no. 466 (2004): 394–414.

Troeung, Y-Dang. "Witnessing Cambodia's Disappeared." *University of Toronto Quarterly* 82, no. 2 (2013): 150–67.

Wake, Caroline. "Through the (In)Visible Witness in *Through the Wire*." *Research in Drama Education* 13, no. 2 (2008): 187–92.

Walcott, Rinaldo. "Against Institution: Established Law, Custom, or Purpose." In *Trans.Canada.Lit: Resituating the Study of Canadian Literature*. Edited by Smaro Kamboureli and Roy Miki, 17–24. Waterloo: Wilfrid Laurier University Press, 2007.

Ziff, Bruce, and Pratima Rao, eds. *Borrowed Power: Essays on Cultural Appropriation*. New Brunswick, NJ: Rutgers University Press, 1997.

Epilogue
The Exceptional and the Ordinary

THY PHU AND VINH NGUYEN

Recently, a Pew Report announced that in 2018 Canada "surpassed" the US for the first time and "now leads the world" in refugee resettlement.[1] The exceptional thus remains a powerful discourse for the Canadian nation-state at a time when concerns about border security have intensified and calls for national protectionism are especially strident. Throughout this book, we have analysed the complex operations of exceptionality in Canada, tracing, in our exploration of *historicization*, how its emergence in and entanglement with settler colonialism and the British Empire stretches commonplace definitions and timelines of refuge(e);[2] and illuminating, in our examination of *convergences*, how exceptionality overlaps with and shapes categories of social organization.

Our contributors demonstrate how the discourse of exceptionality unfolds in three integrally related ways: through the state of exception, humanitarian exceptionalism, and the exceptional refugee. Because exceptionality lies at the core of the state in the sense famously theorized by Agamben, this discourse has been an important mechanism in the construction of Canadian reactions to refugees, whether it be in the denials of entry to Jewish asylum seekers ("none is too many") in 1939 or magnanimous rescues of Indochinese boat people (the often touted number sixty thousand), in detention and deportation of "irregular" migrants or celebrations of entrepreneurial and successful refugees, in the Safe Third Country agreement or the private sponsorship program. The state of exception also undergirds humanitarian exceptionalism, a logic that develops in a Manichean mode, calcifying polarities of good and evil, tolerant and intolerant, and human and alien. This logic, in turn, replicates a meta-narrative about refugees, wherein a before/after structure emphasizes progress from stateless dispossession to safe resettlement, from oppression to liberation.[3]

Significantly, this meta-narrative produces a key figure, namely the exceptional refugee. Refugee exceptionality names the phenomenon in which the extraordinary successes of a few refugees are held up as special cases that prove the rule that all refugees can and should succeed – thereby obscuring the unseemly fact that the infrastructures which determine success are inaccessible to most refugees. For example, under the auspices of the Resettlement Assistance Program, the Canadian government provides only limited financial support and temporary housing to refugees, with the expectation that they will be self-sufficient just a year after arriving in Canada.[4] One of the most notable of these exceptional figures is Ahmed Hussen, who, after fleeing Somalia and coming to Canada with his family when he was a teenager, went on to a distinguished career as a community organizer and activist, before being appointed as minister of immigration, refugees, and citizenship in 2017.[5] In drawing attention to public celebrations of this remarkable story, we seek neither to discredit nor diminish its personal significance for Hussen. Rather, we wish to highlight the conspicuous ways that these celebrations deploy the now familiar conventions of exceptionality so that the refugee who became the minister charged with the safeguarding of Canadian citizenship – and entrusted with the power to determine the direction of refugee policy – is a potent symbol that refuge in Canada makes anything possible and attainable. Indeed, these celebrations frame Hussen's impressive trajectory as one of progress and uplift – from suffering and obscurity to settlement and success – in ways that emblematize the opportunities afforded to refugees in a liberal state like Canada.[6]

For a more fraught account of refugee exceptionality, consider the case of Phan Thị Kim Phúc, the so-called "girl in the picture." After the end of the war in Vietnam, Phan was exploited by the communist state of Vietnam as an emblematic victim of American aggression, and during a layover in Canada in 1992, she defected from the country. Phan's decision to claim refugee status in Canada serves to burnish the nation's self-image as peaceable and benevolent, in notable contrast with the US, whose imperial ambitions, as manifest in its role in the war in Vietnam, have been widely condemned. Because the story behind Phan's journey to Canada aligns neatly with humanitarian exceptionalism, it appears to shore up the discourse's overarching themes of nation-building. And yet, as Vinh Nguyen points out elsewhere,[7] Phan's explanation of her decision to publish her biography suggests that she is not as faithful to the script of humanitarian exceptionalism as it might seem, or, perhaps more accurately, that she has adapted this script to suit her own needs and not just those of the state.[8] At a telling moment in the biography,

Phan acknowledges that she was moved to tell her story not just out of gratitude to the nation for welcoming her but also because, otherwise, she could not economically afford to build a life in Canada.

In this regard, she is not alone, as most refugees require far more resources than the modest assistance made available to them. Here, humanitarian exceptionalism is invoked not just by Canada but also by the refugee. So, while this double invocation on the part of the state and the refugee serves different, by no means mutually exclusive, ends, it would be a mistake to dismiss refugee collaboration in celebratory, state-sanctioned versions of their story as naïve or misguided. Careful attention to the figure of the refugee enables us to discern the subtle yet resounding critique implicit in stories that, at first glance, merely seem to rehearse meta-narratives.

By foregrounding refuge(e) – that is, by attending to the concerns of refugees and taking seriously their desires and objectives – this volume explores the potential for "narrative plenitude," to invoke scholar and novelist Viet Thanh Nguyen's provocative term for ways of expanding the politics of representation to encompass multiplicity and a range of stories.[9] While *Refugee States* emphasizes narrative plenitude in relation to discourses of exceptionality, our contributors also point to notions of the ordinary as a counter to these discourses. As Gada Mahrouse's chapter compellingly shows, consideration of the ordinary is an important means of challenging the constraints posed by exceptionality. Moreover, Peter Nyers's discussions of "haunting" Canadian citizenship, Edward Ou Jin Lee's thinking on refusal as an everyday practice of survival, and Jennifer Adese and Malissa's Phung's dialogue on genealogical emplacement all speak to the specificity of ordinary acts where refuge(e) emerges. How might our understanding of refuge(e) be enhanced if we were to look not to spectacles of crisis and catastrophe but to the mundane and the everyday, phenomena that are often disregarded? Given that the conditions which produce refugees are anything but exceptional – critic Georgina Ramsay points out that the global refugee regime is characterized by what she describes as "ordinary displacements" – the ordinary offers potential insights into narrative plenitude.[10] *Refugee States* provides a glimpse into these possible quotidian experiences through its adumbration in discourses of exceptionality, which we hope will inspire further study into ordinariness.

By foregrounding the concept of refuge(e) and drawing attention to Canada as a key discursive site, this volume thus demonstrates the manifold ways that the nation needs refugees even as it announces itself as answering to refugee needs. At the same time, *Refugee States* has not sought to be comprehensive, recognizing that refuge(e) is a transnational phenomenon and concept whose complexities cannot be exhausted in a single study. Instead, our objectives here are more modest in scope: to further develop critical refugee studies for a Canadian context and, relatedly, to consider how awareness of this context advances this multidisciplinary field. Our contributors contextualize and examine the ways that Canada cultivates and projects its image as an international leader in human rights and refugee resettlement as a means of nation-building and of mediating transnational relationships. The individual chapters unpack how narratives of Canadian humanitarian exceptionalism are constructed and their social, political, and cultural implications.

In highlighting the insights of historicization and convergences, our contributors reveal the disquieting legacies of the British Empire and the ongoing impact of settler colonialism in shaping refuge(e) experiences to and in Canada as a means of sparking further inquiry into the relationship between militarism and humanitarianism, which unfold in still other empires. Taken together, the volume provides a critical refugee studies framework to nuance "refugees" as agential subjects rather than simply passive objects of study, thereby explaining how "refuge" marks an intersectional process imbricated with the politics of race, gender, sexuality, and class, and illuminating the varied forms with which the concepts of "refuge" and "refugee" are articulated.

NOTES

1 That this report disregards the fact that 80 per cent of the current 70.8 million displaced people in the world live in neighbouring countries in the global South demonstrates how Canada continues to receive a disproportionate share of the humanitarian spotlight when the assistance it actually extends is meagre compared to less wealthy nations such as Lebanon, Jordan, and Turkey. See Radford and Connor, "Canada Now Leads the World in Refugee Resettlement."
2 Notably, the legacies of French colonialism, a pivotal part of Canada's history as well as the impetus for many forced migrations, need extensive investigation.
3 Murray, *Real Queer?*
4 "Financial Help – Refugees."
5 Other examples include prominent musician K'naan (Somali-born Keinan Abdi Warsame); award-winning novelist Kim Thúy; Adrienne Clarkson and Michaëlle Jean, who, in 1999 and 2005, respectively, were appointed to the post of governor general, the British monarch's symbolic

representative in Canada; and Peter C. Newman, the influential Czech-born publishing magnate, among many others. This list, though by no means exhaustive, attests to the popular visibility of the figure of the exceptional refugee.

6 See, for example, Porter, "In Canada, an Immigration Minister Who is Himself a Refugee"; "Ahmed Hussen: From Somali Refugee to Canada's Immigration Minister."
7 Vinh Nguyen, "Vietnamese Canadian Refugee Aesthetics." *The Oxford Encyclopedia of Asian American Literature and Culture* (forthcoming).
8 Chong, *The Girl in the Picture*.
9 Viet Thanh Nguyen, "Asian-Americans Need More Movies, Even Mediocre Ones."
10 Ramsay, "Humanitarian Exploits."

REFERENCES

"Ahmed Hussen: From Somali Refugee to Canada's Immigration Minister." *CBC The Current* (2017). https://www.cbc.ca/radio/thecurrent/the-current-for-june-19-2017-1.4164543/ahmed-hussen-from-somali-refugee-to-canada-s-immigration-minister-1.4164622.

Chong, Denise. *The Girl in the Picture: The Story of Kim Phuc, the Photograph, and the Vietnam War*. New York: Penguin, 2001.

"Financial Help – Refugees." Government of Canada. https://www.canada.ca/en/immigration-refugees-citizenship/services/refugees/help-within-canada/financial.html.

Murray, David A.B. *Real Queer?: Sexual Orientation and Gender Identity Refugees in the Canadian Refugee Apparatus*. Lanham: Rowman and Littlefield, 2015.

Nguyen, Viet Thanh. "Asian-Americans Need More Movies, Even Mediocre Ones." *New York Times*, 21 August 2018. https://www.nytimes.com/2018/08/21/opinion/crazy-rich-asians-movie.html.

Porter, Catherine. "In Canada, an Immigration Minister Who Is Himself a Refugee." *New York Times*, 6 September 2017. https://www.nytimes.com/2017/09/06/world/canada/ahmed-hussen-canada-immigration-minister.html.

Radford, Jynnah, and Phillip Connor. "Canada Now Leads the World in Refugee Resettlement." Pew Research Centre, 19 June 2019. https://www.pewresearch.org/fact-tank/2019/06/19/canada-now-leads-the-world-in-refugee-resettlement-surpassing-the-u-s/ Accessed 27 June 2019.

Ramsay, Georgina. "Humanitarian Exploits: Ordinary Displacement and the Political Economy of the Global Refugee Regime." *Critique of Anthropology* (2019).

Contributors

Jennifer Adese (otipemisiwak/Métis) is the Canada Research Chair in Métis Women, Politics, and Community, and an Associate Professor in the Department of Sociology at University of Toronto Mississauga (UTM). Adese's current research examines the contemporary history of Métis women's political organizing, for which she is also the recipient of a SSHRC Insight Development Grant (2019–21) for the project "'No one else can speak for us': Métis Women's Political Organizing, 1970s–Present." Adese is also co-editor of two edited volumes: *New Directions in Contemporary Métis Studies* (with Chris Andersen) from University of British Columbia Press, and *Indigenous Celebrity* (with Robert Alexander Innes) from University of Manitoba Press. Her work has been published in journals such as *TOPIA, American Indian Quarterly, SAIL: Studies in American Indian Literatures, MediaTropes, Decolonization: Indigeneity, Education & Society* (*DIES*), *Public*, and appears in select edited anthologies on Indigenous art, activism, and resistance.

Donald Goellnicht was a Professor of English and Cultural Studies at McMaster University. During a distinguished career that spanned more than three decades, he inspired and mentored a generation of scholars in fields such as Asian North American literature and culture, African American literature, diaspora studies, queer studies, critical race and ethnic studies, and critical refugee studies. Through his numerous publications on Asian North American writers and artists, and collaborative projects – including a special issue of *Essays on Canadian Writing* on "Race" (2002); *Asian North American Identities: Beyond the Hyphen* (2004); and a special issue of *Modern Fiction Studies* on "Theorizing Asian American Fiction" (2010) – he helped establish and build the field of Asian North American studies. His legacy of generous mentorship and committed scholarship is felt throughout Canada and beyond.

222 Contributors

Jennifer Hyndman is currently Associate Vice-President Research at York University, and former Director of the Centre for Refugee Studies from 2013 to 2019. Her research focuses on the geopolitics of forced migration and refugee camps, humanitarian responses to displacement, and refugee resettlement in North America. Current projects focus on private sponsorship (funded by SSHRC), the social determinants of well-being among newcomers (funded by CIHR), and the politics of intersectionality in refugee reception contexts (SSHRC). Hyndman's most recent book is *Refugees in Extended Exile: Living on the Edge*, with Wenona Giles (Routledge, 2017). Hyndman is author of *Dual Disasters: Humanitarian Aid after the 2004 Tsunami* (2011) and *Managing Displacement: Refugees and the Politics of Humanitarianism* (2000), and co-editor with W. Giles of *Sites of Violence: Gender and Conflict Zones* (2004).

Edward Ou Jin Lee is an Associate Professor at the School of Social Work at the Université de Montréal. With a focus on QTBIPOC (queer and trans, Black, Indigenous, and other People of Colour) and migrants, their research projects engage in critical, participatory, community-based, and digital research methodologies, and draw from critical race feminist theories, intersectionality, and queer/trans diasporic and decolonial critique. Ed's practice interests include critical, anti-oppressive, and anti-racist decolonizing social work, particularly within the context of social policy advocacy and community organizing.

Laura Madokoro is a historian and Associate Professor in the Department of History at Carleton University. Her research explores the entangled history of migrants, refugees, humanitarians, and state authorities in shaping the possibilities and experiences of refuge. She is the author of *Elusive Refuge: Chinese Migrants in the Cold War* (Harvard University Press, 2016) and co-editor of *Dominion of Race: Rethinking Canada's International History* (University of British Columbia, 2017). Her work has appeared in a number of journals, including the *Journal of Refugee Studies*, *Refuge*, and the *Canadian Historical Review*, and she also contributes regularly to print and social media, including www.activehistory.ca where she is a member of the editorial collective.

Gada Mahrouse is an Associate Professor at the Simone de Beauvoir Institute at Concordia University in Montreal. Her interdisciplinary work is informed by critical race studies, transnational feminist cultural studies frameworks, and post/anti-colonial theories. Mahrouse's areas of research have focused on sites including transnational solidarity activism; political, ethical, or alternative tourism; humanitarian and social justice awareness-raising campaigns; feminist pedagogies; and race in Quebec. Her book, *Conflicted Commitments: Race, Privilege and Power in Transnational Solidarity Activism* (McGill-Queen's University Press, 2014), explored anti-racist challenges to transnational solidarity movements. It won the *Women's and Gender Studies et Recherches Féministes* Outstanding Scholarship Prize in 2016. Her work has been published in a number of journals, including *International Journal of Cultural Studies*, *Citizenship Studies*, *Race and Class*, and *ACME: An International E-Journal for Critical Geographies*.

Vinh Nguyen is an Associate Professor of English at Renison University College, University of Waterloo. He specializes in Asian North American literature and culture and critical refugee studies. He held a SSHRC Vanier Canada Graduate Scholarship, a Sir James Lougheed Award of Distinction, and a Harry Lyman Hooker Fellowship, among other honours. He is the 2017 recipient of the John C. Polanyi Prize in Literature. His writing can be found or is forthcoming in *Social Text*, *MELUS*, *ARIEL*, *Canadian Literature*, *Life Writing*, and *Canadian Review of American Studies*.

Peter Nyers is University Scholar and Professor of the Politics of Citizenship and Intercultural Relations in the Department of Political Science at McMaster University. His research focuses on the social movements of non-status refugees and migrants, in particular their campaigns against deportation and detention and for regularization and global mobility rights. He is the author of *Irregular Citizenship, Immigration, and Deportation* (Routledge, 2019) and *Rethinking Refugees: Beyond States of Emergency* (Routledge, 2006). He is also a chief editor of the journal *Citizenship Studies*.

Thy Phu is a Professor at the University of Toronto. She is the author of *Picturing Model Citizens: Civility in Asian American Visual Culture* (2012) and co-editor (2014) of *Feeling Photography*. In addition to this book, coedited with Vinh Nguyen, she has completed two others, *Warring Visions: Photography and Vietnam* and an edited volume entitled *Cold War Camera* (both forthcoming from Duke University Press). Her research explores the intersections between visual studies, critical race studies, transnational American studies, and transpacific critique. She is also Principal Investigator for The Family Camera Network, which collects and preserves family photos and stories about them (familycameranetwork.org).

Malissa Phung is honoured and privileged to live and work as an uninvited guest on the territories of the Huron-Wendat, Mississauga, Haudenosaunee, and Anishnaabe peoples. She is a second-generation settler descendant of Sino-Vietnamese refugees who have resettled on the territories of the Cree, Blackfoot, Métis, Nakado, and Tongva peoples. A professor in the School of Communication and Literary Studies at Sheridan College, she currently teaches Communications, Composition, and Rhetoric, Popular Literature, and Cultural Studies. Her teaching and research interests focus on Indigenous and Asian relations, Asian diasporic culture, decolonial advocacy, and anti-racism in an intersectional framework. Some of her writing has been published in academic journals such as *Postcolonial Text*, *Canadian Literature*, *Asian Diasporic Visual Cultures of the Americas*, and *Verge*, as well as in the 2011 volume of the Aboriginal Healing Foundation series entitled *Cultivating Canada: Reconciliation through the Eyes of Cultural Diversity*.

Johanna Reynolds is a research and project coordinator at York University's Centre for Refugee Studies and an affiliate of the Centre for Oral History and Digital Storytelling at Concordia University. Johanna's research focuses on discursive and spatial strategies of exclusion within Canadian refugee and border policies and practices. Her work is informed by feminist and political geography, critical refugee studies, and critical border studies scholarship. She has published in *Refuge: Canada's Journal on Refugees* and the *International Journal of Migration and Border Studies* and has co-created a multi-media digital archive that centres the experiences of people displaced across multiple borders. Johanna is actively involved in refugee advocacy and migrant rights networks.

Alia Somani is a professor of English at Sheridan College, and she holds a PhD from Western University. Her research project explores the intersections between memory and nation-formation and considers two events in Canada's past that symbolize the exclusion of racialized minorities from the nation: the 1914 *Komagata Maru* Incident and the 1985 Air India bombing. Alia's publications have appeared in various journals, including *South Asian Diaspora*, *Postcolonial Text*, and *TOPIA: Canadian Journal of Cultural Studies*. In addition to her academic work, Alia has written and directed a play about the *Komagata Maru* Incident, and she organizes regular events around South Asian history and culture at Sheridan College.

Index

Page numbers in italics denote tables and figures.

academia, 126, 134, 139–40n40
Adese, Jennifer, 122–4, 126, 129–30
advertisements, 65
Afghans, 27
Africans, 30, 40–1, *40*
Agamben, Giorgio, 4–5, 9, 207, 215
agency, 5, 131–2
Al Moulia, Hani, 177–9, 181
Albright, Madeleine, 87–8
American exceptionalism, 10
American Revolution, 105
anger, 61, 62
anti-Black logics, 160
anti-sex laws, 151, 164nn45–7
Antonio (migrant), 155–6, 157–8
Arafeh, Lina, 183
Arat-Koç, Sedef, 149
Arendt, Hannah, 9
Ariel (migrant), 154–5
arrivant, defined, 137n1
assimilation, 134–5, 139n40, 149, 182
asylum seekers: choosing truths, 203; vs. chosen refugees, 25; definition, 25; deterring, 42–3; and feelings of officials, 180; legitimacy, 25–6, 30–1; number of applications (2012/13), 43; as "queue jumping," 32; vs. refugees, 29, 34, 37; Safe Third Country Agreement (STCA), 26; Singh Decision, 47n49; UN Convention Relating to the Status of Refugees (1951), 28–9; as uninvited, 25
autoethnographic methodology, 138n10

Bacchetta, Paola, 161
Balanced Refugee Reform Act (BRRA), 32, 35
Balibar, Etienne, 40
Bannerji, Himani, 24
banning refugees, 3, 173, 185n1. *See also* exclusion
belonging, 85
benevolence, 62, 147
"Beyond Human Rights" (Arendt), 207
Biden, Joe, 27
Bilge, Sirma, 145–6
biometric visas, 27, 29, 38, 41–3, *42*, 166n73
Black, Richard, 8
Black Lives Matter Toronto, 161
blended visa office-referred refugees (BVORs), 30, 39
The Boat (Le), 207
"boat people," as term, 63

"bogus," as term, 35
"bogus refugees," 30–1, 33–5, *33*
book overview, 4–10, 13–16, 215–16, 217–18
borders extended, 44
Brand, Dionne, 196–205, 206–8, 209–10n23, 209n21
British Empire: Asia and Africa, 159; and humanitarian exceptionalism, 17–18n23, 166n64; and Indigenous peoples' suppression, 13; subjects right to settle, 55, 67, 81; subjects vs. citizens, 81; treatment of Indians, 62; whitewashing Budge Budge and Canada, 60
British immigrants, 12, 81. *See also* imperial citizenship; *Komagata Maru* Incident
British Raj, 56, 63
Brydon, Diana, 200
Buddhism, 195
Budge Budge massacre, 56, 60, 62
Byrd, Jodi, 137n1, 159

Cader, Fathima, 58
Cambodia, 68n14, 196–7
Canada and/vs. United States: #WelcometoCanada, 3–4; asylum seekers, 25; resettlement numbers, 27, 215; Safe Third Country Agreement (STCA), 26, 66, 157; Smart Border Accord, 29; Vietnam war, 216
Canada Border Services Agency (CBSA), 29, 42, 155
"Canada Knows How to Respond to Refugees" (Clarkson), 88
Canadian Citizen Act, 91n8
Canadian Committee of the Red Cross, 91n14. *See also* International Committee of the Red Cross
Canadian Council for Refugees, 39

Canadian Immigration, Refugees and Citizenship Canada (IRCC), 41
Canadian Temporary Resident Biometrics Program (TRBP), 38. *See also* biometric visas
"Canadians First," 148–50, 158–9
cannibalism, 133–4
capitalism vs. communism, 28
Caruth, Cathy, 210n28
Castaneda, Claudia, 186n7
Central Agency of Information, 76
Chileans, 28
Chimni, B.S., 8
China, 76–7
Chinese Exclusion Act. *See* Chinese Immigration Act
Chinese Immigration Act, 12, 75, 79, 84
Chinese people: 1999 boats, 23, 30–1, 36, 37; head tax, 65, 75–6, 85–6; stowaways, 4; and white settler masculinity, 164n44. *See also* Clarkson, Adrienne; Poy family
Chouliaraki, Lili, 179
Chrétien, Jean, 37
cisnormativity, 162–3n29. *See also* heterocisnormativity
citizenship: as "gift," 145 (*see also* gratitude); haunting, 101, 107; as political, 99, 103; vs. refugees, 99; vs. "uncivilized New Canadians," 148–9; weaponization of citizenship, 119–20, 134–5. *See also* imperial citizenship
Citizenship and Immigration Canada (CIC), 150, 153, 165–6n64
civic duties, 182
civilian exchanges, 78–9, 81, 91n8, 92n23–4, 93nn26–7
civility. *See* white civility

Clarkson, Adrienne: overview, 73, 74–5; civilian exchange, 92n23; minimizing systemic racism, 83–4, 85–6, 88, 89; refugee narrative, 71–2, 88–9. *See also* Poy family
Coleman, Daniel, 13, 61–2
Coletu, Ebony, 120
colonialism/colonization: classifications and power, 145; history of, 133; and refusal, 144; term and immigration law, 151; transnational, 146. *See also* settler colonialism
communism vs. capitalism, 28
Community Historical Recognition Program of Citizenship and Immigration Canada (CHRP), 64
Comprehensive Plan of Action, 27
constative/performative acts, 105
consumption, 206
Continuous Journey Regulation, 12, 40, 55, 66. *See also* Safe Third Country Agreement
Convention Relative to the Treatment of Prisoners of War (1929), 76
credibility, 195
Crépeau, François, 195
criminalization: "irregular arrivals," 32, 36, 44; LGBTQI people, 149, 163n41, 164nn45–7; and precarious status, 150–1; and safety, 164–5n52; Sri Lankan Tamils, 31. See also *Komagata Maru* Incident
Critical Disability Studies (CDS), 173–4, 175–6, 178, 184–5
critical humanitarian scholarship, 179
critical multiculturalism, 199, 209n21
Critical Race Theory (CRT), 175–6
Critical Refugee Studies (CRS), 8–11, 16, 44, 101–2, 146–7, 174–6

cross-racial kinship, 198, 204, 206–8
cultural appropriation, 198

Dawson, Carrie, 194
Day, Iyko, 137n5
decolonization, 132, 136, 145, 161
"Decolonizing Antiracism" (Lawrence and Dua), 132
de-indigenization, 119
Deleuze, Gilles, 109
Department of Immigration and Colonization, 146
Derrida, Jacques, 105, 111
"Desegregating American Literary Studies" (Fishkin), 198–9
designated class, 28
designated countries of origin (DCO), 32, 35, 41–3
Designated Foreign Nationals (DFN), 36, 41, 44
detention, 31, 155–6, 195. See also *Komagata Maru* Incident; Tamils
disability, 173–4, 175–9, 181, 184, 187n38
discrimination, 13, 75–6. *See also* racism
displacement, 13, 133–4. *See also* Indigenous peoples
Dobson, Kit, 201, 209–10n23
Dogs at the Perimeter (Thien), 196
Douglass, Frederick, 132
draft dodgers, 4
Dua, Enakshi, 132

East Asia, 63
Eastmond, Marita, 194
Echlin, Kim, 210n34
echo effect, 39
economic migrants, 7
Edkins, Jenny, 109
Elleman, Bruce, 78, 92n18, 93n26

empathy/sympathy, 175, 180, 182–3, 204–6, 210nn34–5
Erevelles, Nirmala, 175
Espiritu, Yến Lê, 6, 9, 130–1, 139n22, 174, 182
exceptionalism, 5, 10. *See also* humanitarian exceptionalism; state of exception; super-refugees
exceptionality, 5. *See also* exceptionalism; exclusion; state of exception
exclusion: "bogus refugee," 31–2, 150, 151, 152, 153–4 (*see also* illegality); and "bogus refugee" term, 35; capping PSRs, 39–41, *40*; critical studies examining, 175–6; "dangerous regions," 41, 42–3, *42*; deterring refugees, 42–3; erasing, 59, 60, 64–6, 68n14, 72, 85, 90; history of Chinese people, 75–6, 84; and living as undocumented, 154–5; persons with disabilities, 181; POWs in Philippines, 92n23; and public opinion, 26; visas and Chileans, 28. *See also* head tax; *Komagata Maru* Incident; Tamils

fake passports, 156
Fassin, Didier, 185
fast-tracking, 32
fear, 28–9. *See also* securitization
"First Nations," as term, 159
Fishkin, Shelley Fisher, 198–9
Five Country Conference, 42
Flaminio, Anna, 121–2
Fleming, Melissa, 177, 178, 182–3
Forbes, Jack, 133–4
Foucault, Michel, 163n33
Foxen, Patricia, 195, 210n34
Freud, Sigmund, 210n28
fugitive slaves, 4

Gabi (refugee), 153–4
Galbraith, David, 186n2
Gaudry, Adam, 159
gender, 30–1, 118, 187n26
genealogical disclosure, 120–1, 122–6, 131, 138n10
geopolitics, 28
Ghadarites, 56
The Gift of Freedom (Nguyen), 85
global North, 28
Gordon, Avery, 109
Gordon, P.H., 91n14
Gorman, Daniel, 68n1, 81
government-assisted refugees (GARs), 30
Graff, Rayne, 129
gratitude, 72, 85, 90, 90n4, 183
Grech, Shaun, 175
Grue, Jan, 184
Guattari, Felix, 109

Hadhad family, 178–9, 181, 188n58
Halberstam, Jack, 143
Harper, Stephen, 37, 39–40, 163n32
haunted citizenship, 107, 109–11
havens vs. honeypots, 26
Hayden, Bridget, 205
head tax, 55, 65, 75–6, 85–6
Heart Matters (Clarkson), 77, 81, 83
heterocisnormativity, 148–52, 158–9, 162–3n30
history erased, 59, 60, 64–6, 68n14, 72, 85, 90
homophobia, 145
honest relationships, 135–7
Honig, Bonnie, 100
Houle, France, 195
human rights, 207
humanitarian exceptionalism: and British Empire/settler colonialism, 17–18n23; vs. economic priorities, 145, 151, 165, 181; and hero tropes,

184; and heterocisnormativity, 156; vs. Indigenous dispossession, 72; invoked by refugees, 217; in social media, 3–4; and state of exception, 215; and suppressing racist memories, 57, 59; Trudeau welcoming Syrians, 3, 178, 180–1; truth of, 4, 16n5, 218n1 (see also *Komagata Maru* Incident; Tamils); and *Voyage of the Komagata Maru, or India's Slavery Abroad* (Singh), 61–2
Hungarians, 27
Hussen, Ahmed, 216
Huysmans, Jeff, 29
Hyndman, Jennifer, 39–41
hypocrisy, 67. *See also* humanitarian exceptionalism

identity fraud, 42
illegality, 149, 150, 152–7
"immigrant," as term, 7
Immigrant and Refugee Community Organization of Manitoba (IRCOM), 128–9
immigrants, 12, 65, 123. *See also* Chinese Immigration Act; migrants; refugees
Immigration, Refugees and Citizenship Canada (IRCC), 41
Immigration Act (1976), 6, 28, 33, 151
Immigration and Refugee Board (IRB), 31, 152, 210n34
Immigration and Refugee Protection Act (IRPA), 25, 33, 37, *42*, 150, 165n56
imperial citizenship, 12–13, 55, 68n1, 75, 91n8. *See also* British immigrants
imperialism, 9, 10, 63, 132–4
India, Indian people, 55, 80. See also *Komagata Maru* Incident

Indian Act (1876), 134, 139n40
Indian Act (1951), 135
Indigeneity, 130
Indigenous kinship, 121–2. *See also* decolonization
Indigenous peoples: assimilation, 134–5, 139n40, 149; vs. Canadian sovereignty, 11–12; decolonization, 132, 136, 145, 161; dispossessed, 12, 66, 72, 159–61; enfranchisement, 134–5; and "First" people, 159; and *Komagata Maru* Incident, 66; and LGBTQI migrants, 159–61; LGBTQI/Two Spirit people, 91n5, 149, 163n41; and Macdonald, 90n5; Missing and Murdered Indigenous Women, 91n5; 1905 Saskatoon photo, 66; prioritizing, 117; refusal/resistance, 143, 144; survivance, 118, 137n3; as term, 138n8; and universities, 134, 139–40n40; weaponization of citizenship, 119–20, 134–5
Indigenous peoples and refugees: and authority of settler nation-state, 118; conceptual divisions, 13, 119; decolonization, 132; de-indigenization, 119; genealogical disclosure as solidarity building, 131–2; and imperialism, 132–3; and LGBTQI migrants, 159–61; new pathways together, 128, 129, 135–7; as opposites, 117–18; tensions between, 128–9
Indigenous Studies, 139–40n40
individualism, 89, 128, 181–2, 182. *See also* super-refugees
Indochinese Designated Class Regulation, 28
Industrial Revolution, 133

inspirational stories. *See also* super-refugees
internally displaced people (IDPs), 82
International Committee of the Red Cross (ICRC), 76–8, 92n15. *See also* Canadian Committee of the Red Cross
international refugee regime, 74
internment camps, 93n26
intersectionality, 8, 146–7, 175–7, 200
invasions, 64–5
"irregular arrivals," 32, 36, 44
irregular petitions, 106. *See also* Non-Status Women's Collective

Jacobs, Harriet, 206
Japan, 76–7, 91n14, 92n18, 92n24, 93nn26–7
Jewish people, 4, 165n54, 215
Jimenez, Shauna, 39–40
Jobs, Steve, 173, 186n2
Johnston, Basil H., 133
Johnston, David, 148, 163n32
Johnston, Hugh, 55

Kahnawakero:non, 143
Kana, Amit, 187n38
Kazimi, Ali, 59, 63–8
Kenney, Jason, 33–5, 36, 39, 154
kiyokewin, 121–2
Knudsen, John Chr., 195
Komagata Maru Incident: overview, 55–8; memorializing, 59; and MV *Sun Sea*, 58; passengers as refugees, 56–7, 58–9, 60; *Undesirables: White Canada and the Komagata Maru* (Kazimi), 59, 63–8; *Voyage of the Komagata Maru, or India's Slavery Abroad* (Singh), 59–63, 67–8
Kurdi, Aylan, 30, 88
Lamb, Christine, 187n31

land acknowledgments, 124–5
language: and policy making, 36–7, 83; and protection, 26; and victim narratives, 25–6
Lather, Patti, 205
Lawrence, Bonita, 132
Le, Nam, 207
Lebanon, 41
legal categories: in Canadian law, 82; as limited, 45, 82; vs. lived experience, 56, 84; and Poys as refugees, 74–5
legislation/policy making: and asylum seekers, 26–7; asylum seekers vs. refugees, 25; and "bogus refugee" term, 34, 35, 36–7; deterring asylum seekers, 42; and fear, 28–9; "on the fly," 23; and language, 36–7, 83; and mechanisms of state violence, 44; and public opinion, 26, 37, 41; and racialization, 38, 39–41, 40, 134; since 9/11, 37–8; sponsorship, 39 (*see also* privately sponsored refugees)
Leow, Joanne, 201
Leroux, Darryl, 159
lesbian, gay, bisexual, trans, queer, and intersex (LGBTQI): overview, 144–7; Antonio's experiences, 155–6, 157–8; criminalization, 149, 163n41, 164nn45–7; dominant narratives, 152; Gabi's experiences, 153–4, 158; and Indigenous dispossession, 159–61; refusal, 156–8, 159; Sage's experiences, 156–7, 158; Shayma and Ariel's experiences, 154–5, 158; SOGIE, 152
Levine-Raskin, Cynthia, 34
liberal nationalism, 3. *See also* white nationalism
liberalism, 17n9, 72, 90n4

Literature in the Ashes of History
 (Caruth), 210n28
luck/chance, 84, 89, 92n23
Lye, Colleen, 199

Macdonald, John A., 90n5
Macdougall, Brenda, 121–2
Macklin, Audrey, 26, 57
Madokoro, Laura, 137n5
Malkki, Liisa, 9
Manifest Manners (Vizenor), 137n3
Mann, Alexandra, 56
masks, 109
Massaro, Toni, 205
Mawani, Renisa, 62–3
McGranahan, Carole, 158
media outlets, 176–9. *See also* newspapers
memories: forgetting racist incidents, 57, 59, 60, 64–6, 68n14, 85, 90; haunting, 201, 203; and photographs, 65–7; strategic use of, 59
Métis people, 138n18, 159. *See also* otipemisiwak/Métis people
Mexicans, 35, 153–4
"migrant," as term, 7, 26
migrants: British subjects, 12, 81 (see also *Komagata Maru* Incident); non-status, 106, 145 (*see also* illegality; Non-Status Women's Collective); precarious status, 144, 150, 154; and/vs. refugees, 7, 26, 118, 144. *See also* immigrants; lesbian, gay, bisexual, trans, queer, and intersex; refugees
migration narratives. *See* genealogical disclosure; super-refugees; victim narrative
Missing and Murdered Indigenous Women (MMIW), 91n5
Mongia, Radhika, 40

Montoya, Nico, 181
Moulin, Carolina, 183
multiculturalism, 17n9, 199, 200. *See also* critical multiculturalism
Multiple Borders Strategy, 29
Muslim Ban/Travel Ban, 3, 173, 185n1
Mustafa, Nujeen, 176–9, 187nn30–1

Nansen Refugee Award, 4, 188n55
narrative plenitude, 217
narratives, 71–2, 88–9. *See also* refugee fiction; super-refugees; victim narrative
nationalism, 3. *See also* white nationalism
nation-states, 118, 145, 159, 207
Nayeri, Dina, 183
neoliberalism, 182–3
New Canadians, 148–9
newspapers: and "bogus refugee" term, 33–5, *33*; *Komagata Maru* Incident, 64–5; propaganda, 93n29; and "queue jumping" term, 35–7, *36*. *See also* media outlets
Nguyen, Mimi, 72, 85, 90n4, 175
Nguyen, Viet Thanh, 217
Nguyen, Vinh, 61, 101, 180, 184
9/11, 29, 37, 165n56
non-status people, 99, 106. *See also* Non-Status Women's Collective
Non-Status Women's Collective: overview, 99–100, 101; haunting protest, 107, 109–10; petition, 106–9
nuclear family, 148, 150, 151
Nyers, Peter, 5, 10, 118, 174

MV *Ocean Lady*, 31–2, 34, 57, 68n2, 68n10
"On Ethnographic Refusal" (Simpson), 143

Ong, Aihwa, 195
Operation Syrian Refugees, 30
ordinary acts, 217
Otherness, 205, 206. *See also* racism
otipemisiwak/Métis people, 121–4

Palestinians, 41, 45n18
Payne, William, 39–40
Peace by Chocolate. *See* Hadhad family
Peeren, Esther, 110
Peers, Danielle, 178, 180
persecution and refugee status, 7, 83
petitions, 100–9
Phan Thị Kim Phúc, 216–17
Phung, Malissa, 124–6, 126–7, 129–30
Pinochet, Augusto, 28
Pisani, Maria, 175
policy-oriented research, 8
positivity, 179–80, 185. *See also* super-refugees
Post Ref Racism, 180
power: and dispossession of Indigenous peoples, 12; duality of, 9; and empathy, 206; and refugee voices campaigns, 182; as subjection, 90n4; transnational, 62–3
Poy family: and Chinese Immigration Act, 72, 89; departing Hong Kong, 79–80; head tax, 85–6; and imperial citizenship, 91n8; intelligence information, 80; loss of material goods, 80–1; and official refugee definition, 83; and racism, 83–4, 85–6, 88; as stateless, 81. *See also* Clarkson, Adrienne
Prague Winter (Albright), 87
precarious status, 144, 150, 154
pre-emptive screening, 29

prisoners of war (POWs), 76–7, 80, 91–2nn14–15, 92n18, 92n23–4, 93nn26–7
privately sponsored refugees (PSRs), 30, 39, 41
Protecting Canada's Immigration System Act, 32, 35
protection and language, 26
protests, 107, 109–10, 161. *See also* petitions
protracted displacement, 27
protracted refugee situations (PRS), 27
Puar, Jasbir, 175–6, 180, 182
public opinion and exclusionary policies, 26
Punjabi migrants. See *Komagata Maru* Incident

"Québec's First Peoples," 159
Queer, Trans, Black, Indigenous, and other People of Colour (QTBIPOC), 143. *See also* lesbian, gay, bisexual, trans, queer, and intersex
"queue jumping," 32, 33–4, 35–7, *36*

race and authorship, 199
racialized people: and anti-Black logics, 160; cross-racial kinship, 198, 204, 206–8; and disability, 175–6; model minorities, 182; question of origins, 121, 126; and the temporary resident visa (TRV), 165–6n64; and white civility, 61–2
racism: anti-Black, 160; Clarkson experiences, 83–4, 85–6, 88; "dangerous" regions, 38, 41, 42–3, *42*; as disease, 62; hidden by language, 64; hidden by legalities, 61; as isolated events, 64; obscured policies, 55; question of origins,

121, 126; racialized British subjects, 12 (see also *Komagata Maru* Incident); without races, 40–1. *See also* Chinese Immigration Act; exclusion; *Komagata Maru* Incident; Tamils

Rajaram, Prem Kumar, 181

Ramsay, Georgina, 217

Razack, Sherene, 205–6

Red Cross. *See* Canadian Committee of the Red Cross; International Committee of the Red Cross

"REF Talks," 173

"refugee," as term: in Canadian law, 82; as complex, 11; intersections, 7; *Komagata Maru* passengers, 56–7, 58–9, 60; and "migrant" label, 26; and status/power, 87–8. *See also* legal categories; refugees: definition

refugee claimants. *See* asylum seekers

Refugee Convention, 56

refugee fiction, 196–7, 198–205, 206–8, 209n21, 209n23

"refugee state," as term, 6, 7–8

refugees: vs. asylum seekers, 25, 29, 34, 37; binary of, 34; books by Clarkson on, 71; and Canadian citizenship, 120; Canadian overview, 27–30, 135; chosen and unchosen, 24; vs. citizens, 99; as colonizers, 12, 132; continuation of label, 101; and continued intervention, 90n4; definition, 11, 45, 81–4, 118–19, 137n5 (*see also* legal categories; "refugee," as term); and disability, 175, 176–9, 181, 187nn30–1; expectations of, 26, 178, 185, 216 (*see also* super-refugees); history of, 74; inspirational (*see* super-refugees); and migrants, 7; vs. migrants, 26, 144; non-status, 99, 106; number in 2020, 27; numbers in/from Syria, 30; as ordinary, 185, 217; percentage in global South, 16n5; permanent regime, 82; and political ends, 4; and political engagement, 99–100, 102 (*see also* Non-Status Women's Collective); as "problems," 6, 8; profiting from, 182–3; reduction in, 66–7; research on, 8–10, 16, 44; as speechless emissaries, 72; state complicity, 85; as terrorists, 28, 31; transnational power/injustice, 62–3; as ungrateful, 183; UNHCR definition, 11; universalized notions of, 73. *See also* Indigenous peoples and refugees; super-refugees

refugees, denied. *See* exclusion

"refugeetude," 101–2

refusal, 143–6, 156–8

remembering, 59–66

rescue, 72

Réseau Education Sans Frontières (RESF), 106

resentment, 180

resettlement: and colonization, 128; and designated class, 28; number in 2017, 27; prioritizing regions/nationalities, 30; as protection, 25; of protracted refugee situations (PRS), 27

Resettlement Assistance Program, 216

resilience/determination, 86, 179–80, 183–4

resources, 216, 217. *See also* Hadhad family

responsibility, 175

revolution, 105

risk management, 29, 36, 42
Roma, 34, 35
Room for All of Us (Clarkson), 84
Rousseau, Cecile, 195, 210n34
Royal Canadian Mounted Police, 42

Safe Third Country Agreement (STCA), 26, 66, 157
Sage (migrant), 156–7
Schalk, Sami, 178, 181, 184
Schlund-Vials, Cathy, 59, 68n14
Second World War, 4, 76–81, 91n8, 91n14, 92n18, 92n23–4, 93nn26–1
securitization, 28–9, 37, 150–1, 158
segregated curriculum, 199
settler colonialism: and British Empire, 12, 13; and Canada as diverse, 117; "Canadians First," 147, 148–9, 158–9; classifications and power, 145; as consumptive sickness, 134; and global colonialism, 146; and humanitarian exceptionalism, 10–11, 17–18n23; and refusal, 144; weaponization of citizenship, 119–20, 134–5. *See also* colonialism/colonization
settlerhood, 136
Sexual Orientation and Gender Identity and Expression (SOGIE), 152
Seyhan, Azade, 138n10
Shayma (migrant), 154–5, 157
Signatures of Citizenship (Zaeske), 103
signatures on petitions, 105–6, 108
Sikhs. See *Komagata Maru* Incident
Simpson, Audra, 143, 144
Singh, Gurdit, 55, 59–63, 67–8, 68n2
Singh, Karissa, 180
Singh Decision, 47n49
Smart Border Accord, 29, 37
smuggling, 31, 32, 35, 37, 43

Somalis, 27
South Sudanese, 27
Southeast Asia, 28
sovereignty: and British Empire, 12; and exceptionalism, 5; Indigenous vs. Canadian, 11–12; and settler colonialism, 12, 13
Speech from the Throne, 148, 150, 163n32
sponsorship, 39, 41. *See also* privately sponsored refugees
Sponsorship Agreement Holders (SAH), 39
spontaneous arrivals. *See* asylum seekers
MS *St. Louis*, 4
Standing Rock Indian Reservation, 161
Starcevic, S
eb, 185
"state," as term, 6
state of exception, 5, 215. *See also* sovereignty
statelessness, 81
"Stealing the Pain of Others" (Razack), 206
stereotypes, 43. *See also* exclusion
Stoler, Ann Laura, 109–10
stowaways, 4
success narratives. *See* super-refugees
Sudanese, 27, 106
Sullivan, Jack, 79
MV *Sun Sea*, 31–2, 34, 57–9, 68n10
supercrips, 173–4, 178, 184, 187n38
super-refugees: Al Moulia, 177–9, 181; debt and gratitude, 182–3, 185; Hadhad family, 178–9; Hussen, 216; Jobs as, 173; media and political narratives, 178–9; Mustafa, 176–9, 187nn30–1; and power, 182; and privilege, 181; and war, 179–80

surveillance, 109
survivance, 137n3
Syrians: and Clarkson, 88; Operation Syrian Refugees, 30; as prioritized, 40; as protracted refugee situations (PRS), 27; restricted, 173, 185n1; and Trudeau, 3, 40, 178, 180–1

"Tamil, Tiger, Terrorist?" (Cader), 58
Tamils, 31–2, 34, 57–9, 68n10
t-discourses, 163n33
TEDTalks platform, 177, 179, 182–3
Temporary Resident Biometric Program (TRBP), 41–3, *42*. *See also* biometric visas
temporary resident visa (TRV), 145, 152, 165–6n64
temporary workers, 154
terrorism, 28, 29, 37, 165n56
Terry, Jennifer, 179
testing laws, 56
Thien, Madeleine, 196
Toews, Vic, 31, 32, 58
tolerance, 17n23
transgressive texts, 199, 204
trauma: as drive for life, 210n28; and refugee narratives, 194–5, 197; stealing and consuming, 206; suppressing, 60; in *What We All Long For* (Brand), 199, 201, 202–3
tribunals, 196
Troeung, Y-Dang, 195
Trudeau, Justin: after 2015 election, 89; Hadhad family story, 178, 180–1; and Non-Status Women's Collective, 106–8; welcoming Syrians, 3, 40
Trump, Donald, 3, 27, 87–8, 173, 185n1
truth telling, 194–5, 197, 202–3
Turkey, 41

Uganda, 145
UN Convention Relating to the Status of Refugees (1951): on authorization, 33; and conservative climate, 137n5; definition of refugee, 81–4; designated class, 28; legal obligations, 28–9; signed by Canada, 5
Underground Railroad, 4
Undesirables: White Canada and the Komagata Maru (Kazimi), 59, 63–8
United Nations High Commissioner for Refugees (UNHCR): and BVOR, 39; definition of refugee, 11; expanding, 82; Fleming TEDGlobal talk, 177, 182–3; Nansen Refugee Award, 4, 188n55; and Palestinians, 45n18; Sudanese petition, 106
United States: civilian exchanges, 78, 92n24, 93n26; forgetting racist incidents, 68n14; Muslim Ban/Travel Ban, 3, 173, 185n1; number of refugee resettlements, 27; refugees after 9/11, 37. *See also* Canada and/vs. United States
US Refugee Admissions Program, 3

van Dijk, Jan, 25–6
victim narrative, 25–6, 187n26, 194–6, 197, 210n34. *See also* super-refugees
Vietnam war, 4, 130–1, 139n22, 216
visas, 27, 29, 41–3, *42*, 166n73. *See also* Temporary Resident Biometric Program (TRBP)
Vizenor, Gerald, 118, 137n3
Vowel, Chelsea, 125
Voyage of the Komagata Maru, or India's Slavery Abroad (Singh), 59–63, 67–8

wahkohtowin, 121–2. *See also* Indigenous kinship
Wake, Caroline, 205
Walcott, Rinaldo, 160, 209n21
war, 4, 10, 30, 130–1, 139n22, 179, 216. *See also* Second World War
War, Genocide, and Justice (Schlund-Vials), 68n14
war on terror, 29, 37, 165n56
Ward, Rowena, 78
weendigo, 133
#WelcomeToCanada, 3–4
wétiko psychosis, 133–4
Wettergren, Åsa, 180
What We All Long For (Brand), 198–205, 206–8, 209n21, 209n23
white civility, 61–2
white nationalism, 17–8n23, 134, 135
white supremacy, 200
whiteness: and anti-Black logics, 160; and desirability, 65, 134, 165n54 (*see also* nuclear family); read as white, 126, 130
"The Wild Beyond" (Halberstam), 143
Winnipeg, MB, 128–9
Wirch, Jenna "Liiciious," 129, 132
witnessing, 205
WorldPride, 145

Yousafzai, Malala, 187n31

Zaeske, Susan, 103–5

Cultural Spaces

Cultural Spaces explores the rapidly changing temporal, spatial, and theoretical boundaries of contemporary cultural studies. Culture has long been understood as the force that defines and delimits societies in fixed spaces. The recent intensification of globalizing processes, however, has meant that it is no longer possible – if it ever was – to imagine the world as a collection of autonomous, monadic spaces, whether these are imagined as localities, nations, regions within nations, or cultures demarcated by region or nation. One of the major challenges of studying contemporary culture is to understand the new relationships of culture to space that are produced today. The aim of this series is to publish bold new analyses and theories of the spaces of culture, as well as investigations of the historical construction of those cultural spaces that have influenced the shape of the contemporary world.

General Editor: Jasmin Habib, University of Waterloo

Editorial Advisory Board

Lauren Berlant, University of Chicago
Homi K. Bhabha, Harvard University
Hazel V. Carby, Yale University
Richard Day, Queen's University
Christopher Gittings, University of Western Ontario
Lawrence Grossberg, University of North Carolina
Mark Kingwell, University of Toronto
Heather Murray, University of Toronto
Elspeth Probyn, University of Sydney
Rinaldo Walcott, OISE/University of Toronto

Books in the Series

Peter Ives, *Gramsci's Politics of Language: Engaging the Bakhtin Circle and the Frankfurt School*
Sarah Brophy, *Witnessing AIDS: Writing, Testimony, and the Work of Mourning*
Shane Gunster, *Capitalizing on Culture: Critical Theory for Cultural Studies*
Jasmin Habib, *Israel, Diaspora, and the Routes of National Belonging*
Serra Tinic, *On Location: Canada's Television Industry in a Global Market*
Evelyn Ruppert, *The Moral Economy of Cities: Shaping Good Citizens*
Mark Coté, Richard J.F. Day, and Greg de Peuter, eds, *Utopian Pedagogy: Radical Experiments against Neoliberal Globalization*
Michael McKinnie, *City Stages: Theatre and the Urban Space in a Global City*
David Jefferess, *Postcolonial Resistance: Culture, Liberation, and Transformation*
Mary Gallagher, ed., *World Writing: Poetics, Ethics, Globalization*
Maureen Moynagh, *Political Tourism and Its Texts*
Erin Hurley, *National Performance: Representing Quebec from Expo 67 to Céline Dion*
Lily Cho, *Eating Chinese: Culture on the Menu in Small Town Canada*
Rhona Richman Kenneally and Johanne Sloan, eds, *Expo 67: Not Just a Souvenir*
Gillian Roberts, *Prizing Literature: The Celebration and Circulation of National Culture*
Lianne McTavish, *Defining the Modern Museum: A Case Study of the Challenges of Exchange*
Misao Dean, *Inheriting a Canoe Paddle: The Canoe in Discourses of English-Canadian Nationalism*
Sarah Brophy and Janice Hladki, eds, *Embodied Politics in Visual Autobiography*
Robin Pickering-Iazzi, *The Mafia in Italian Lives and Literature: Life Sentences and Their Geographies*
Claudette Lauzon, *The Unmaking of Home in Contemporary Art*
Kyle Conway, *Little Mosque on the Prairie and the Paradoxes of Cultural Translation*
Ajay Heble, ed., *Classroom Action: Human Rights, Critical Activism, and Community-Based Education*
Jason Demers, *The American Politics of French Theory: Derrida, Deleuze, Guattari, and Foucault in Translation*
Gaoheng Zhang, *Migration and the Media: Debating Chinese Migration to Italy, 1992–2012*
Kyle Wanberg, *Maps of Empire: A Topography of World Literature*
Vinh Nguyen and Thy Phu, eds, *Refugee States: Critical Refugee Studies in Canada*